بسم الله الرحمن الرحيم

Great Books
of
Islamic Civilization

GREAT BOOKS OF ISLAMIC CIVILIZATION

N. A. Baloch

KITAB BHAVAN
NEW DELHI-110002

Kitab Bhavan
Publishers, Distributors, Exporters & Importers
1784, Kalan Mahal, Darya Ganj
New Delhi - 1100 02 (India)

Phone : (91-11) 23277392/93, 23274686, 30906494
website : www.kitabbhavan.com
Email : nasri@vsnl.com
Fax : (91-11) 23263383

Ist Indian Edition : 1997
Reprinted : 2006

ISBN : 81-7151-236-4

Published in India by :
Nusrat Ali Nasri for Kitab Bhavan
1784, Kalan Mahal, Darya Ganj
New Delhi - 1100 02 [India]

Printed in India at :
Lahooti Fine Art Press
1711, Sui Walan, Darya Ganj
New Delhi - 110002 (India)

CONTENTS

MATHEMATICAL SCIENCES

SCIENCE AND ART OF HEALING

APPLIED SCIENCE AND TECHNOLOGY

INTRODUCTION

In the history of world civilizations, Islamic Civilization has been essentially a faith-cum-knowledge based civilization. The Quranic revelation simultaneously strengthened the foundations of Faith and Knowledge. The genesis of search for knowledge and achievement of excellence, the distinctive characteristics of the early Islamic society, may be explained briefly.

History of the Islamic Peoples (*the Ummah*), and of Islamic Education, started with the Quranic imperative 'Read!' which made learning compulsory. The Quran in itself became an inexhaustible source of knowledge, and also the revelation established the undisputed superiority of knowledge and strongly motivated the believer to seek *more and more of knowledge*. Consequently, the Prophet (*sal'am*) declared that learning was compulsory for every 'believer' (*muslim*), man and woman, and that knowledge was to be sought for even though it be in China— i.e. wherever it was available, through any language, any teacher, and in any country. There was a further elaboration that knowledge for mankind must multiply with the instrument of writing—the tip of the pen, and that mankind had been destined to know the unknown. Human beings were called upon to see, to observe, to ponder, to think, to reflect, to understand and to learn. In effect, ISLAM became a way of living and learning, QURAN the book, and PROPHET the teacher. Primacy of knowledge was affirmed and the concept of compulsory learning and education was confirmed.

As the early Islamic community took to education, 'Childhood Education' (*Ta'līm al-Atfāl*) came to be viewed by the Muslim educator as the fundamental and foundational stage of education. As a result, the first organized educational institution—the universal primary school–was born. The *Kuttāb* (Primary School) was held under any roof that was then available — such as mosques, houses of teachers and of learned men, palaces, bookshops, literacy salons, tents and open air in the desert. In the eastern world of Islam this elementary school became known as *Maktab* and in the Fareast (Malaysia - Indonesia) as *Pondok*. With further development of formal system of education, *madrasahs* were established as the more distinct higher educational institutions outside the mosques in the 5th century A.H.

From believers' dedicated effort to understand the meaning of Quran, emerged the different 'Quranic Studies' (*'Ulūm al-Quran*) which is the subject of Suyuti's work. The 'Quranic Studies', in turn, paved the way for emergence of other studies which eventually developed into independent sciences. Hadith and Sunnah were complimentary to the comprehension of the divine revelation and therefore, Hadith was studied intensively. This study developed into an independent science, and Ibn Salāh's work is an introduction to the 'Science of Hadith'. Efforts at integrating faith and knowledge, the spiritual and the rational attitudes in belief and behaviour, culminated in al-Ghazali's expositions in his different works, mainly *Ihyā' 'Ulūm al-Din* and *Kimyā-i Sa'ādat*.

• • • • •

The Quranic revelation had motivated mankind to read, to observe, to think and rethink, to search and research, and to seek more and more of knowledge to be able to grasp the reality not only of the Creator's existence but His presence permeating the whole universe, both the world of Humans and the world of Nature. The more gifted among the believers responded to the Quran's call more seriously: they began to observe, think and reflect in order to understand and learn more and more about God's creation. Their researches extended the frontiers of knowledge at a rate not known before in history, and led to the development of different studies and sciences.

As 'knowledge' was to be sought for from all possible sources, the Muslims researchers spared no pains to seek knowledge through translation from Greek, Indian, Iranian and possibly Chinese sources. By the first quarter of the 2nd Hijra century, the Muslim scholar had gained acquaintance with the literary traditions of the non-Muslim peoples.

With the Qur'ānic emphasis on importance of knowledge, and the Prophet's motivation to *muslims* to acquire knowledge, pursuit of knowledge became a living ideal with the early Islamic community. It gained *momentum* in the first century of the Hijra, and led to considerable *expansion* of knowledge during the 2nd and 3rd centuries. Beginning from the 4th century and continuing on for the next few centuries, there was an *explosion* of knowledge, the first one in human history. This necessitated comprehension of the ever growing orbit of knowledge.

• • • • •

To meet this end, Fārābī (d. 339 A.H.) was the first to write his *Ihsā' al-'Ulūm* ('Enumeration of Sciences') to classify the known quantum of knowledge. His approach was essentially philosophical. Khwārazmi (365 A.H) in his *Miftāh al-'Ulūm*, Brethren of Purity in their *Rasā'il* and Ibn Sina (d. 428 A.H.) in his encyclopedic *AL-SHIFĀ* as also in his important treatise 'Categories of Rational Sciences' (*Aqsām al-'Ulūm al-'Aqliyah*) conceived an exposition and categorization of the different sciences on philosophical basis. The general approach of all these pioneers was to encompass Knowledge in all its dimensions. Khwārazmi divided sciences into two broad categories–those generated under Islam and the rest, but his main objective was to develop a clear understanding of the different sciences by clarifying the meanings and concepts underlying their terminology/phraseology. In 377 A.H., al-Nadīm undertook to compile his *Al-Fihrist* ('The Catalogue') in which bibliography became an essential feature of classification. Some authors instead of attempting to encompass the entire range of Knowledge preferred to discuss and describe in their works a specific number of subjects and sciences. For instance, Fakhr al-Dīn al-Rāzī in his *Hadā'iq al-Anwār fi Haqā'q al-Asrār* brought under discussion sixty sciences; al-Dawwāni in his *Unmūdhij*, ten; al-Suyūti in *al-Niqāyā*, fourteen. In these works, mainly a general presentation was made of each science instead of adding any relevant bibliographical information. An exception to this was the work entitled *Irshād al-Qāsid fi Aqasa al-Maqāsid* of Muhammad b. Ibrahīm al-Akfānī (d. 749 A.H/1348) who, after a general introduction on learning, education and knowledge, discussed sixty disciplines/sciences and also brought under reference, in their context, four hundred books. Subsequently, Ibn Khaldun, not in a separate work but in the sixth chapter of MUQADDIMAH, classified sciences into two main categories–the natural ones which are the direct product of human thought and the transmitted ones which are borrowed from their original source; the former are not associated with any particular people but the latter belong to the Islamic community. In essence, Ibn Khaldun's categorization was similar to that of Khwārazmi, but more mature in generalization, concepts and details under the two categories.

Thus, beginning with *'Ihsā' al-'Ulūm* of Fārabī numerous works were written to enumerate and classify sciences with different approaches and objectives. The process reached its climax in Tāshkopruzāde's *Miftāh al-Sa'ādah* in which he presented the best synthesis of all the main approaches. In his introduction, and subsequently, he has rationalized the principles and concepts underlying his scheme of classification. Secondly, the work is encyclopedic in scope attempting to encompass 'Knowledge' in all its dimensions. Thirdly, his presentation of a subject/science is not general or theoretical, but is invariably supplemented by bibliographic information about authors and their books.

Tāshkopruzāde's work has other merits of its own. It preserves the intellectual legacy of Islamic civilization following the destruction of its nerve centre of Baghdad by the Mongols. It includes the achievements of the contemporary Ottoman period. His work had great impact on classification of knowledge subsequently. Haji Khalifa based his encyclopedic *Kashf al-Zunūn* essentially on the same principles.

In his work, the process of classification of knowledge reached the mature stage of being formulated into an independent discipline. Tāshkobruzāde gave it the name *'Ilm Taqāsīm al-'Ulūm* which, keeping in view his further observations, would mean 'The Science of Systematic Classification of Knowledge'. His definition (p.40) clearly indicates that Tāshkobruzāde conceived the classification of knowledge in itself as an independent science with a methodology of its own.

Though the books laid under reference in this publication constitute a representative cross-section of great Islamic books in all important areas of knowledge, (as reflected in the list of contents), they do not necessarily represent a unique selection in any manner. Also their presentation does not bring in any new information that is not already available in the different sources; neither the object is to give an exhaustive information on each book and its author. Only a brief introduction of each book and author has been attempted, and to make each account readable it has not been loaded with references and footnotes. An attempt has been made to note the full correct name of the author, the years of his birth and death or the period during which he flourished, his educational background and professional work so that the perspective of the authorship of the book can be better appreciated. The description has been confined to essential details. Wherever original statements and opinions have been cited, or their purport and substance provided, such expressions have been placed in single or double inverted commas.

It is necessary to clarify that this work is neither research oriented nor planned as a text book correct to a comma and a colon. The main objective is to introduce the author and the book as briefly as possible. For this purpose relevant information has been brought together and compiled in a simple readable form. As for as possible, information has been drawn from the original texts or their translated editions, and also from secondary sources and reference works.

The originality and the pioneering quality of the great books stand out prominently in the time frame, i.e. when their contribution is compared with previous or contemporary record. What may appear to be familiar and common place in this last quarter of the 20the century was entirely original representing great advance in human knowledge when these works were authored centuries ago. However, without any evocation of nostalgia, it may be stated that the great books of Islamic thought, culture and civilization, which are partly covered in this publication, present an achievement record of the early investigators and researcher, both scholars and scientists, which is absorbing enough to motivate modern inquisitive minds, particularly of the young, to higher intellectual attainments.

I am indebted to all those eminent authors whose works have enabled me to prepare the script of this book. Assistance received from different institutions, particularly the Suleymaniye Public Library Istanbul, the Zāhriyyah Library Damascus and the Royal Palace Library Rabat is gratefully acknowledged. My very best thanks are due to Sayyid Nafis Raqam, the most eminent *Kātib* of Pakistan, for having calligraphed the book titles.

N. A. Baloch

THE STANDARD WORK IN QURA'NIC STUDIES.

Al-Suyūtī

الإتقان في علوم القرآن

جلال الدين عبد الرحمن السيوطي

Jalal al-Dīn,' Abd al-Rahmān b. Abu Bakr al-Kamāl b. Muhammad Ibn Sābiq al-Dīn al-Suyūtī of Egypt, an encyclopedic versatile author, was born in Cairo in 949 A.H. (1445 A.D.) and died there in 911 A.H. (1505 A.D.). He received his education in Cairo, achieved reputation as *'fiqih,'hafiz* and *muhaddith,* and excelled his contemporaries in the compass of his knowledge. At the age of forty, he isolated himself, took his abode in Rauzat al-Miqyās on the Nile, and devoted himself to studying and writing. He would not accept invitations even from those in high authority, and would return with thanks if any gifts were received from them. Thus, in a state of single mindedness he authored as many as six hundred works on different subjects, Often he has included in his books relevant information from earlier sources which are now lost, and hence the importance of his works.

The Holy Quran, as the word of God revealed to the Holy Prophet, became centre of all attention by the believers during the life-time of the Prophet. All the verses revealed were written down and also committed to memory. The whole text was later meticulously transcribed and sent to all parts and provinces by the commandment of Caliph Uthmān (23-35 A.H.). Being the most authentic revealed book that placed all emphasis on KNOWLEDGE, the believers set their hearts on studying Holy Quran in detail. It became a source of knowledge by itself, and also simultaneously motivated the believer *to think, search and research, and seek more and more of knowledge.*

A beautifully transcribed manuscript of
AL-ITTIQĀN FI 'ULŪM AL-QURAN
(Amja Zade Huseyn, No. 4)
Suleymaniye G. Kutuphanesi,
TURKEY

وظلموا بأمر الحق مستكبرة ، واتفقوا لا دفعة بينهم مغترات مزورة ، كلما هديتهم الى الحق
كان اصم واعمى لهم ، كأن آيات الله لم تنزل كأنهم [illegible] يبسطون افواههم واشداقهم فالعالم
بينهم موجوم تتلاعب به الجهال والصبيان ، والكامل عندهم [illegible] والخليق لغة
النقصان ، وايم الله ان هذا هو الزمان الذي يلزم فيه السكوت ، والمصير حلسا
من احلاس البيوت ، ورد العلم الى العالم لولا ما ورد في صحيح الاخبار من علم علما
فكتمه الجمه الله بلجام من نار ، ولله در القائل

اداب على جمع الفضائل جاهدا ، وادوم لها تعب القريحة والجسد
واقصد بها وجه الاله ونفع من ، بلغته ممن جد فيها واجتهد
واترك كلام الحاسدين وبغيهم ، هملا فبعد الموت ينقطع الحسد

وانا اتضرع الى الله جل جلاله
وعز سلطانه كما من باتمام هذا الكتاب ان يتم النعمة بقبوله
وان يجعلنا من السابقين الاولين من اتباع رسوله ، وانه لا يخيب سعينا فهو الجواد
الذي لا يخيب من امله ، ولا يخذل من انقطع عمن سواه واملّه آمين آمين آمين

وهذا آخر الكتاب

قال مؤلفه رضي الله تعالى عنه وغفر عنه فرغت من تأليفه يوم السبت ثالث
عشر شوال سنة ثمانية وسبعين وثمانمائة [illegible]
[illegible] بعد ذلك والله تعالى الموفق للصواب
ولا حول ولا قوة الا بالله العلي العظيم
وصلى الله على سيدنا محمد واله
وصحبه وسلم تسليما
كتبه [illegible]

Colophone

AL-ITTIQĀN FI ‘ULŪM AL-QURAN

The Holy Quran came to be studied assiduously, and with devotion, from different angles, and this contributed to the development of 'Quranic Studies' which multiplied in number to such and extent that it called for more comprehensive works to encompass and systematize them. *Kitāb al-Murshid al-Wajīz ila 'Ulūm Tata'allaq bi Kitāb al-Azīz* (The Precise Guide to the Studies Related to the Sacred Book) was the first important work which was authored in the 7th century A.H. by Abu Shāmah al-Maqdisī (d. 665 A.H./1266 A.C.). In the next century, a more advanced work entitled "*al-Burhān fi 'Ulūm al-Qurān*" (A Clear Exposition of the Quranic Sciences) was written by Badr al-Din Al-Zarkashī (d. 794/1392). This book motivated al-Suyūtī to produce the much more comprehensive AL-ITTQIĀN about one hundred years later.

Al-Suyuti had given more time and special attention to the studies centering on Holy Quran, and authored more than half a dozen books in this field. Of these, his most important work was "*al-Ittiqān fi 'Ulūm al- Qur'ān*" ('The Standard Work on Qur'ānic Sciences'). He had first planned to write a voluminous commentary on Holy Qur'ān to be entitled as *Majma' al-Bahrayn wa Matla'al-Badrayn*, for which he first prepared an introduction entitled *al-Takhbīr fi 'Ulūm al-Tafsīr* and published it in 872 A.H./1367 A.C. Thereafter, when al-Zarkashī's work *al-Burhān fi 'Ulūm al-Qur'ān* came to his notice he revised and enlarged his *AL-TAKHBĪR* into *AL-ITTIQĀN*.

AL-ITTIQĀN deals elaborately with all those studies which concern the reading, writing and the understanding of Holy Quran. He gives a detailed exposition of *Hurūf*, *Kalimāt*, *Nuzūl*, *Awqāt*, *Arbāb*, the places of *Nuzul* (revelation), *Kitābat*, *I'jāz*, *I'rāf*, *Tajwīd*, *Nāsikh* and *Mansūkh*, and other disciplines derived from Holy Quran, and all those principles which help in understanding the Qur'anic laws. Finally, the science of *tafsir* and the grades of *mufassirūn* (commentators of the Holy Writ) are discussed. Thus, AL-ITTIQĀN excells all other works of this category in so far as it is comprehensive and covers all those studies which have been treated individually by other scholars.

THE MIRACLE OF THE QURAN.

Al-Baqillāni

إعجاز القرآن

القاضي أبو بكر بن محمد الباقلاني

Qadi Abū Bakr b. Muhammad b. al-Tayyib b. Muhammad b. Ja'far b. al-Qāsim al-Baqillāni (338-403 A.H.) was an illustrious scholar, a brilliant polemicist, Asha'arite theologian, Malikite Jurisconsult, and a prolific writer. He was born in Basra, flourished during the later half of the 4th century A.H., and died on 20 Dhu'l-Qa'dah 403/(5 June, 1013).

He authored fifty two books, of which six have survived. These works show that he took a bold stand on strengthening the Asha'arite theology of Islam and the Sunnite position on the Caliphate/Imamate. He was according to Ibn Taimiyya "the best of the Asha'arite *Mutakallimin* unrivalled by any predecessor or successor". In his book *Bayān*, he underlined the importance of validity of tradition and made an original contribution to the concept of apologetic miracle which vindicates the claim to prophethood. He devoted three of his works to the expsosition of the different aspects of the Holy Quran. His *Insāf*, besides defining the Sunnite theology, contains a comprehensive discussion of the increation of the Quran, while his another work *Intisār* deals mainly with the textual integrity of the Quran.

His *I'JAZ AL-QUR'AN* demonstrates the miracle of the Quran in its unexcelled power of expression and superb meaning for universal guidance. Qadi Abū Bakr's influence was profound and the impact of this particular work great. It has been cited continuously for centuries after him.

INTRODUCTION TO THE SCIENCE OF THE HADITH

Ibn al-Salāh

معرفة أنواع علم الحديث أو مقدمة ابن الصلاح

ابو عمرو عثمان بن عبد الرحمن المشهور بابن الصلاح

Taqi al-Din, Hafiz, Abu 'Amr 'Uthmān b. Salāh al-Din 'Abd al-Rahman b. Musa b. Uthmān al-Kurdī al-Shahrzūrī was born in 577 A.H./1181 A.D. at Sharkhān, a village of Irbil near Shahrzūr in Northern Iraq, and died in Damascus on the 24th of Rabi- II, 643 A. H. (1245 A. D.). His father 'Abd al-Rahmān was known by the title 'Salāh al-Din', and hence Abu 'Amr 'Uthmān later on became known as 'Ibn al-Salāh'. Personal attention of Abd al-Rahman Salāh al-Din who was himself an eminent scholar motivated his brilliant son to aspire for higher educational achievements. His father accompanied him to Mausal where he studied under eminent teachers. From there commenced his long pursuit of knowledge and the young scholar travelled to Baghdad, Hamadan, Nishapur, Merv, Damascus and Halb gaining advanced knowledge of the Hadith from highly qualified teachers.

Ibn Salāh finally returned to Damascus and was appointed as Professor of the Hadith at the Nāsirī College. Subsequently he also taught at the al-Ruwāhiya College in al-Quds, but when king al-Malik al-Ashraf established *Dār al-Hadīth*, a special institute for the teaching of the Hadith, in Damascus, Ibn al- Salāh was appointed as Rector and he held that position for thirteen years.

Abū 'Amr 'Uthmān Ibn al-Salāh excelled in *Tafsīr, Hadith, Fiqh, Rijāl* and other subjects. But it was mainly due to his accomplishment in the Hadith that only he was recognized as *al-Shaikh* so much so that this venerated title became synonymous with his name. Said al-Irāqī in a verse of his *Alfiya* says:

Whenever I use the word 'al-Shaikh'
I mean none else but Ibn al-Salāh.

Often, his highly qualified contemporaries turned to Ibn al-Salāh to acquire advanced knowledge of the Hadith from him. He was essentially an educator whose foremost concern in life was to disseminate knowledge, of the Hadith in particular. Ibn Salāh authored ten books of which the one that received universal recognition was *Ma'rafat Anwā'Ilm al- Hadīth* (literally 'Knowledge of the Different Aspects of the Science of the Hadith'). He completed this work on the last Friday of the month of Muharram in 634 A.H., and began teaching and dictating it two days later, with effect from Sunday the 2nd of Safar, so that he finished dictating the whole of it in the Ashrafiyya Hadith Institute (*'Dar al- Hadith').*

'The Hadith' being the record, reports and accounts of what the Prophet himself (*sal'am*) had said, done or approved, these were meticulously preserved by his Companions (Sahāba) who transmitted the same to the younger generation and they, in turn, to the succeeding generations. The Qur'ān and the Hadīth were the two indispensable and inseparatable sources of divine guidance to enable the growing Islamic community to manage their affairs; but, while the text of the Qur'ān was available in writing, the Hadith accounts were being transmitted orally. Therefore, it became necessary not only to codify the Hadith in its entirety, but also to subject the process of transmission as well as the transmitted texts to severe evaluatory criticism in order to identify those records and reports which were absolutely authentic. Accordingly, studies were conducted on the different aspects of the subject to determine the veracity of the reports and the authenticity of the reported texts. Those studies which led to fruitful conclusions were recognized as *'Ulūm al-Hadīth*, i.e. the specific knowledge areas or studies falling within the domain of *'Ilm al-Hadith* or 'Science of Hadith'. Through intensive inquiries and painstaking research by the most knowledgeable scholars, the different disciplines (e.g. *'Ilm al-Rijāl* or biographical knowledge of the Hadith reporters, *Isnād* or the continuity of the chain of reporters, and *Jurh wa Ta'dīl* or screening and confrontation) were evolved and the whole apparatus

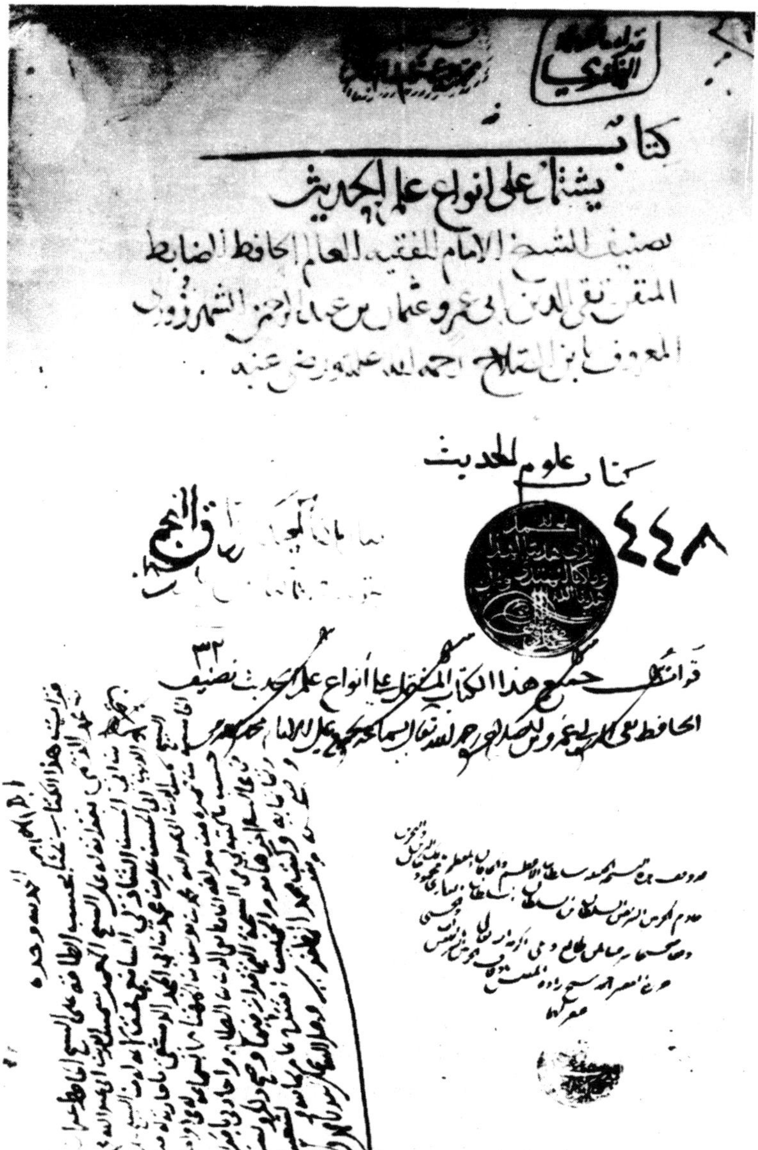

One of the earliest manuscripts of
MUQADDIMAH IBN AL-SALĀH
dated 8 Shaʿban 640 A.H.
(Ayasophia, No. 448)
TURKEY

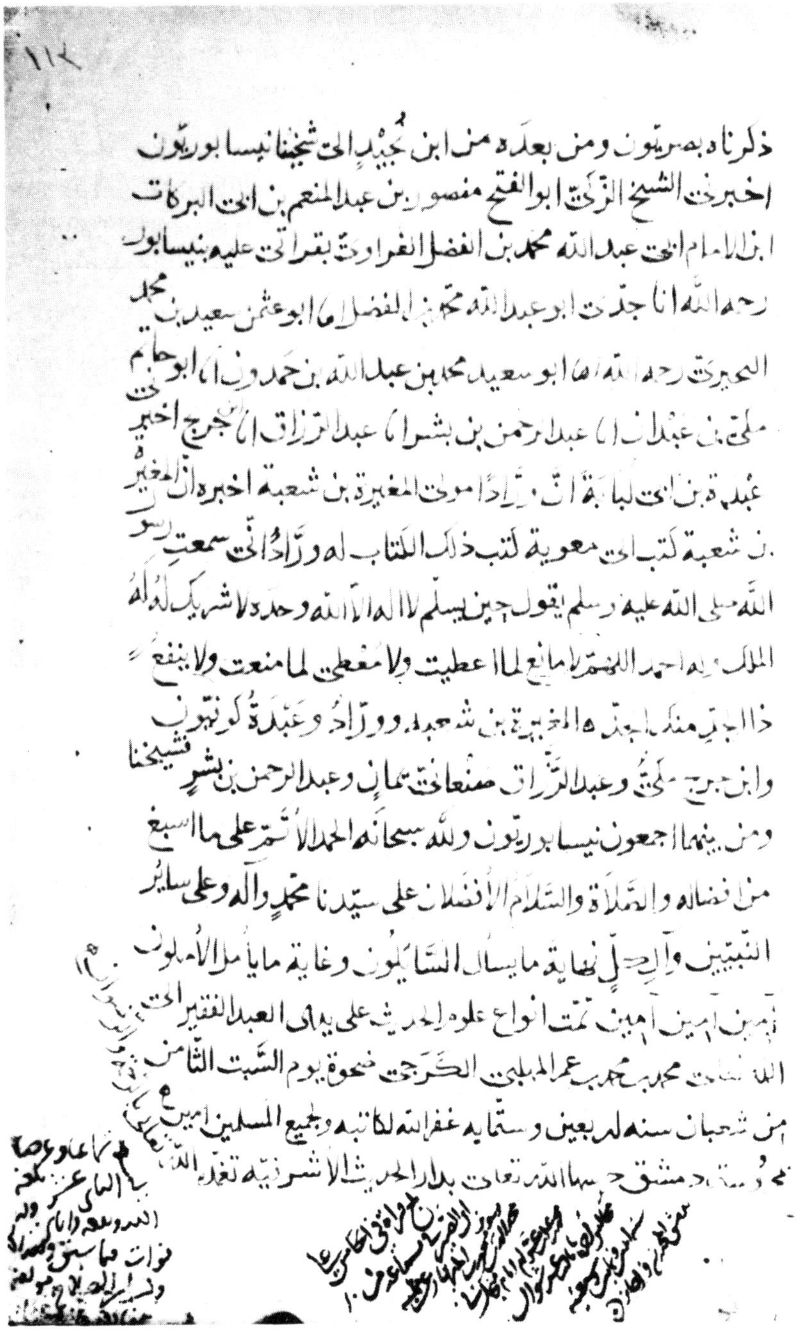

١١٧

ذكرناه بصريون ومن بعده من ابن جريج الى شيخنا نيسابوريون
اخبرني الشيخ الزكي ابو الفتح منصور بن عبد المنعم بن ابي البركات
ابن الامام ابي عبد الله محمد بن الفضل الفراوي بقراءتي عليه بنيسابور
رحمه الله انا جدي ابو عبد الله محمد بن الفضل انا ابو عثمن سعيد بن محمد
البحيري رحمه الله انا ابو سعيد محمد بن عبد الله بن حمدون انا ابو حامد
مكي بن عبدان انا عبد الرحمن بن بشر انا عبد الرزاق انا ابن جريج اخبرني
عبدة بن ابي لبابة ان ورادا مولى المغيرة بن شعبة اخبره ان المغيرة
بن شعبة كتب الى معوية كتب ذلك الكتاب له وراد اني سمعت رسول
الله صلى الله عليه وسلم يقول حين يسلم لا اله الا الله وحده لا شريك له له
الملك وله الحمد اللهم لا مانع لما اعطيت ولا معطي لما منعت ولا ينفع
ذا الجد منك الجد المغيرة بن شعبة ووراد وعبدة كوفيون
وابن جريج مكي وعبد الرزاق صنعاني يماني وعبد الرحمن بن بشر فشيخنا
ومن بينهما اجمعون نيسابوريون ولله سبحانه الحمد الاتم على ما اسبغ
من افضاله والصلاة والسلام الافضلان على سيدنا محمد واله وعلى ساير
النبيين وال كل نهاية ما يسال السائلون وغاية ما يامل الاملون
امين امين امين تمت انواع علوم الحديث على يدي العبد الفقير الى
الله تعالى محمد بن محمد بن عمر الحنبلي الكرجي ضحوة يوم السبت الثامن
من شعبان سنة اربعين وستماية غفر الله لكاتبه ولجميع المسلمين امين
بمدينة دمشق حرسها الله تعالى بدار الحديث الاشرفية تغمد الله

Colophone
MUQADDIMAH OF IBN AL-SALĀH

of criticism was established to identify the specific evaluatory criteria, to apply them judiciously, and to differentiate and classify the Hadith record and reports in terms of their authenticity.

Some of the 'Principles' which had been enunciated in the early juridical works, such as *al-Risālah* of Imam *al- Shāfi'ī* and *Kitāb al-'Ilal* of al- Tirmidhī, laid the foundation for the later independent studies with which developed a full-fledged 'Science of the Hadith' known as *'Ilm Usūl al-Hadīth* or *Mustalah al- Hadīth.*

Ibn Hajar in his *Nukhbat al-Fikr* has referred to the developmental history of this science. The book *al-Muhaddith al-Fāsil bayn al-Rāwī wa al-Wā'ī* authored by Qadi Abu Muhammad al-Hasan b. 'Abd al-Rahmān b. Khalād al- Rāmhurmuzī (d. circa 360 A.H.) was the first independent work which brought together all that had been said before him on the subject. Thereafter al-Hākim, Abu Abdullah Muhammad b. Abdullah (d. 405) of Nishapur wrote his *'Ulūm al-Hdīth* in which he identified fifty graded types of the Hadith on the basis of the evaluatory criteria. Abu Nu'aym Ahmad b. Abdullah al-Sūfī al- Isbahānī (336-430 A.H.) examined al-Hākim's work and included relevant material from it in his own book *al-Mustakhraj*, but he had his shortcomings which came under criticism subsequently. In the latter half of the 5th century, the eminent al-Khatīb Abū Bakr Ahmad b. Ali al-Baghdādi (d. 463 A.H.) wrote two important works, *al-Kāfiya fi Qawānīn al- Riwāyah wa Qawā'idhā* and *Al- Jāmi' li Adāb al-Shaikh wa al-Sāmi* which subsequently became the main source of reference for the later scholars. Then, in the 6th century Qazi Iyād (d. 544 A.H.) in his *Kitāb al-Ilmā'* and Abu Hafs 'Umar al-Mayānaji (d. 580) in his *Mā lā Yasma'al-Muhaddith Jihlhu* advanced the studies further.

In 634 A.H. (1236 A.D.), Ibn Salāh authored his standard work on the subject which became popularly known as *Muqaddimah Ibn Salāh*, i.e. 'Ibn Salāh's Introduction' (to the Science of the Hadith). Ibn Salāh had studied the works of his predecessors, particularly of al-Khatīb, and brought together in his book all the relevant material on the subject which was hitherto scattered in different sources. He differentiated and classified sixty five types of the Hadith with reference to the criteria of authenticity. Because of its comprehensiveness and clarity, scholars set their heart on his *Muqaddimah*, studied it assiduously, and wrote their own books in the footsteps of Ibn al-Salāh. Thus, *al-Nu'awi* produced two scholarly summaries *(al-Irshād* and *al-Taqrīb)* of the *Muqaddimah,* al-'Irāqī (Zayn al-dīn) versified it in his *Alfiyah*, others elaborated upon the *Muqaddimah* suggesting improvements (thus, Hafiz al- Mughaltā'i in his *Islāh Ibn al-Salāh)*, and still others brought it under reference raising questions and seeking clarifications. Then came Ibn Hajr (743-852 A.H.) who did what Ibn Salāh had done earlier. In his *Nukhbat al-Fikr*, Ibn Hajar reproduced the substance of Ibn Salāh's *Muqaddimah* as well as of all the other works authored subsequently, edited the whole material systematically with his own annotations and observations. His *Nukhbat* became popular and was studied and commented upon subsequently, and yet Ibn Salāh's *Muqaddimah* remained a standard work on the subject, a landmark in the history of the Science of the Hadith.

THE BOOK OF FLASHES OF SUFISM.

Abu Nasr al-Sarrāj

كتاب اللمع في التصوف

أبو النصر عبد الله بن علي السراج الطوسي

Abu Nasr, 'Abdullah b. 'Ali b. Muhammad b. Yahyā, al-Sarrāj al-Tusi, whose family had a long line of Sufis, was a highly admired and revered Sufi of his times, affectionately called *Tāwūs al-Fuqarā'* ('The Peacock of the Poor'). He flourished in the 4th century and died in the month of Rajab, 378 A.H. (988 A.D.).

Abu Nasr Abdullah studied with his father and other eminent teachers, became a teacher himself, and other scholars studied with him. He endeared himself to all by his simple and sincere living and his complete devotion to the *Shari'ah*. Other Sufi *Mashā'ikh* (Guides) of his times considered him as their *Faqqīh*.

His book Al-Luma' is of great merit for its brief exposition of the doctrines of *tasawwuf* in the light of Holy Quran and the Sunnah of the Holy Prophet. According to him, strict adherence to the *Sharī'ah* laws enables one to attain the status of a true sufi. His illuminating discourses make *Al-Luma'* one of the earliest and the most reliable works on Sufism.

In *Kitāb al-Luma'* al-Sarrāj has given a comprehensive exposition of the Sufi attitude and way of life by presenting the widest possible concensus in the views of as many as forty-one respectable authorities. This much quantum of knowledge of the Sufi way of life is not to be found in any other contemporary sources - a distinctive feature that makes *Kitāb al-Luma'* the most valuable sources of early information on Sufism. According to al-Sarrāj, the term 'Sufi' was derived from sūf, the course woollen cloth worne by the Sufis. He regards Holy Quran and the Sunnah as the foundational source of Sufism.

The work contains highly mystical expressions which cannot be elucidated by logical reasoning but which can only be realized in experience by those who are spiritually advanced. This work has been used as a very precious source of guidance in the later works of the Sufis.

THE ALCHEMY OF HAPPINESS

Al-Ghazzālī

کیمیای سعادت

ابو حامد محمد ابن محمد الغزالی

Abu Hāmid Muhammad al-Ghazzali was born in Tūs in 450 A.H. (1058).Left as an orphan in his childhood, he took to schooling seriously. He studied under different teachers of whom the most eminent was *Imam al- Harmayn* al-Juwayni with whom he continued his studies until the great teacher died in 478 (1085). Further, through self education, he became an accomplished theologian and jurist, original thinker of great vision, and religious reformer with an unequalled power of pursuation. For sometime he served as Rector at the Nizamia College of Baghdad, but then chose to be by himself to advance in his own spiritual development. He spent eleven years in meditation and self-appraisal, and through deep personal experience opted for the Sufi way of life. This period was not of retirement from work for him but of intensive creative activity. Of about 404 books ascribed to him, many were written during this period. On being persuaded to return to academic life, he taught for sometime at the Nizamiyyah College at Nayasbur (499/1106). Later he returned to Tus where he had founded a *Khānqah*, and undertook to educate and guide disciples in the Sufi way of life. He died there in Jumada II, 505 (December, 1111).

It was during the decade of his independent studies after departing from the Nizamiyyah College, that he authored his monumental work *Ihyā' 'Ulūm al-Dīn*, ("The Revival of the Religious Sciences"). Essentially a great teacher excelling in the art of communication and power of pursuation, it became a life mission for al-Ghazzali to educate and enlighten his fellow beings in the most fruitful and spiritual-

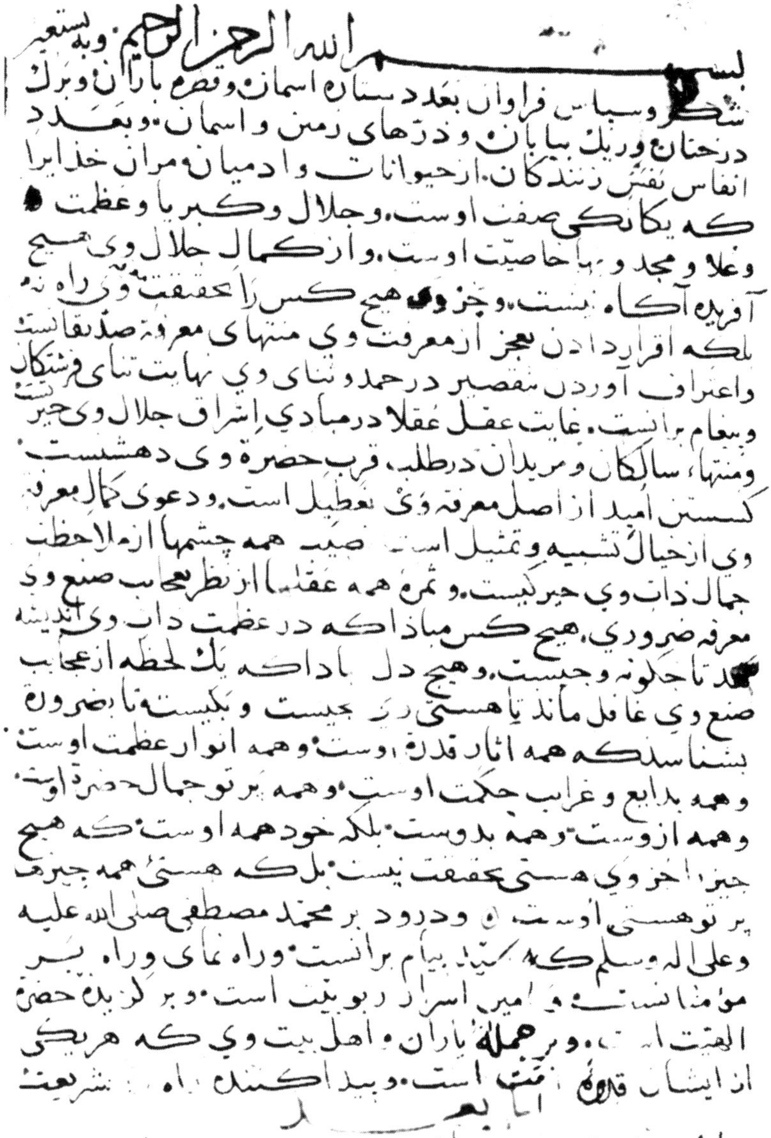

بسم الله الرحمن الرحيم وبه نستعين
شکر وسپاس فراوان بعدد ستارگان آسمان وقطره باران وبرگ
درختان وریگ بیابان وذره‌های زمین وآسمان، وبعدد
انفاس نفس زنندگان از حیوانات وآدمیان، مر آن خدای را
که یگانگی صفت اوست، وجلال وکبریا وعظمت
وعلا ومجد وبها خاصیت اوست، واز کمال جلال وی هیچ
آفریده آگاه نیست، وجز وی هیچ کس را حقیقت معرفت وی راه نه
بلکه اقرار دادن بعجز از معرفت وی منتهای معرفت صدیقانست
واعتراف آوردن بتقصیر در حمد وثنای وی نهایت ثنای فرشتگان
وپیغامبرانست. غایت عقل عقلا در مبادی اشراق جلال وی حیرت
ومنتهای سالکان ومریدان در طلب قرب حضرت وی دهشت
گسستن امید از اصل معرفت وی تعطیل است، ودعوی کمال معرفت
وی از خیال تشبیه وتمثیل است. نصیب همه چشمها از ملاحظت
جمال ذات وی خیرگیست، وثمره همه عقلها از نظر عجایب صنع وی
معرفت ضروری. هیچ کس مبادا که در عظمت ذات وی اندیشه
کند تا چگونه وچیست، وهیچ دل مبادا که یک لحظه از عجایب
صنع وی غافل ماند تا هستی وی چیست وبکیست تا بضرورت
بشناسد که همه آثار قدرت اوست، وهمه انوار عظمت اوست
وهمه بدایع وغرایب حکمت اوست، وهمه پرتو جمال حضرت اوست
وهمه از وست، وهمه بدوست، بلکه خود همه اوست، که هیچ
چیز را جز وی هستی بحقیقت نیست، بلکه هستی همه چیز
پرتو هستی اوست. ودرود بر محمد مصطفی صلی الله علیه
وعلی آله وسلم که سید پیغامبرانست، وراه نمای وراه بر
مؤمنانست، وامین اسرار ربوبیت است، وبرگزیده حضرت
الهیت است، وبر جمله یاران واهل بیت وی که هریکی
از ایشان قدوه امت است، وپیدا کننده راه شریعت
اما بعد
بدانکه حقیقت آدمی را ببازی وهرزه نیافریده اند

A beautifully transcribed manuscript of
KĪMYĀ-i SA'ĀDAT
(Chelebi Abdullah, No. 185)
Suleymaniye G. Kutuphanesi,
TURKEY

ly satisfying way of life. This mission was adequately fulfilled in the precious pages of AL-IHYA, a great work of all times which he had written mainly for advanced readers. Later he wrote a complimentary work, *Iljām al-Awwām* for the general reader.

Ihyā' 'Ulūm al-Dīn is authored according to a well planned scheme of the four main parts, each one further sub-divided into ten books. The four quarter parts deal with *Ibādāt* (worship and prayers), *'Adāt* (social customs), *Muhlikāt* (the destructive acts), and *Munjiyat* (the virtuous acts leading to salvation). Thus, it is a complete guide on all aspects of religious life - prayers and worship, daily social conduct, avoidance of vice and error and self-purification, and the virtuous *sufi* way of life. In main, AL- IHYA was intended to lift the believer from the mere form of religiosity to the true spirit of religious life.

The substance and mission of AL-IHYA was important but, as was seen by al- Ghazzali himself, it was voluminous enough for the average reader. Therefore, he made a digest of it in his *Kitāb al-Arba'īn* which is divided into forty sections comparable to the forty books of AL-IHYA though not corresponding with them sequence-wise. The main abridgment*, as such, of AL-IHYA was made by the author later in its Persian version entitled *Kīmyā-i- Sa'ādat* (The Al-chemy of Happiness). This work is not a literal translation of AL-IHYA but a sort of new edition presenting substance and essence of AL-IHYA as visualized by the great author himself.

The complete original manuscript of AL-IHYA has not survived, and the present text based on the extent manuscripts is only as complete as it could be. In comparison, *Kīmyā-i Sa'ādat* is a complete text in itself and, as such, a more authentic presentation of al-Ghazzali's teachings.

---

* Al-Ghazzali's brother Ahmad, and an eminent scholar and Sufi in his own right, had also prepared an abridged version of AL-IHYA, which has not survived.

THE BOOK ON REFINEMENT OF CONDUCT.

Ibn Miskwayh

تهذيب الأخلاق

ابو علي احمد بن محمد بن يعقوب مسكويه

Abu Ali Ahmad b. Muhammad b. Ya'qūb Miskawayh was born some time during the second quarter of the fourth century of Hijra (10th A.C.) in (the province of?) Rayy and flourished in Isfahan at the court of the Buwayhid rulers, and rose to prominence particularly during the reigns of 'Adud al-Dawlah and Bahā' al-Dawlah. He died in Isfahan at a very old age in 421 A.H. (1030 A.D.).

Initially Ibn Miskawayh devoted himself to philosophy, logic, alchemy and medicine, but then turned to history, penmanship and literature. His voluminous work *Kitāb Tajārib al-Umam* ('The Book of Experiences of Nations') is a universal history down to the death of 'Adud al-Dawlah (982-83 A.H./372-73 A.D.). It was noted for its comprehensive use of all available sources, and it greatly stimulated further development of Islamic historiography.

As a thinker, Ibn Miskawayh made the best of his contribution in Ethics by authoring his *Kitāb Tahdhīb al- Akhlāq* (The Book on Refinement of Conduct).

Islamic ethical literature is rich and varied, and *Tahdhīh al-Akhlāq* occupies an important position in a particular branch of ethical literature. One stream of this literature belongs specifically to the religious and legal tradition and is based on Holy Quran and the Prophet's precepts. The other is of a literary nature and is embodied in poems, sayings and fables, derived from the different traditions of the Muslim society-its aim being cultivation of *adab* in the broad sense of culture and also refinement of manners. Another stream springs from the mystical attitude and experience and is represented by the Sufis' way of life as enunciated particularly in the works of the Sufis. Still anothor stream, and an important one, is philosophical in character and is historically related to the Greek philosophico-ethical tradition. In the earlier terminology this branch came to be specifically called *'ILm al-Akhlāq* (The Science of Ethics), and was reckoned as a part of *al-'Hikmat al-Amaliyah* (Practical Philosophy). Ibn Miskwayh's work is a *Tahdhīb* or a streamlining and reconstructuring of the traditional *'Ilm al-Akhlāq* in the light of Islamic precepts and ideals.

As seen by George Sarton, Ibn. Miskwayh's work is "the best specimen of Neo-Platonic ethics composed by a Muslim".* As explained by the author himself, the main objective of this work is to train the soul and mind to produce all good actions with ease and comfort. Such a training urges us to know our souls as to what they are, what is their nature, for what purpose they have been brought into being, and the extent of perfection and the faculties and innate habits they can achieve so that when we employ them properly we can achieve success and high positions as Allah Himself may guide us.

The book is divided into five parts. To begin with Ibn Miskwayh explains that SOUL is of a spiritual nature and, therefore, as an independent and immortal entity it stands on a higher plane than the mutable substance of the body. Besides having desire, impulse and reason, the Soul has four principal virtues: prudence or temperance, courage, wisdom, and the combination of the three. The second part treats of man's natural disposition of habituation and education, and the rules of good breeding. The third part treats of the supreme good and happiness. It is most rewarding to live a moral and happy life in the community and the state. The fourth part deals with justice. In the fifth part the themes are love and friendship. The models of worship prescribed by Islam foster the sense of brotherhood and universal love of mankind. The concluding section discusses health and sickness of the Soul.

---

* Sarton, George: *History of Science*, Vol. I. p. 687.

THE BOOK ON RELIGIOUS SECTS AND SCHOOLS.

Al-Shahrastānī

كتاب الملل والنحل

محمد بن عبد الكريم الشهرستاني

Abu'l-Fath Muhammad b. Abd al-Karim Ahmad al-Shahrastānī was born in 469 A.H. (1076/1077) at Shahrastān in the province of Khurāsān. He received his education in Jurjāniyah and Nishapur, and as a scholar he excelled in his knowledge of Hadith, Law and Jurisprudence, became a distinguished theologian in the Asha'arite system, and was respected and honoured as 'Imam'. He was also a leading philosopher of his times. He taught for three years at the Nizamiyyah college of Baghdad, but then returned to Shahrastān where he died in the year 548 A.H. (1153 A.D.).

Al-Shahrāstānī authored a number of books on different subjects, of which atleast 17 are known. Mainly he wrote on Islamic faith and belief *(aqā'id),* dialectics *(kalām)* and comparative religion. In philosophy, he wrote three works:(i) 'Doubts of Aristotle and Ibn Sina And Their Critique' (*Shubhāt Aristātālis wa Ibn Sina wa Naqduhā*), (ii) 'Disputations among Philosophers' (*Musāra'at al- Falāsifa*), and (iii) History of Philosophy (*Tarīkh al-Hukamā'*).

Al-Shahrastānī's contribution in the field of comparative religion was most advanced and important. As a devoted Muslim of strong faith, he was much concerned with the purity of Islamic belief, and as a philosopher with the belief and faith of mankind. To dispel superstitions, he wrote two works 'Sutlities of Superstitions' *(Daqā'iq al-Auhām)* and "Extremity of Superstitions" *(Nihāyat al- Auhām).* On Comparative Religion, besides his famous *al- Milal wa Nihal,* he also wrote another work "A Brief Classification of Religions of Mankind"

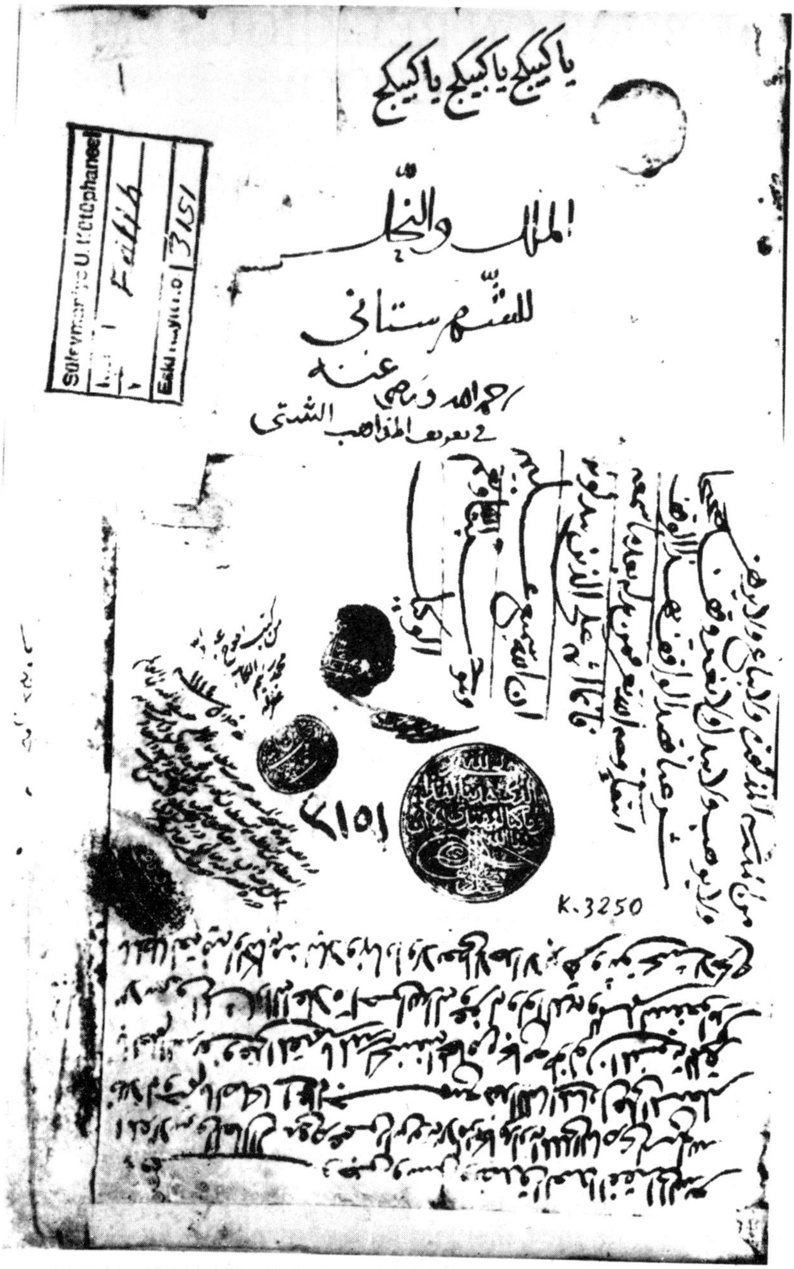

One of the earliest manuscript of
KITAB AL-MILAL WA AL-NIHAL
Transcribed in Ramadan 593 A.H.
(Fātih, No. 1351)
Suleymaniye G. Kutuphanesi,
TURKEY

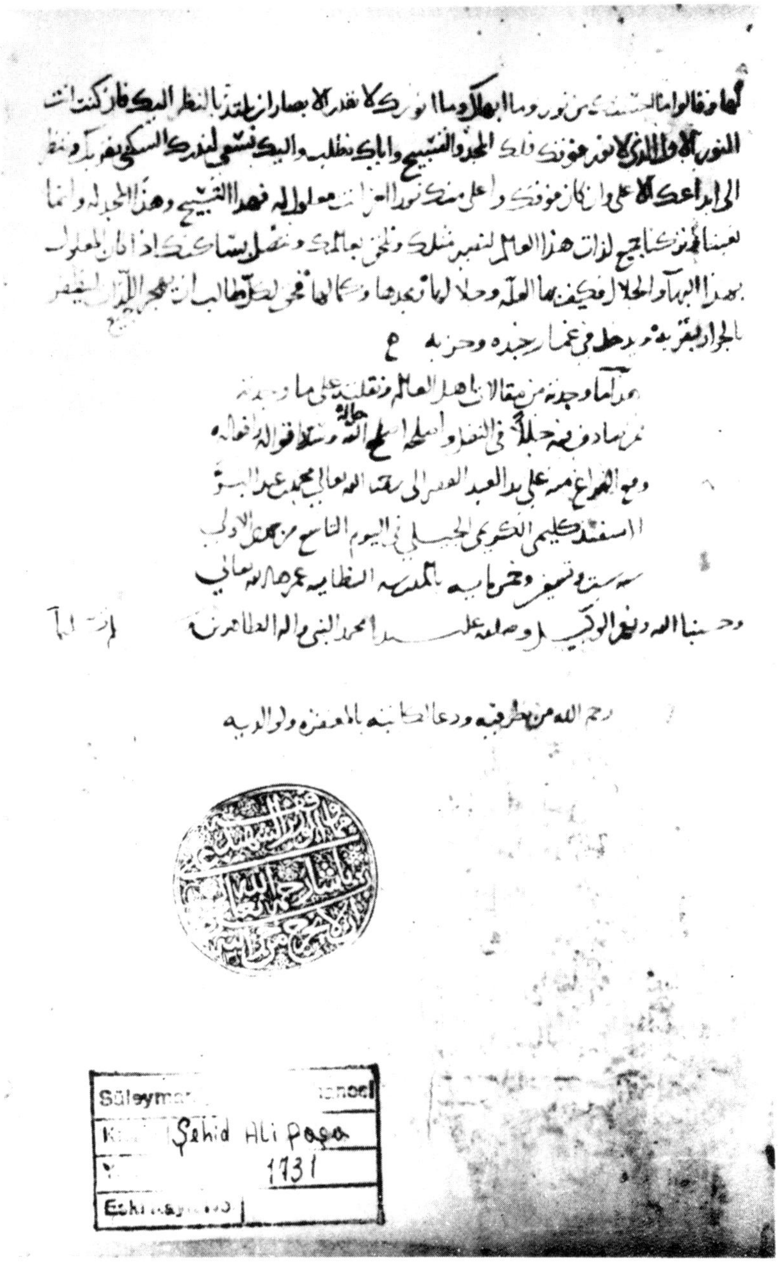

Another copy of
KITAB AL-MILAL WA AL-NIHAL
9 Jumada-I 596 A.H.
(Shahid Ali Pasha, No.1731)
TURKEY

(Talkhīs al-Aqsām li Madhāhib al- Anām).

His chief work "The Book of Religious Sects and Schools" was written in 1127-28 A.D. The first part of the text contains an account of the sects of Islam; then of the peoples of scripture, the Jews and Christians; and lastly of those of dubious revelation, the Madgians and the Manichaeans. The second part deals with the Sabians, Greek, Muslim, Chiristian, and the Arabic philosophy, specially the system of Ibn Sina; and finally with the religions of the Arabs before Islam and of the people of India.

Comparative studies of religious sects had been made earlier by some qualified scholars such as Baghdadi in his work 'Difference Between Different Sects', but these studies reached their climax in al-Shahrastānī's work. In his *Tabaqāt al- Shāfi'iya al-Kubrā*, the venerable author Subki has recorded his unqualified opinion to the effect that al- Shahrastānī's *Kitab al-Milal wa al-Nihal* was in his view "the best book in this field".

THE DETAILED TREATISE ON MATTERS CONCERNING LEARNERS AND GUIDELINES FOR TEACHERS AND LEARNERS.

Al-Qābisī

الرسالة المفصلة لأحوال المتعلمين وأحكام المعلمين

ابو الحسن علي بن محمد بن خلف القابسي

The author Abu al-Hasan Ali b. Muhammad b. Khalaf was born in Qairawān (Tunisia) on 6 Rajab, 324 A.H. (May, 936 A.D.). His family originally belonged to the village of al-Mu'āfirīn in the suburbs of the town of Qābis (not very far from the city of Qairawān). As such, he became more widely known as al- Qābisī, but was also referred to by the *nisba* of his village as *al-Mu'āfirī al- Qābisī*, or even as *al-Qairawānī* since he was born and brought up in Qairawān. He completed his studies under eminent teachers of Qairawān which was then an important educational centre. Thereafter, as a mature scholar of 28 he travelled to 'Mashriq' (the Muslim East), performed pilgrimage in 353 A.H., and engaged himself in advanced studies in the Hadith under renowned teachers, first in Makka Mukarrama and then on return in Sikandariya in Egypt. He was back in Qairawān in Sha'bān 357 A.H. where he took to the teaching profession. A large number of pupils who studied under him became eminent scholars of their times. He died on Wednesday night, the 3rd of Rabi-al-Ākhar, 403 A.H. (1012 A.D.). He was a man of good faith and piety, devoted to prayers, friendly to all and helpful to the needy and poor.

In his biographical notices, Qābisī has been mentioned as being "the foremost in different sciences" (*taqaddumhu fi al- 'ulūm*, according to al-Dhahbī), and excelling particularly in the science of Hadith.

He authored a number of books (13 or 14 as mentioned by some) of which at least nine or ten are more certainly to have been composed by him on different subjects such as Hadith, Fiqh, Correct Belief, Education and Pilgrimage.

By vocation, Qābisi was essentially a teacher who taught for about five decades and gained insights and understandings into the process of teaching and learning as also into the needs and requirements of students and teachers. Besides, the tradition of pedagogy and professional education had already been established in *Maghrib* (the Muslim West) a century earlier, under the leadership of the Mālikite Jurists. Abd al- Salām b. Sa'īd b. Habīb known as 'Sahnūn' (d. 240 A.H.) had authored *Kitāb al-Mudavvana,* the foremost code of Malikite Jurisprudence, and set an example in 'Maghrib' in the realm of higher learning and scholarship. His son Muhammad who died in 256 A.H., wrote a treatise on 'The Responsibilities of Teachers' (*Ādāb al-Mu'allimīn*) which gave an impetus to further development in the field of pedagogy. Sahnūn's work inspired Qābisi who elaborated upon the subject in his own book in the light of his long teaching experience and practical observations.

Qabisi wrote *al-Risāla al-Mufissila li Ahwāl al-Mua'llimīn wa al-Muta'llimīn* (The Detailed Treatise on Matters Concerning Learners and Guidelines for Teachers and Learners) in which he placed special emphasis on childhood education, the main educational objective being to enable the pupil to develop as a good Muslim in belief and in action. The entire text and the ideas involved are presented in a 'Question-Answer' form. As an accomplished teacher, al-Qabisi used to emphasise that questions be raised by the students. He would cite the example of great teacher Abu al- Abbās who during his lectures used to analyse the issues involved threadbare, who preferred student-teacher discussion in order to advance knowledge, and who would always say "Relieve us from mere listening: come up with the problems" *(da'onā min al-simā': alqao al- masā'il).*

Qabisi's work is divided into three parts as under:-

Part-I. Introduction. Explanation as to what is *Īmān, Islām* and

Ihsān; what is *Istiqāma* and what is the definition of *Salāh*. Excellences of the Quran, and the formalities to be observed in its learning.

Part-II. Teaching of the Quran and the parents' responsibility. Instruction in poetry, calligraphy, grammar, recitation. Remunerating the teacher. Teacher's conduct. Importance of teacher's personal attitude to pupils. The different aspects of capital punishment, and being lenient to pupils. Maintaining justice and equality between pupils, and looking after their welfare. Preventing them from hurting each other. Friday and other holidays.

Part-III. The teacher and his responsibilities. Gifts for teachers. Full-time attention to teaching. Teacher's illness. Cooperative teaching by the teachers etc., etc.

Thus, besides his other advanced views, Qābisī was the inventor of the concept and practice of 'Co-operative Teaching by the Teachers' which has been realised only in some of the modern educational systems in the 20th century.

INSTRUCTION OF THE LEARNER: THE METHOD OF LEARNING.

Al-Zarnūjī

تعليم المتعلم طريق التعلم

برهان الدين الزرنوجي

The author Burhanuddin belonged to the town of Zarnūj near Bukhara, and hence was known as al-Zarnūjī. He was a pupil of the well-known Hanafite Jurisprudent Burhanuddin al-Marghinānī, the author of HIDĀYĀ. Zarnūjī flourished as an eminent Jurisprudent, but he was a great teacher deeply interested in the problem and process of formal education.

In 1203 A.D., he authored the important treatise *Ta'līm al-Muta -a'llim Tarīq al-Ta'allum* ('Instruction of the Learner: The Method of Learning'). Except for some casual observations (probably arising out of the local lore and folk wisdom*) not directly related to the process of education, this work may be regarded historically as the first significant contribution in the theory and practice of Professional Education.

Zarnūjī's work represents a landmark in the history of Pedagogy in the Muslim East up to the turn of the 12th century. Its popularity in the Islamic countries is attested by the fact that not only has it survived in a large number of manuscripts but also it has been printed again and again (in Istanbul, Cairo, Bombay, etc.). In Europe, it was translated into Latin, and also the text was printed in Leipzig in 1838.

As a work of merit in the field of professional education, it was

---

* E.g. eating of the seeds of coriander and sour apples or passing from in between a file of camels being the causes of foregetfulness. Obviously, the first was not good for health while the second impaired one's safety.

studied as a text book by teachers for four centuries. During the 10th century A.H. (16th A.D.), as many as three commentaries were written on it. The book is divided into the following thirteen chapters:-

I. The nature and merit of knowledge and study.

II. Purpose of study.

III. The student's choice of the subject, the teacher, and of the student associates in continued companionship.

IV. Respecting knowledge and those who possess it.

V. Effort and perseverance in study.

VI. Undertaking the study: its method and organization.

VII. Placing one's faith in God.

VIII. The time for acquisition of knowledge.

IX. Helping and counselling.

X. The means which promote attainment of knowledge.

XI. Abstinence from evil during pursuit of learning.

XII. What creates memory and what brings about forgetfulness.

XIII. Factors which promote or prevent earning of livelihood and those that prolong or diminish one's longevity.

The author's concept underlying the scheme of this treatise is that of the 'whole' education of the learner rather than his mere academic attainment. He recognizes and extols moral purpose in learning. His presentation clearly distinguishes between 'Knowledge' and 'Education', the former as a general quality of mind and the latter as a 'teaching-learning process', and also underlines some of the important concepts of educational psychology. The role of effort, aspiration, pursuit and persistence in student achievement is underlined and stressed.

THE DISCOURSE OF LISTENER AND SPEAKER ON THE ETIQUETTE OF LEARNING AND LEARNER.

Ibn Jamāʻah

تذكرة السامع والمتكلم في أدب العالم والمتعلم

القاضي بدر الدين بن أبي إسحق إبراهيم ابن جماعة

The author Qādī al-Qudāt, Shaikh al-Islām, Badr al-Din Muhammad b. Ibrahim b. S'adullah Ibn Jamā'ah was born in the family of the Arab stock of Kinānahat Hamā (Syria) in Rabi- II, 639 A.H. (1241 A.D.). Hence he is also known as 'al-Kinānī al-Hamavī'. He was educated at Hamā, achieved excellence in religious studies and jurisprudence, and became an exponent of the Shafi'ite legal system (hence known as 'al-Shafi'ī). Eventually, he attained the high status of *Shaikh al-Islam* and held the high position of Chief Justice (*Qadi al-Qudāt*). Dhahbi has observed that Qadi Ibn Jamā'ah was well versed both in prose and poetry, and had left copious notes *(ta'āliq)* on *Fiqh, Hadith, Usul al-Fiqh,* and *Tarikh*. He commanded respect and influence, and had a large number of students and followers. He died at Cairo in Jumada-I in the year 733 A.H. (1332 A.D.), aged 94, and was buried by the side of the great Imam Shāfi'ī.

Not much is known about his biographical details but the study of his book *Tadhkirat al-Sāmi' wa al-Mutakallim fi Adab al- 'Ālim wa al-Muta'allim* ('The Discourse of Listener And Speaker on the Etiquette of Learning and of Learner') would indicate that he was closely associated with the teaching profession and was fully aware of academic life and work of teachers and pupils in educational institutions. It was in the year 672 A.H. (1273 A.C.) that Qādī Ibn Jamā'ah completed his

TADHKIRAH as a guide for students and teachers to help improve quality of their academic life and work.

The book is divided into the following five chapters:-

I. Superiority of knowledge and the exalted position of those who possess it, and of the learned.

II. Qualifications of the teacher - how he should conduct himself and his classes, and treat his students.

III. The manner of the student - by himself, and in his relationship with the teacher who guides him and with his fellow-students.

IV. Being in company of books and the related obligations.

V. Etiquette of residence in the Madrasahs, for the beginners and for the seniors.

Ibn Jamāʻah places a high premium on personal and professional qualifications of the teacher, his main responsibility being the promotion of student welfare and advancement of knowledge. He must shun pride and arrogance, should meet people with a smiling face, help the needy and hold students in affection.

In methodology of teaching, Ibn Jamāʻah has attached special importance to the teacher's class discussion - and hence, probably, 'Speaker' and 'Listener' being the two key words in the title of his book. He recommends that the teacher should encourage students to ask questions, and help them to formulate their questions properly. He urges the student that when he asks a question he should do so politely without any affront to the teacher. The teacher should not be satisfied merely by giving a lecture but he must assure himself that the students have followed. However, to ascertain this he should not put direct questions: rather during the course of a new lecture he should raise questions the answers to which would involve previous knowledge. If a student is shy and sensitive, response may be elicited by indirect questions, so that the student does not feel that he is being subjected to a test.

Instruction should commence with simple manuals. The teacher should motivate students in the best possible manner and create in them love for knowledge.

When a student comes for admission, the teacher should first assess his capacity. Also the teacher must fix the class hours according to the convenience of students, and that the teacher should not be paid if he would teach either before sun-rise or in late afternoons.

Appointment of the teacher should be made very carefully. No person other than an authority in the subject should be permitted to teach it. If any leniency is shown in this matter, it will be a mockery of religion and learning, and a fraud played upon the people.

Sincerity of purpose and clean personal conduct are essential for the student to succeed in the programme of studies. He should exercise moderation both in eating and sleeping. He should accommodate the teacher, should not feel shy in asking questions but should raise questions politely and should not interrupt while the teacher is explaining. The student must see to it that what he commits to memory is correct and authentic. He must be punctual and must stick to the class and to the programme of instruction.

Detailed observations are made on the choice and study of books on lending, borrowing, purchasing and transcribing books.

The fifth chapter deals mainly with the choice of an educational institution by the scholar and the requirements of residential life. The nature of the higher educational institutions (*madāris*) and their curricula for the beginners and the advanced classes are discussed enabling the student to make a judicious choice of the institution and the programme of study. The residential life of scholars and conditions of residential accommodation are explained and the need for a proper choice of a residential companion is stressed. The manner of entry into and exit from the residential institution is brought under discussion.

Each of the five long chapters of the book is sub-divided into a number of 'sections' *(anwā')*, and each section *(nau')* is loaded with considerable detail on the subject concerned as well as the supporting references from the Islamic educational tradition. As such, Ibn Jamā'ah's work is important both from the point of educational as well as cultural development. In the domain of pedagogy, Ibn Jamā'ah may be regarded as a pioneer in the formulation of Question-Answer method as an essential feature of the teaching-learning process.

THE COMPREHENSIVE EXPOSITION OF KNOWLEDGE AND ITS EXCELLENCE.

Ibn 'Abd al-Barr

جامع بيان العلم وفضله

ابو عمر يوسف بن عمر بن عبد البر

Abū 'Umar Yūsuf b. Abdullah, Ibn 'Abd al-Barr was born in Cordova (Spain) in 368 A.H./978 A.C. The city was then the centre of higher Islamic learning and education, and the brilliant young 'Umar studied there under scholars of repute, entered into correspondence with eminent scholars of 'Mashriq' ('the Muslim East', which he did not visit) and travelled all over his native land Spain in search of knowledge. As an accomplished scholar, he became the most distinguished *muhaddith* ('traditionist') of his age and one of the greatest of all times. He was equally distinguished in jurisprudence and in the science of genealogy, and was the foremost upholder and defender of the Sunnah. He held the high position of Q̄adi at Lisbon and Santarem under al-Muzaffar b. al- Aftas, and died at Jātiva (Shātiba) in 463 A.H. (1070 - 1).

Ibn 'Abd al-Barr authord a large number of works and, being an accomplished *Muhaddith* and eminent jurist, he based his discussion and exposition in all that he wrote on Quran and the Sunnah. Of special importance among his works which have been preserved are: *Jāmi' Bayān al-'Ilm* (discussed below); *Kitāb al- Istī'āb fi Ma'rifat al-Ashāb* on the biographies of the companions of the Holy Prophet (*sala'm*); *Kitāb al-Istidhkār fi-Sharh Madhāhib 'Ulamā' al-Amsār fi ma Tadawwanahū al- Mu'atta min Ma'āni al-Rā'i wa al- 'Āthār* with an explanation of arrangement of its chapters. The most scholarly and important work in Hadith written by Ibn Abd al-Barr was his Introduction to the Mu'atta of Imām Mālik, which has fortunately survived and come to light more recently. This is *Kitāb al-Tamhīd li mā fi al-Mu'attā min al-Ma'ānī wa al-Asānīd* in 20 volumes, about which Ibn Hazm said: "I do not know any one *like him* in exposition and understanding of the Hadīth, not to talk of anyone excelling him in it!"

Ibn Abd al-Barr wrote his important book *Jāmi' Bayān al-'Ilm wa Fadlihī wa mā Yanbaghī fī Riwāyatihī wa Hamlihī* (The Comprehensive Exposition of Knowledge And Its Excellence And What Needs to be Done in Its Transmission And Dissemination). He wrote this work specifically to establish the superiority of knowledge. It is divided into two parts after the Introduction (*Khutbah*) in which the Holy Prophet's sayings against concealing knowledge are cited and the reader is urged to seek knowledge in accordance with the Prophet's observation that "Seeking knowledge is obligatory for every believer." As to what knowledge should be acquired, it is explained what is *Fard 'Ayn* (Obligatory Studies) and *'Fard Kifāyat'* (Elective Studies).

Part-I. This part includes chapters on excellence of knowledge, preference of knowledge to a mode of worship; excellences of the learned; the art of writing; correcting a recorded book of knowledge by collation; correcting pronunciations; forbearance and perseverance in achieving knowledge undertaking journey, and dissemination of knowledge; the manner and method of achieving knowledge, and holding discussions and debates; transmission of knowledge to others; seeking honour and position by patronising the learned and the students; propagating Islam and teachings of Qur'an and Sunnah for the sake of Allah and not for any worldly gains and pursuits.

Part-II. This part is devoted to practicing what is learnt and avoiding acts forbidden, principles of knowledge and its nature, its division and limitations. Attention is called to the spurious studies current among the people of different castes and creeds. The 'Peoples of Books' and their traditions are briefly discussed. It is explained what a learned man should do when he is asked about something he does not know. The author deals with *Ijtihād al-Rā'i* (reasoning) on the line of the 'Principles of Fiqh' in the absence of any clear text (*nass*). Emphasis is placed on sticking to the Sunnah and avoiding innovations and evil propensities.

THE CATALOGUE.

Al-Nadīm

كتاب الفهرست

محمد بن إسحق بن محمد بن إسحق النديم

The author of this important work Abu al-Faraj Muhammad b. Ishāq, who later became known as 'al-Nadīm' for being a boon companion of the Buwayhid ruler Mu'izz al-Dawlah (954-967 A.D), was born by about 320 A.H. His father Abu Ya'qūb Ishāq who was himself a *warrāq*, a dealer in paper and books, arranged good education for young Muhammad. Later, he received higher education in different disciplines from most eminent teachers, such as Isma'īl al- Saffār, an authority on the Hadith; Abū Sa'īd al- Sīrāfī, the Jurist; al-Husain b. Ishāq, the theologian and natural scientist; Abū al-Faraj al- Isbahānī, the author of the famous *Al- Aghānī* (a thesaurus of poetry, songs and singers, literature and culture); al-Marzubānī, the literatuer and author of *Tabaqat al-Shu'arā'* (Generations of Poets); al-Hasan b. Sawwār, the logician and translator of scientific texts; Yūnus al-Qass, the mathematician; and Abu al-Hasan Muhammad ibn Yusuf al- Nāqit, a scholar of Greek Sciences. Such an extensive exposure to the different areas of knowledge enabled him to extend independent inquiries into the original source material pertaining to these and other disciplines.

He is said to have commenced his career as a *Kātib*, which may mean either a scribe or secretary well versed in correspondence, or a calligrapher and transcriber of books. Some of his own observations would show that he was associated with book trade and as such became an assiduous researcher and collector of books; he also continued to gain acquaintance of other scholars who either themselves transcribed or produced books, or collected books travelling far and wide. Because of his learning and scholarship, he was taken into service by the Buwayhid rulers and became their trusted court companion. He died on Wednesday, in the month of Sha'bān on the 10th day from the end of it, in the year 380 A.H. (990 A.D.).

With his scholarly pursuit of books as repositories of knowledge and his deep interest in *Kitābat*, the art and technique of writing, which helped in transcribing and producing more and more books, he first authored a book on this subject giving simultaneously the characteristics and comparison of books so produced. It was in the year 377 A.H (987/88 A.D.) that he systematically commenced documenting and describing the books which he then had in his own collection, or which he had once possessed and examined, or about which he had good authentic information. His approach in documentation was encyclopaedic in so far as it purported to bring under reference all the known books of all the nations. He entitled this work as *AL-FIHRIST, (The Catalogue)*. Its complete basic draft was probably completed by him in the year 380 A.H., sometime before his death.

In the preface, he set forth the scope of his documentation as under:-

"This is a catalogue of books of all peoples, Arab and non-Arab, existing in Arabic language and Arabic script, dealing with various sciences together with the accounts of those who composed them and the categories of their authors - their genealogies, dates of birth, length of life, times of death, locations of their cities, and their virtues and faults - from the beginning of each science to this our own time, which is the year three hundred and seventy-seven after the Hijra" (A.D. 987/88).

It is obvious from this statement that AL-FIHRIST was not intended to be a mere book-list. Al-Nadīm had planned it to provide information on (i) each book with its correct title, (ii) the author's name and other necessary details about him, and (iii) the subject matter of the book and the area of knowledge to which it belonged – the three main ingredients essential to the process of cataloguing. With scholarly approach and skill in documentation, al-Nadim laid the foundation of 'Science of Cataloguing' in this work.

An Earliest Manuscript of
KITAB AL-FIHRIST
(Title Page of MS 1934)

Thus, in its scope and presentation, AL-FIHRIST is to be regarded the first standard subject-wise 'catalogue' covering all areas of knowledge. It is divided into ten Parts which are further sub-divided into Sections each dealing with one or more subjects, with a general introduction followed by bibliographical details. The 1st section of the 1st chapter deals with the foundational base for knowledge, viz. languages, scripts, and forms of writing both of Arabs and non-Arabs. Historically, this Section becomes the first ever scientific account in the domain of Paleography. The tenth and the last part contains an account of alchemists and the practitioners of Alchemy, both the ancient and the recent ones.

With each book documented in its essential details, al-Nadīm brought under reference all the books relevant to each discipline by way of bibliography. However, he listed them together, and not alphabetically, an important feature of cataloguing/bibliography which was to develop later in the more advanced work *Kashf al-Zunūn* of Haji Khalifa. But *AL-FIHRIST* has the merit of being a 'Universal Catalogue' of its times in so far as it documents important intellectual achievements during the first four centuries of Islam with an extended frame of reference linking intellectual achievements of several civilizations. The author, being the most knowledgeable scholar himself, succeeded in making AL- FIHRIST a mirror of science, literature and culture-reflecting all important achievements in these areas and much more. In the opinion of a modern scholar "not only is the work extremely valuable for a knowledge of the culture of medieval Islam and of the literary personalities of the period, but it gives important information about the classical material available for transmission through Muslim culture to the Western world. *Al-Fihrist* is thus a true record of civilization."*

* W.T.H. Jackson in his 'Foreword' to *The Fihrist of al- Nadim*, Columbia University Press New York, 1970.

THE KEY TO HIGHEST ATTAINMENT AND LIGHT OF LEADERSHIP.

Tashkopruzāde

مفتاح السعادة ومصباح السيادة

طاش کبری زاده

Abu al-Khayr,'Isām al-Din, Ahmad b. Mustafā b. Khalil Tāshkopruzāde was born in Busra in 901 A.H (1495 A.D), and was educated in Ankara where he attained personal eminence as well as excellence in scholarship. He took to the teaching profession, and taught in a number of institutions. In 958 A.H. (1551 A.D.), he was elevated to the high position of Qadi of Canstantinople. Besides his professional obligations, he was mainly an educator committed to transmitting knowledge both orally and through pen. Although he lost his eyesight in 961 A.H., he began dictating an informative work on the learned men of the Ottoman Empire and finished its dictation in 965 A.H (1557 A.D.). He died three years later in 968 A.H. (1561).

Tāshkopruzāde, with Turkish as his mother tongue, took to Islamic education in the classical tradition and achieved mastery in Arabic language and wrote as many as 37 books and treatises. His works show that he was highly qualified in *fiqh*, *falsifa-cum-tasawwuf*, *Kalām*, academic and curricular subjects, history and biography. As a result of his strong general education and independent studies in the different disciplines, he developed a special interest in determining and defining the different areas of knowledge. He wrote a commentary on the Third Part of al-Sakkāki's *Miftāh al-'Ulūm* (Key to Sciences), a comprehensive treatise defining the scope of useful studies (*al-Risālah al- Jāmia'h li Wasf al-'Ulūm al- Nāfi'ah*). However, his most important contribution, reflecting his erudite scholarship and originality of thought, consisted in his systematic classification of knowledge in his monumental *Miftāh al-Sa'āda wa Misbāh Siyādah* ('The Key to Highest Attainment And Light of Leadership').

In this work, the process of classification of knowledge reached the mature stage of being formulated into an independent discipline. Tāshkobruzāde gave it the name *'Ilm Taqāsim al-'Ulūm* which, keeping in view his further observations, would mean 'The Science of Systematic Classification of Knowledge'. He defined it in terms of its methodology and scope as under:

- This is a science which in its exposition proceeds stage by stage, from the general categories to the specific ones, in order to identify the (specific) category of the subjects/ sciences falling under a general category.
- Since the most general of all the sciences in respect of its subject matter is Metaphysics (*al-'Ilm al-Ilāhī*), 'the science of classification' in itself would become a sub-category under it (Metaphysics). In this respect, therefore, the stage by stage exposition would proceed from 'the specific' to 'the general' contrary to what has been said above. But (on the whole) the former is easier and more convenient.

His definition clearly indicates that Tāshkobruzāde conceived the classification of knowledge in itself as an independent science with a methodology of its own. His approach, underlining the originality of his concepts and ideas, represents a marked advance over the previous approaches and concepts to classify 'Knowledge'.

In *Miftāh al-Sa'āda* Tāshkobruzāde has brought under discussion over three hundred subjects/studies/sciences and placed them under appropriate categories - all under the umbrella of a common frame of reference. The main principle underlying his scheme of classification is unity and integration of knowledge, a categorization in terms of common denominators rather than division or compartmentalization of knowledge. According to him all 'things' (of knowledge) have had their existence/origin in four stages (marātib), viz. Script/Writing (*al-*

Kitābat), Wording/Expression (*al-'Ibārat*), Intellect (*al- 'Adhhān*), and the Corpus (*al-A'ayān*). In this scheme, the first three are obviously the agents which create, among others, the fourth one i.e. the corpus of knowledge. Proceeding on this premise, Tāshkobruzāde classified all the known subjects and sciences under seven main headings, each termed as a *dauhat* 'root- cum-cluster' (of related subject): (1) Script/Writing/transcription, (2) Word/Expression, (3) Intellect, (4) the Corpus, (5) Practical Need, (6) Religious Law, and (7) Esoteric/Spiritual disciplines. This is what he calls *al-haykal*, the general frame for the system of classification on which his book is based.

Tāshkobruzāde's work has other merits of its own. It preserves the intellectual legacy of Islamic civilization following the destruction of its nerve centre of Baghdad by the Mongols. It includes the achievements of the contemporary Ottoman period. His work had great impact on classification of knowledge subsequently. It became an important reference work, and later Haji Khalifa based his encyclopedic *Kashf al- Zunūn* essentially on the same principles. Haji Khalifa defended Tāshkobruzāde's shortcomings and paid "all compliments to him for having dived deep into the oceans of knowledge and brought out the pearls".

ON FIRST PHILOSOPHY.

Al-Kindi

كتاب الفلسفة الأولى

أبو يوسف يعقوب بن إسحق الكندي

One of the intellectual giants of universal fame, Abu Yūsuf Ya'qūb b. Ishāq al-Kindī was the most distinguished scholar, author, mathematician and scientist. He was also a great philosopher with originality of ideas who held his own views on the nature of Greek Philosophy. He flourished during the period extending from the later half of the 2nd century to the end of the 1st half of the 3rd century A.H., and was a contemporary of Caliph Mamun and Caliph Mu'tasim when Islamic thought was at its best. Kindi may appropriately be called "The Philosopher of Islam" for his pioneering work on philosophy.

Kindi "was well acquainted with the main tenets of Greek Philosophy, and even had a translation of a summary version of the Enneads made for him. It was he who initiated the process of formulating a technical philosophical vocabulary in Arabic, and of rethinking Greek philosophy in terms of Islamic doctrines. In both these respects, he was followed by Fārābī, through whom the basis for Peripatetic philosophy became well established in Islam." (Nasr).

As enumerated by al-Nadim in his *Kitab al-Fihrist,* Kindi authored about 250 works on different branches of knowledge such as philosophy, psychology *(al-Nafs),* mathematics, physics, medicine, pharmacology, geography, music, astrology, precious stones, and manufacture of perfumes, glass and weaponry (swords).

Kindi completed his book, *On First Philosophy (Kitab fi al-Falsifat al-'Ūlā*), during the reign of the Abbasid Caliph al-Mu'tasim (218-

27/833-42) to whom it was also dedicated. By defending philosophical thought, Kindi fortified the position of philosophy which was then fondly cultivated by other Muslim scholars and philosophers. His position as philosopher is set forth in the introductory chapter of this important work which underlines the principles of philosophy, the four 'causes' and the four 'scientific questions'. He condemns those who attack philosophy. Though Kindi quotes from Aristotle's Metaphysics, he holds his own views and 'ceases to follow the Greeks where they are in disagreement with Quranic revelation' (E.I.). He holds that 'the truth must be acquired from whatever source it comes', though 'the statements of the philosophers must be re-examined and completed.' According to him, pursuit of philosophy is an Islamic subject par excellence, since 'the knowledge of the essence of things and their true nature' *(Haqāiq al-ashyā' kamā hiya)* is identical with the message of the Prophet–being the science of divine sovereignty and divine unity, the science of morality and ethics'. In his important work, *On First Philosophy,* Kindi laid the foundations of Islamic philosophy, i.e. pursuit of philosophy in the true spirit of Islam, to know the true nature of things and discover unity in universal reality as a reflection of One Creator of all things.

THE RASĀ'IL (TRACTS) OF IKHWĀN AL-SAFĀ: THE TRACT OF SYNTHESIS.

Ikhwān Al-Safa

رسائل اخوان الصفاء وخلان الوفاء: الرسالة الجامعة

اخوان الصفاء

No other work has been ascribed to so many different authors as the *Rasā'il* of *Ikhwān al-Safā*[*] because they were produced and published anonymously. All that can be said with certainty is that by the middle of the 4th century of Hijra a group of learned men of Basra with predominantly philosophical convictions joined together as associate authors-cum-editors and produced a large number of tracts *(rasā'il)* on different themes. They have been named as Abu Sulaiman Muhammad b. Ma'shar (or Mushir) al-Bayusti or Busti (known as al-Maqdisi or Muqaddasi), Abu al-Hasan 'Ali Harūn (or Zahrun) al-Zanjāni, Abu Ahmad al-Mihrjāni, al-'Aufi, and Zayed b. Rifā'ah. Probably, al-Maqdisi was the one who finalized the drafts in the form of approved text. But again the authorship of the *Rasā'il* is attributed to Ahmad b. Abdullah, and also to Maslama al-Majrītī (d. Circa 395 or 398 A.H.).

All the *Rasā'il* were not written at the same time. This 'Brotherly Circle' with its changing members, possibly continued on their intellectual activity over a period of about half a century during which they issued tracts on different subjects. Fifty were however in circulation in the year 373 A.H. when Abu Hayyān al-Tauhīdī wrote his book *al-Imtā' wa al-Mu'ānisā*. Most probably, forming of the scholarly circle

* (1) Rasā'il = Epistles or Tracts. 'Ikhwān al-Safā = Bretheren of Purity, Bretheren of Sincerity, Pure Bretheren, or Sincere Bretheren.

and preparation and circulation of the tracts took place during the period 338 - 373 A.H.

There are conflicting statements about the total number of the *Rasā'il* varying from 50, 51 to 52 plus the very last and the concluding tract called *al-Risālah al- Jāmī'ah.* The actual number of the texts in the complete copies is fifty two. In *al-Jami'ā* itself, the number of the *Rasā'il* summarized is fifty two.

The authors of the *Rasā'il* do not base their discussions and interpretations exclusively or mainly on Islamic beliefs and teachings, and therefore they do not project what may be called as *Islamic* Philosophy. However, they have a place in the realm of Muslim scholarship and, as such, in the history of Muslim philosophy.

Behind a facade of conformity to the Quran and the Tradition, the authors of these tracts attempted to install philosophy as an integral part of religion - their ultimate aim being that by the diffusion of such an integrated learning, a more righteous and Uptopion society will emerge in which the learned would be the leaders. They established a close scholarly circle ostensibly to reform the society by communicating a quantum of knowledge based on integration of Greek philosophy with the Islamic Shari'ah. Though the *Rasā'il* reflect their author's pro- Ismā'ili sympathies, they also occasionally follow anti-Ismā'ilī line. Thus, while Ismā'ilī sympathies are obvious, there is no proof on record that either the formation of the Ikhwān al-Safā circle or the production and publication of the Rasa'il had any relationship with the Ismā'ilī Movement. This relationship developed later when the Rasā'il became popular with the later Ismā'ilī missionaries. The authors of the Rasā'il have rather related themselves to the concept of *Safā* (purity or sincerity of the Sufīs) and also describe themselves as'Sufis'.

Beside their rational approach and philosophic content, the place of the Rasā'il in Muslim educational thought and practice need to be studied, because they had their impact, positive and negative, both in the Sunni and the Shī'i circles.

The *al-Risālah al-Jāmi'ah* (The Tract of Synthesis) is referred to in the *Rasā'il* as if it were the jwell of the crown, to which the readers were urged to look for eagerly. Thus, in the *Rasā'il* it is described by the Ikhwān as a tract that "includes the (substance) of all these (fifty two) previous tracts", written for the purpose of 'elucidating the realities' of all tracts which are mere introductions to it. It is therefore claimed that the secrets of *Al-Jāmi'ah,* which is the ultimate aim of all the others, cannot be revealed except to those who have mastered the other fifty two. No doubt, much importance is claimed for *Al-Jāmi'ah* in its own pages as also in the *Rasā'il.* It is variously described as the crown and essence of the tracts, a philosophic synopsis of their contents, a commentary on these, a residue of esoteric knowledge which should not be given except to the very select, a seret exposition of what has only been hinted at in the tracts, and such other description. All this was probably meant to excite curiousity and hold attention. In its organization and presentation, as also in the exposition of any new thought-content, *Al- Jāmi'ah* does not reveal itself to be the climax to the proceeding series of Rasā'il which it purports to conclude. Its merit has rather been devalued by the advanced inflated pronouncements building up high expectations. One obvious merit of *Al- Jāmi'ah* is that it presents, though in an imbalanced manner, the summary of every one of the fifty two Rasā'il with the addition of two fresh discourses: the first deals with Adam's sin and its allegorical interpretation, while the subject of the second is the controversy between Man and Animals.

THE BOOK OF OBSERVATIONS AND ADMONITIONS.

Ibn Sīnā

كتاب الإشارات والتنبيهات

أبو علي الحسين بن عبد الله ابن سينا

Abu Ali al-Husayn b. Abdullah b. Sīnā, the famous 'Ibn Sīnā' of the Islamic world and 'Avicinna' of the West (370-428/980-1037), was a scholar of vast learning, prodigious memory, brilliant mind, practical approach and penetrating common sense, who wrote a number of works on different subjects. He flourished as a great physician and philosopher, but was also a distinguished scientist, mathematician, logician, and poet at the same time. The historic influence of his scientific thought has come to light more recently with the publication of "*Avicenna, Scientist and Philosopher*" (London, 1952). His stature as a medical scientist and physician is amply confirmed by his *Qānūn fi al-Tibb* ('Canon Medicinae')

Though Ibn Sīnā was the greatest philosopher, he was not isolated from the world and lost in books or wedded only to abstract thinking. He was a busy physician, welded political influence and served as Vezier (Prime Minister) to his patron Princes. His full involvement in the living currents of life lends meaning and validity to his experience and vitality to his reflection.

Besides philosophy and medicine, Ibn Sīnā also wrote on physics, chemistry, mathematics, natural history, astronomy and music. Of his numerous works on philosophy, only a few have survived in their complete authentic text. Among these are his encyclopaedia of natural sciences and philosophy *Kitāb al-Shifā'* ('The Book of Healing' - from ignorance), *Kitāb al-Ishārāt wa al-Tanbihāt* (The Book of Hints and admonitions) and *Danishnama-i-ALa'i* The Knowledge Book for 'Alā'ī', i.e. for Prince 'Alā' al-Dawla). His philosophical encyclopaedia *AL-SHIFĀ* implies the following classification: (1) Theoretical Knowledge sub-divided, with regard to increasing abstraction, into physics, mathematics and metaphysics); (2) Practical Knowledge (ethics, economy, politics).

In *al-Shifā'*, Avicenna embraces the totality of the sciences according to the following plan:

1-Logic; 2. Physics; 3. Mathematics; 4. Metaphysics.

In *'The "Logic" of the Orientals',* which has survived partly, he proposed to present, for the elite, the "Oriental Philosophy". Avicenna repudiated his own earlier works, which are chiefly Aristotelian, as being suitable for the common people; instead, he proposed to present, for the elite, the "Oriental philosophy". His trilogy - Hayy Ibn Yaqzan (Living Son of the Awake), al-Tair (The Bird), and Salaman and Absal -- deals with the complete cycle of the gnostic's journey from the "world of shadows" to the Divine Presence, the Orient of Light (Nasr.). Within the limits of metaphysics Avicenna includes all the 'revealed' data contained in the Qurān. He establishes that God, the only necessity , is good, all-powerful, creator of all things, provident.

Another work of Ibn Sīnā, much shorter than *al-Shifā'* but of great importance, is *Kitāb al-'Ishārāt wa al- Tanbīhāt.* This impressive title may be translated literally as Hints And Warnings, or meaningfully as Directives and Remarks, Remarks and Admonitions, Observations and Admonitions, or Briefings and Criticism. It consists of four independent and self-containing parts, each dealing with a single discipline. These are:

Part-I	Logic	Part-III	Metaphysics
Part-II	Physics	Part-IV	Sufism

The scheme followed by Ibn Sīnā in the treatment of each subject is that first he fives his own views and observations on the subject and then a critical evaluation of the views of others, both the predecessors and the contemporaries, correcting and admonishing them on their mistakes and misgiving. In his very brief preface Ibn Sīnā says:

"I have formulated principles and generalities of wisdom in this work, 'Observations and Admonitions', for you who are anxious to discern the truth. Guided by your own intelligence, it should be easy for you to differentiate (the principles and generalities) and determine the more specific details."

The merit of *Kitāb al-Ishārāt wa al- Tanbīhāt* is twofold. Firstly it is of one of the complete works of Ibn Sīnā, and secondly in its being the latest and the most mature exposition of the four significant dimensions of Ibn Sīnā's philosophical system. He wrote it for the most informed and advanced students of philosophy in his times, and hence couched it is concise, terse and abstruse style. According to him logic is a science or academic discipline in itself and at the same time also a basis or instrument for philosophical thought.

Regarding Ibn Sīnā's system of philosophy it has been observed: "He is the only one among the great philosophers of Islam to build an elaborate and complete system of philosophy - a system which has been dominant in the philosophical tradition of Islam for centuries, because that system had features of remarkable originality displaying a type of genius-like spirit in discovering methods and arguments whereby he sought to reformulate the purely rational and intellectual tradition of Hellenism, to which he was an eminent heir, and, to an extent, within the religious system of Islam" (Fazlur Rahman).

BOOK ON THE SOUL.

Ibn Bājjah

كتاب النفس

أبو بكر محمد بن يحيى ابن باجة

Abū Bakr Muhammad b. Yahyā b. al-Sā'igh, known as Ibn Bājjah, was born in Saragossa in the north of Spain during the years 475-80 A.H., and died in Fez (Morocco) in Ramadan, 533 A.H. (1139 A.D.) Besides philosophy and mathematics, Ibn Bājjah was well-versed in botany, astronomy, logic, grammar, literature and music. He was a poet of great merit, and also composed music and excelled in playing upon the 'Ūd. Ibn Bājjah wrote several commentaries on Aristotle as well as independent works on astronomy, philosophy and music.

The early sources usually mention him as "al-Wazīr al-Hakīm" (The Philosopher Prime Minister). Politically, Ibn Bājjah had gained name and fame, having held the post of Wazīr for two rulers. First it was at Saragossa which had been annexed by the Almorvids (Al-Murābitūn) in the year 503/1110 and where their Governor Abū Bakr Ibn Ibrāhīm al-Sahrāwī, known as Ibn Taifulwīt ruled. There after, Ibn Bājjah was appointed to the highest post of the Vazir by the ruler Yahyā b. Yūsuf b. Tashufīn which he held for 20 years.

According to Ibn Khaldun, Ibn Bājjah was as great as Ibn Rushd in the Maghrib (West) and Farabi and Ibn Sīnā in the Mashriq (East). Ibn Bājjah's original Arabic writings have survived in a Compendium which was edited and transcribed by his pupil Ibn al- Imām,* and in a few Hebrew translations. His philosophical thought is reflected in

* Of its two later copies, the one is preserved in the Bodleian Library, Oxford, while the other which was in the Berlin Library was lost during World War-II. A third manuscript, containing Ibn Bājjah's writings on Logic has survived in a mass. in Escurial. A forth one, containing one more treatise not to be found in the Bodleian and the Berlin manuscripts, is preserved in the Tashkent State Library in Uzbekistan, USSR.

Risāla Ittisāl al-'Aql bi al- Insān (Treatise on the Unison of the Intellect with Man), *Kitab Tadbir al-Mu'tawahhid* (The Regime of the Solitary). The more celebrated and the more complete of his works which has survived is *Kitāb al-Nafs* (The Book on the Soul), a philosophical treatise on psychology which influenced later scholars including Ibn Rushd.

Ibn Bājjah exercised great influence on contemporary thinkers, Ibn Tufayl (d. 581/1185) and Ibn Rushd (d. 595/1198) in particular and the Latin scholars of the Middle Ages in general. His Latinized name 'Avempace' was popular among the Hebrew and Latin scholars in those days. His treatises, the *Tadbīr al-Mutawahhid*, the *Risālat al-Ittisāl*, and the *Risālat al-Wadā'* were translated into Hebrew, and widely read in Europe. Ibn Rushd acknowledges in his *Talkhīs Kitāb al-Nafs* that what he has expressed concerning Mind is the view of Ibn Bājjah. However sometime Ibn Rushd also re-examines and criticises the philosophical views propounded by Fārābi, Ibn Sīnā and Bājjah as well.

The text of *Kitāb al-Nafs* was originally complete but, later on, Ibn Bājjah's friend and disciple al-Wazīr Abu al- Hasan Alī Ibn al-Imām, through whom his writings have survived, lost a few pages from the end of the book. Like his *Kitāb Tadbīr al-Mutawahhid*, Ibn Bājjah refers to *Kitāb al-Nafs* in terms that clearly indicate that it is his original and independent work, while he refers to some other works of his as notes or commentaries on the works of Aristotle.

In this book, Ibn Bājjah has given his exposition of the nature of the Soul under eleven discourses (chapters) each of which is intended to explain a specific dimension of it. These are:

I. Nature of the Soul.

II. The Nutritive Faculty.

III. Faculty of Sense-Perception.

IV. Faculty of Seeing.

V. Faculty of Hearing.

VI. Faculty of Smell.

VII. Taste, the faculty of perceiving flavour.

VIII. Touch, the faculty of perceiving the tangible body.

IX. Common Sense, a sense composite of the five faculties, from Sight to Touch.

X. Faculty of Imagination.

XI. The Reasoning Faculty.

Ibn Bājjah's *Kitāb al-Nafs,* as a philosophical treatise on psychology, is the earliest text known so far that gives the gist of all the three books of *De Anima* of Aristotle. Besides, Ibn Bājjah refers to Plato, Alexander of Aphrodisias, Galen and Themistius. Of the Muslim philosophers, he refers to Farabi admiringly and also mentions Ghazzali with respect and reverence.

In *Kitab al-Nafs* Ibn Bājjah offers for the first time, a complete and comprehensive survey of peripatetic psychology as well as the Islamic view of the Soul and its faculties. Ibn Bājjah has relied on the works of Fārābi in dealing with philosophy and logic, but has made considerable additions. He has adopted an entirely different method of philosophical investigation, in so far as he has based his metaphysics and psychology on physics. He brings his discussion of the soul by stating that bodies, natural or artificial, are composed of matter and form, their form being the permanent acquisition or the entelchy of the body. According to him, knowledge in man means his seeing the existents together with their perfect existence in his intellect through the insight of his soul which is a gift of God. The 'gift of God' is of different grades in different men, the greatest insight being that of the Prophets who perfectly know Him and His Creations.

Thus, in his philosophical system, Ibn Bājjah began by describing 'Aristotleian Psychology' and finally arrived at the concept of prophecy and revelation -- as was arrived at by Ibn Sīnā. Imām Ghazzali dealt with the subject in his *Mishkāt al- 'Anwār.*

TREATISE ON 'THE ALIVE SON OF THE AWAKE'.

Ibn Tufayl

حَيِّ بْنِ يَقْظَان

أبو بكر محمد بن عبد الملك ابن طفيل

Abū Bakr Muhammad b. 'Abd al-Malik b. Muhammad b. Muhammad b. Tufayl belonged to the Arab *qabila* of 'al-Qays' and hence called 'al-Qaysi. He was born in the 1st decade of the 6th century A.H. in Wādī Āsh (the modern Guadix, 40 miles N.E. of Granada) in Andalus (Spain) and passed some years of his life in Qurtuba (Cordova) and Ishbil (Seville). He died in Marrakush (in Morocco) in 581 A.H. (1285- 86 A.D.).

Though a philosopher and physician, he also held original ideas on Astronomy and was a poet. Besides his contributions in medicine, he is best known for his treatise *Hayyu Ibn Yaqzān* ('The Alive' son of 'The Awake'). Ibn Sina also wrote a treatise by the same title, but Ibn Tufayl's work has a different setting and a different end. The story is of a child who is left alone in wilderness comprehends through his keen observation and reasoning not only the facts and phenomena of physical nature but also proceeds beyond the visible universe into the realm of metaphysics and realises the existence of an omnipotent Creator of all. Thus the allegory is employed to demonstrates quest of knowledge and the human capacity to realise the highest truth. The work also exemplifies a theory of 'Naturalisim in Learning and Education'.

Through this remarkable, all absorbing and philosophically oriented treatise, Ibn Tufayl became widely known in Europe (as

'Abubacer', i.e. Abū Bakr). The text* was first published by Edward Pococke Sr. (1604 - 1691), together with a Latin translation by Edward Pococke Jr. (1648 - 1727) as philosophus autodidactus sive Epistola Abi Ja'far Ibn Tophall'. The romantic setting of Ibn Tufayl's work inspired De Foe to make his own story after it, shorn of any philosophical implications and yet with the comparable title 'Robin son Crusoe' (Robin son of Crusoe).

---

* The Arabic edition publis had four times in Cairo beginning from 1299 H./1881-82 and twice in Constantinople. Latest edition based on a new MS. and re-examination of the others by Leon Gauthier, with French translation (Alger, 1900). English translations by Aswell, by George Keith, and by Simon Ocklay (London, 1708, and reprinted in 1731, Cairo 1905, and London 1929).

THE SUBSTANCE OF THE IDEAS OF CLASSICAL AND LATER PHILOSOPHERS AND THEOLOGIANS.

Fakhr al-Din al-Rāzī

محصل أفكار المتقدمين والمتأخرين

فخر الدين الرازي

Abu 'Abdullah Muhammad b. 'Umar b. al-Hasan b. Al Husayn al-Rāzi belonged to a Qureshite family that had migrated from Tabaristan to Rayy where he was born in 543/544 A.H. (1149/50 A.D.). Because of his sound education, advanced knowledge and superior ability to communicate convincingly, he emerged as an unrivalled scholar and one of the greatest exponents of Islam and defender of faith. As such, he was called *'Fakhr al Din'* (the Pride of Religion), an honorific title by which he became widely known. He played a leading role in strengthening the foundations of faith and came to be regarded as *Imām,* and also as *'Hujjat al-Islam'* (Proof of Islam) after Ghazzali. Imam Fakhr al-Din Rāzi's studies were not confined only to the domain of religion but extended to many other branches of knowledge. He was an encyclopaedist, being a theologian, exegist, philosopher, historian, mathematician, astronomer, and physician at the same time. He also excelled in Arabic literature and wrote a commentary on al-Ma'rri's *Saqt al-Zand.* He lectured both in Arabic and Persian and also composed in Persian. He visited, stayed and taught in Khwarizm, Transoxiana and finally in Khurasan where he died in Herat aged about sixty three on Sunday 21 Muharram 606 A.H. (26 July 1209).

Fakhr al-Dīn Rāzi authored a large number of important works, his magnum opus being the commentary of Holy Quran *al-Tafsīr al-Kabīr* (The Great Commentary) but he also wrote treatises on mathematics and natural science. He successfully countered the influence of the Peripatetics who had continued on the tradition of Aristotalian Philosophy, by writing a criticism of Avicenna's *al- Ishārat wa 'al-Tanbīhāt* (The Book of Hints and Remarks). Imam Razi's criticism exerted a more enduring influence than that of his predecessor, al-Ghazzali.

His *Kitāb Muhassal Afkār al- Mutaqaddimīn wa al-Muta'akhirīn min al- Falāsafa wa'al-Mutakallimīn* (The Substance of the Ideas of Classical and Later Philosophers and Theologians) is an important work in which he evaluates philosophical and theological themes and doctrines of his predecessors, under 'Four Pillers' *(arkān)* of *Ilm al-Kalām* which he discusses systematically.

The First Rukn deals with three preambles *(maqaddamāt),* the ancient sciences, the preliminary sciences, conceptions *(tasawwurāt)* and judgments *(tasdīqāt).* Under *tasdiqāt,* it is pointed out that the world consists of four kinds of peoples: those who admit both the 'perceptibles' and the necessary 'evidents' *(al- hissiyāt* and *al-badīhiiyyat),* those who deal with the 'perceptibles, 'those who consider the 'perceptibles' but not the 'evidents', and the sophists. The second preamble concerns 'Speculation' *(al-Nazr),* and the third pertians to 'Indication' (al- Dalil).

The Second Rukn explains the division of the known objects as the 'existents' and their functions *(ahkām al- maujūdāt),* the non-existents *(ma'dūm),* and the absence of an intermediary between *mawjūd* and *ma'dūm* dealing with all aspects of *Wujūd* (the existence). *The Third Rukn deals with Metaphysics (al-Ilahiyāt). The Fourth Rukn* concerns the *Sama'iyāt,* that is what depends on reports and traditions, such as the matters related to Prophethood, Resurrection, Souls, Grave Sins, Reward and Punishment, and Imāmat.

THE CONCLUSIVE DIVINE PROOF.

Walīyyullāh Al- Dihlivī

حجة الله البالغة

قطب الدين أحمد بن عبد الرحيم ولي الله الدهلوي

An Arab Qurashite family, with tradition of learning and scholarship, which had migrated from Iran to India by about the 7th/13th century after the foundation of the Sultanate of Delhi, gradually attained prominence and eventually settled in Delhi. Among a long line of eminent ancestors was Waliyyullāh's grandfather Wajīh al-Dīn and father Shaikh Abdal Rahim (1644-1719) who was a religious scholar, sufi, physician and eminent educator being the founder of the Rahīmiyyah College of Delhi. Waliyyullāh was born on Wednesday, the 4th of Shawwāl 1114 A.H. (21 February 1703) in the house of his maternal grandfather in Phulat, of the district of Muzaffarnager, India. He was descended from Caliph Umar from his father's side and Caliph Ali from his mother's side.

Young brilliant Waliyyullāh received sound education at the Rahīmiyyah College under personal guidance of his learned father whom he also later took as his own spiritual guide. He was 17 years old when his father died, and Waliyyullāh succeeded him as Rector of the College where he taught and lectured devoting special attention to the personal and spiritual development of students. In 1143 A.H., he performed his first pilgrimage and stayed over for the second in 1144 A.H. During this period, he took to advanced studies under eminent scholars and also collected considerable literature particularly on the Hadith.

After his return to Delhi in 1145 A.H. began an intensively active period of his life which continued on for the next thirty years until his death on 29 Muharram, 1176 A.H. (1762 A.D.). As Rector of the

Rahimiyyah College, scholarly Waliyullāh gave much attention to its development. In particular, he revised the course of studies so that direct study of Quran (not through the medium of traditional *tafsir)* and of the Hadith became the core of the reformed curriculum. He administered the College, taught and lectured, and also carried an considerable correspondence with an ever-expanding circle of those who sought his guidance and to whom he conveyed his ideas on reforming the society.

Waliyyullāh lived in difficult times during the period of decline of the Muslim political power. He struggled valiantly to contribute his best to arrest this decline both in political and social spheres. Indeed, he lived an active life of *Jehād* and *Ijtihād*. He used his pen as powerful weapon and continued to write treatises and books in response to the challenges posed by socio-political conditions as well as by his own developing insights and understandings which unfolded to him the higher realities of life and universe. Of the works authored by him, more than fifty which are known and extant deal with different subjects including Quranic Study, Exegesis, the Hadith, Scholasticism, Law, Jurisprudence, Comparative Law, Sufism, History, Biography, Grammar, Education and Philosophy. He also produced considerable composition in his own verse.

On all these, he has left an imprint of his individuality and originality, both in thought content and presentation. To communicate new ideas in a new thought process, he created new phraseology/terminology embellishing his loaded concepts. He did not write for casual readers but for the advanced, because, the subjects being dealt with by him were of a higher import.

The *magnum opus* of Waliyyullāh is his monumental *Hujjatullah al-Bālighah* (The conclusive Divine Proof) which he completed sometime after 1163 A.H. He had already written a number of works in Persian, but this one he wrote in Arabic to reach the wider world of Islam. Among others, it was one of his main objectives to give a clear convincing exposition of the injunctions of Islam to show that the religious law did not conflict with reason. Thus, he began to unravel the wisdom underlying religious injunctions, in order to remove doubts about the truth of the religion. He observes in his autobiography, *al-Juz' al-Latīf,* that 'he has been raised for the scientific age and to him are entrusted the reins of the future'. Elsewhere he says that it is for the searchers of truth to study his *Hajjatullāh al- Bālighah* and estimate the value of the contribution he has made towards the science of religion (Cf. *al-Sirr al- Maktūm).*

Waliyyullāh undertook to write the *Hujjat* in order to unfold the wisdom and the rationale behind the Shari'ah law. According to him the Hadith is the most important source for developing a correct understanding of Islam, and though the Hadith has been studied elaborately and from different angles, its paramount importance consists in the guidance it gives and the insights it provides for a correct understanding of Islam and Islamic Law.

The book is composed in two main Parts. *Part - I* consisting of seven 'Discussions' *(mabāhith)* which are further subdivided into eighty chapters, deals with the exposition and elaboration of the Universal Laws/Universal Principles *(al-Qawa'id al-Kulliyah)* from which are derived from common agreements *(al-Māslih al- Mara'iyy)* for (formulating) the Shariah Laws. The seven main 'Discussions' centre on the following main themes: (1) The nature and compulsions of human creation. (2) Consequences of human action in this life and after death. (3) Adoption of ways and means for one's own benefit, which is implicit in human nature. (4) Happiness and Misfortune in relation to the earthly life of the humans and in relation to their life in the hereafter. (5) The commonly agreed concepts of Right and Wrong. (6) Political concepts and conditions for the corporate community life (Ummah) (7) The nature of deriving Shari'ah laws from the Tradition. The exposition under this Part is based mainly on the guidance gained from the Quran and the Sunnah. A 'Complimentary Completion' *(Tatimmah)* follows this Part in which the points already covered are further elucidated in the light of the differing opinions of Companions *(sahāba)* and those of the succeeding generation *(tābi'in).*

Part-II consists of thirteen chapters, in which the author explains, particularly in the light of the Hadith, the following aspects of Islamic faith and practice: Belief, Knowledge, Cleanliness, Prayer, Zakat, Fasting, Pilgrimage, Equity *(ihsān)*, Mutual Relations and Transactions *(mu'āmalāt)*, Home or Family Life *(tadbīr al-Manāzil)*, Politics, Ethics, and the *Sīrah* of the Prophet *(sala'm)* as a model.

Basically, the *Hujjat* epitomizes a faith-based rationalism in explaining the edifice of the Islamic Shari'ah. Waliyyullāh begins his introduction with an important observation: "It is generally thought" says he, "that the Shariah Laws are not based on any rationale and that there is no relationship between performance/practice/actions/ deeds (required by Shari'ah and their consequences". In other words, the laws are ordained and have therefore to be observed irrespective of any questions and consequences. Waliyullāh rejects such a concept of the Shariah Laws.

PHILOSOPHY OF ILLUMINATION.

Al-Suhrawardi

حكمة الإشراق

شهاب الدين المقتول السهروردي

Yahya b. Habash b. Amīrak was born in Suhraward in the district of Zanjān in 549/1154. He received his education in Marāgha, and grew up to be a scholar of immense learning. He authored a number of books and was also a poet of merit, his *hā'iyyah qasīdā (abdan tuhinn ilaykum al- arwāhū*) having gained much popularity.

In the realm of ideas, he first followed the path of Sufism, but then turned to philosophy and mysticism.

After his very best intellectual achievements as reflected in his works, his life style as well as thoughts titled towards mystic abnormality. He left his hair and nails to grow, and would not wash his body or clothes. While in Aleppo, he persisted in propagating mystical views which smacked of earlier heresies and for which he was condemned to death (587/1191). Ibn Khalliqān has aptly observed that Suhrawardi was a man whose 'knowledge far exceeded his common sense' *(wa kān ilmhū akbar min 'aqlihī*).

At the height of his creative genuis, combining intellectual-cum-intuitive insights, Suhrawardi gave an exposition of his philosophic thoughts in his two works, *Hayākil al-Nūr* (Temples of Light) and *Hikmat al-Ishrā*q (Philosophy of Illumination). His *Hikmat al-Ishraq* not only opened up a new chapter in the realm of philosophic thought but gave Islamic philosophy a new lease of life. Qutb al-Din Shīrāzī (d.710/1131) in his commentary (*Sharh*) on *Hikmat al-Ishrāq* further illuminated the ideas of Suhrawardi. Among the later thinkers who were influenced by Suhrawardi the most prominent was Sadr al-Dīn

Shīrāzi (Mullā Sadrā) who further advanced philosophic thought under Islam.

The inspirational source for the conception and development of Suhrawardi's 'philosophy of illumination' was the beautiful enlightening verse of the Holy Quran: "God is the light of the heavens and of the earth ...... light upon light" *(wa Allah nūr al-samāvāt wa al-Ard - - - nūrun 'alā nūr*: xxiv: 35). Since the source divine is One, there is only one light, one wisdom, and one mystic truth expressed by saints and sages throughout the ages in different times and climes. According to Suhrawardi: "The Essence of the First Absolute Light, God, gives constant illumination, whereby it is manifested and it brings all things into existence, giving life to them by its rays. Everything in the world is derived from the Light of His Essence and all beauty and perfection are the gift of His bounty, and to attain fully to this illumination is salvation". According to him *'Essence' (dhāt)* is the primary reality, while 'existence' is only a derivative or 'mental' phenomenon.

In *Hikmat al-Ishrāq,* Suhrawardī questioned some of the basic doctrines of the Peripatetic/Neo-Platonic philosophy as it was developed by Ibn Sina. Nāsir al-Din Tūsi who followed the peripatetic tradition was influenced to some extent by Illuministic doctrine. The Illuministic critique of the Peripatetic tradition consisted mainly in "the *Ishrāqī* attack on Ibn Sina's conception of God's knowledge as forms or accidents inhering in God's mind, but later grew in other directions as well - the most important being the view that existence is an unreal mental concept to which nothing corresponds in external reality". (Fazlur Rahman).

By his *Hikmat al-Ishrāq,* Suhrawardi "founded a major philosophical perspective in Islam, the School of Illuminationism, which became a rival of the earlier Peripatetic school and soon even overshadowed it". In his work, Suhrawardi "discusses at length the question of knowledge, ultimately basing it on illumination .... He combines the way of reason with that of intuition, regarding the two as necessary complements of each other. Reason, without intuition and illumination is, according to Suhrawardi, puerile and half-blind and can never reach the transcendent source of all truth and intellection; whereas intuition, without a preparation in logic and the training and development of the rational faculty, can be led astray, and furthermore cannot express itself succinctly and methodically. That is why the "Theosophy of the Orient of Light" *(Hikmat al-Ishrāq)* begins with logic and terminates with a chapter on ecstasy and the contemplation of the celestial assences" (Nasr).

THE SIGNS OF DIVINE GRACE.

Mullā Sadrā

شواهد الربوبية

صدر الدين بن إبراهيم الشيرازي، ملا صدرا

Sadr al-Dīn, Muhammad b. Ibrāhīm b. Yahyā al-Shirāzī, known as 'Mullā Sadrā', was born in Shirāz by about 980 A.H. and died at Basra while he was on his 7th pilgrimage journey in 1050 A.H. (1641 A.D.).

While still young he left Shirāz and went to Isphahan for education. There he studied with eminent teachers such as the mathematician Baha al-Din al-'Āmilī (d. 1031/1622), peripatetic philosopher Mir Fendreski (d. 1050/1631) and the more famous thinker and theologian Muhammad known as Mir Dāmād (d. 1041/1631). Even as student, he was deeply interested in theosophy (philosophical theology) and would assiduously study the early authoritative sources to develop his own understanding of the fundamental questions involved. Being, confident of his own reasoning and perceptions he authored a treatise, *Tarh al- Kaunayan,* in which he argued for the pantheistic doctrine of existence *(Wahdat al-Wajūd)*. This created strong resentment against him in the orthodox circles. He therefore retired to seclusion for a long period of fifteen years, - a period of potential incubation during which he realised the limitation of the mere intellectual power and logical reasoning and turned to God for His grace and guidance, with the result that he gained much deeper insight and intuition whereby he transcended the Peripatetic and the Illuminist. His rational philosophic perceptions had been "lived through" and transformed.

Mulla Sadra was to grow up as a religious scholar but through process of self-realization he turned into a philosopher with originality of ideas not met with earlier in the domain of Muslim philosophy. He authored about 32 to 33 books, treatises, and commentaries - religious and philosophical. Most of these are essentially philosophical in content while application of his philosophical ideas is also reflected in his religious works such as the commentary on the Quran and *Usūl al- Kafi.*

Among his philosophical treatises, the first important one was *Tarh al- Kaunayn* in which he established that the only true existence is God's while all else is mere appearance. His another treatise *Sarayān al-Wujud* reflects 'transitional stage of Sadra's doctrine of essence and existence'. Among commentaries on earlier works, the two are of particular importance: his commentary on Metaphysics of Ibn Sina's *AL-Shifā* and his commentary on *Hikmat al- Ihshrāq* of al-Suhrawardi. But the magnum opus of his philosophic thought is the most comprehensive *al-Hikmat al-Muta'aliya fi al-Asfār al-Arba' al-'Aqliya* ('The Sublime Wisdom in Four Journies of Wisdom). The four parts ('Journies') or the Asfār deal with

(i) the Doctrine of Being,

(ii) Substance and Accidents

(iii) God and His attributes, and

(iv) Man and His Destiny.

Later on, he presented his philosophical ideas, which he had elaborated in *al-Asfār al-Arba'*, in a somewhat concise form in two of his works *al-Mabda'wa al-Ma'ād* and *al- Shawāhid al-Rubūbiya* (The Signs of Divine Grace).

Al-Shawāhid, being Sadra's last work, may be regarded as incorporating the last full statement of his own philosophical thought. Here he does not enter into the elaborate discussions and criticism of the philosophical views of his predecessors as he had done earlier in *al-Asfār al-Arba'a.* Therein he had asserted himself somewhat forcefully while in *al-Shawāhid* he presents his thesis with equanimity. For instance, whereas in *al- Asfār* he criticises "al-Ghazzali's view of the after life", in *al- Shawāhid* "he seeks support from al- Ghazzali and agrees with the latter's interpretation of physical resurrection". This is pointed out by Fazlur Rahman in his scholarly monograph "*The*

Philosophy of Mulla Sadra" as a significant example of the mellowing down of the earlier "hypercritical attitude" of Sadra.

Evaluating Sadra's philosophy, Fazlur Rahman has observed that the three main strands of thought consciously combined by Sadra to yield a "grand synthesis" are (1) the Peripatetic tradition of Ibn Sina, (2) the illuminationist tradition of al-Suhrawardi, and (3) Ibn al-Arbi's theosophy. However this "synthesis is not brought about by mere "reconciliation" and superficial "compromise", but on the basis of a philosophical principle which he both propounded and expounded for the first time in Islamic history. He discovered the principle of the primordiality (sole reality) of existence and its infinite systematic ambiguity despite it or, rather, as Sadra insists, *because* of it. He expounded it and applied it to the entire range of the problems of Islamic philosophy-the nature of God, the nature of the World, and the nature and destiny of man".*

---

* Fazlur Rahman: *The Philosophy of Mulla Sadra,* State University of New York Press Albany,1975, 'Introduction'.

THE ESSENTIAL PREMISES OF THE VIEWS OF THE CITIZENS OF THE IDEAL CITY (STATE).

Al-Farabi

رسالة في مبادئ آراء أهل المدينة الفاضلة

أبو نصر محمد الفارابي

Abu Nasr Muhammad b. Muhammad b. Tarkhan b. Awzlagh/Uzlagh was born in a Turkish family of Wasīj near Fārāb in Turkistan by about 260 A.H. and died aged eighty or more in 339 A.H. (950 A.D.) in Damascus.

Being the son of a *Qāid al-Jaish,* an army officer belonging probably to the Caliph's bodyguard, Farabi grew up and was educated in Baghdad, but then he devoted himself purly to scholarly pursuits. In 330 A.H. (942 A.D.), he accepted invitation from the enlightened Hamdānid ruler of Aleppo, Saif al-Daula, and joined his court and continued to live there in company of eminent scholars for the rest of his life.

Farabi was also a physician, mathematician and musician. His pioneering work *Kitāb al-Musiqī al-Kabīr* (The Great Book of Music) proves him to be a great music theorist. He also excelled as a performing musician. The eminent biographer Ibn Khallikān has noted that in the presence of his patron Sayf-al- Dawlah, Fārābī played on his lūte skilfully so as to send his listeners into ecstasy, to put them to laughter, to draw tears from their eyes or set them all asleep, even the door keepers. Ancient chants attributed to him are still sung by the Mawlwi dervishes (Hitti).

As the most distinguished thinker of his times, he wrote on Physics, Metaphysics, Logic, Music, Ethics, Politics, and the curricular classification of Knowledge.

In this context, he authored important works which also distinguish him as a pioneer of great ideas in the domain of Ethic and Politics. Of these, the following ones are known and published, some having been studied for centuries in Europe: *al-Tanbih 'alā Sabīl al-Sa'ādā* (Reminder for the Way of Happiness); *Mabādi 'Arā' Ahl al-Madīna al- Fādila);* 'On the Principles of the Views of the Inhabitants of the Excellent City State' "On Political Government" *(al-Siyāsa al-Madaniyya);* and "Aphorisms of the Stateman" *(Fusūl al-Madanī*).

Farabi is one of the leading philosophers of all times. He wrote scholarly commentaries on Aristotle's discourses, and also an important work on *Harmony Between the Views of Plato And Aristotle (al-Jama, bain ra'yai al-Hakim al-Aflatun al-Ilahi wa Aristutalis).* For his unexcelled exposition of the Aristotalian philosophy, he became known as *al- Mu'allim al-Thānī*, THE SECOND (GREAT) TEACHER (after Aristotle). He not only defended philosophy but intended "sovereign position to be given to philosophy within the realm of thinking and with the organiszation of the perfect society and philosopher king". (E.I.)

Mabādi Ārā' Ahl al- Madīna al-Fādilā ('The Essential Premises of the Views of the Dwellers of the Ideal City', i.e. Citizens of an Ideal State') is Farabi's most known and admired work in which through detailed and systematic philosophical exposition of the concepts covering the Supreme Creator and the heirarchicel species of creation-Man being the best among them. He then underlines man's need for association resulting in the development of community/society, and the societies closing together to live harmonously in a City State. The book is divided into 19 chapters of which the following brief and inadequate headlines here should all the same give an ideal of the contents of this great philosophical work.

1. Nature of the Being to be believed and worshipped-Allah, and the First Cause of other existents.

2. The nature of heavenly existents, Angles, and their relationship with the First Cause.
3. The heavenly existent. all-inclusive and listed together to interact-scheme-wise harmoniously.
4. Sub-heavenly material existents and their nature.
5. Matter and Form.
6. Explanation of the nature of the existents taken to be Angels.
7. The way heavenly bodies can be described.
8. Arising of the material natural bodies - 'man' being the last among them.
9. Species of the natural bodies - the continuity of their existence, their relationships, and which occurs to them based on perfection and justice.
10. Man and the faculties of the human soul.
11. Limbs, and organs of human body - their relative position with reference to their coming into being and importance.
12. Male and Female - their nature and the nature of their offspirings.
13. The rational part of the soul and its intellegibles. The different intellects - passive, active, potential. Active Intellect and its function.
14. The important part of the soul, soul's functions, the nature of dreams etc.
15. Development of Society from Man's need for association, kinds of societies and the excellent ones, the way they are bound together; the Ideal City (State) and the Ideal Ruler. Excellences in an ideal ruler, importance of his training from childhood to full maturity. In constrast, the nature of the astray and ignorant city, and its relationships.

16. The *sa'ādā* (bliss and fecility) attained by the souls of the dwellers of the ideal city.
17. The environment and customs which should prevail in the ideal city to promote ideas the dater false impressions and notions.
18. The views arising from ignorance, which cause ignorant actions and from which arise ignorant societies and cities.
19. The destructive principles (*al-usūl al- fāsidah*) and the views based on them giving rise to misguided sectarian communities.

METHODS OF JUDGEMENT IN THE ADMINISTRATION OF SHARĪ'AH LAWS.

Ibn Qayyim al-Jawziyyah

الطرق الحكمية في السياسة الشرعية

أبو عبد الله محمد بن أبي بكر المعروف بابن قيم الجوزية

Shams al-Din Muhammad b. Abu Bakr was born in Damascus on 7 Safar 691. (1292). Young Muhammad's father being the superintendent *(Qayyim)* of the Jawziyyah College which then served as Court of Law, the son came to be called as "Ibn Qayyim al-Jawziyyah". He studied under eminent teachers of whom the renowned reformer Ibn Taymiyyah's teachings influenced him the most. He stood by his reformer teacher through thick and thin, and even suffered imprisonment with him (726 - 728 A.H). In 731 A.H., Ibn Qayyim proceeded on pilgrimage to Makka. He then took to teaching as his career, and on 6 Safar 743 A.H. (1342) he gave his first lecture at the Sadriyya College. He continued to teach at this institution until his death on 23 Rajab 751 A.H. (1350). Some of his pupils became eminent scholars in their own right.

Having acquired sound education with special knowledge of *Tafsir, Hadith* and *Fiqh,* Ibn Qayyim advanced the ideas of his great teacher though he maintained an individuality of his own. Unlike Ibn Taymiyyah, Ibn Qayyim was influenced by Sufism, and yet he followed his teacher (Ibn Taymiyyah) in refuting the ideas on prophecy and pantheism which had spread under the doctrine of Ibn al-'Arabi (d. 638 A.H.).

Besides being a highly qualified theologian and jurisconsult, Ibn Qayyim was a man of great learning. He held independent views which he expressed and substantiated ably. Even when the eminent Shāfi'ī jurist and Chief Justice of Damascus Taqī al-Dīn al-Subkī had disagreed with him, Ibn Qayyim held that introduction of a third rider *(muhallil)* was not necessary in order to legalise a horse race between the two bate horses. In an altogether different domain, he refuted the validity of Alchemy and the claim of its practitioners of converting the base metal into gold. To this end, he brought forth forty arguments in his treatise *Butlān al-Kīmiyā'win Arba'īn wajhan,* establishing falsehood of Alchemy.

Ibn Qayyim wrote a large number of books and treatises and left an imprint of his independent views on all of them. About 68 of his works which are known, cover a wide range of subjects such as Quranic Studies, Tafsir, Hadith, Dialectics, Theology, Sīrah, Grammar and Sufism. Following the footsteps of his teacher Ibn Taymiyyah, Ibn Qayyim undertook to counter the trends in the domain of belief and faith *(al- Aqā'id* and *Usūl al-Dīn),* which were against the true spirit of Islam and the rationale of Islamic injunctions.

Thus in two of his books he countered the views held by the *Ittihādiya* (claimants for Ibn al-'Arabi) and others of Jahmiyya-cum-Mu'atazila pursuasions. Ibn Qayyim upheld sincerity in faith and clean living which were implicit in the Sufi way of life, and his *Madārij al-Sālikīn,* a commentary on *Manāzil al-Sā'irīn* of the great *Sūfī* al-Ansārī, represents the best Hanbalī exposition of Sufism. His literary genius is reflected by his *Fawā'id,* a landmark in the history of rhetoric. In the domain of law and politics, he authored his important book *Kitāb al-Turaq al-Hukmiyyah fi al-Silsilat al-Shara'iyyah* (Methods of Judgement in the Administration of Sharī'ah Laws).

Besides substantive Law *(Fiqh)* and Jurisprudence *(Usul al-Fiqh),* both of which were elaborately developed under Islam, there was the third dimension of the day-to-day governance and administration requiring rules and regulations to be made and enforced by the competent authority to ensure public welfare and public good. Ibn Qayyim's teacher Ibn Taymiyyah had in some of his works dealt with the obligation of the governing authority to the governed in this regard. In his treatise *al- Hisbah fi al-Islam* he discussed the duties and functions of the *Muhtasib* (Ombudsman) and in his more elaborate treatise *Al- Siyāsah al-Shara'iyyah fi Islāh al- Rā'ī wa al-Ra'iyyah* he dealt with the duties and responsibilities of the ruler and the ruled, public transactions, dispensation of justice, and enforcement of the *hudūd* laws (punishments for crimes under the injunction of Holy Quran.)

Ibn Qayyim made a further advance in this field when he authored *Al-Turaq al-Hukmiyyah* in response to a question presented to him by a contemporary ruler. The book may perhaps be regarded as the most original and qualitative one on the subject of administration of justice and crime investigation ever written by an early Muslim jurist. Ibn Qayyim deals with circumstantial evidence and gives a score of examples based on the Hadith literature and from the practices of the Prophet's Companions and their followers wherein circumstantial evidence was admitted and cases of criminal as well as civil nature were decided on the basis of that evidence. Ibn Qayyim has also dealt with other important issues such as preventive detention and the modes to be followed for investigation of crimes. His approach is highly practical coupled with a deep insight into the legal concepts and juridical principles of Islam.

Eversince it was written, the book was regarded as the most important source on the subject and, as such, it deeply influenced subsequent writings in this field. In particular, the Mālikī jurist Ibn Farhūn and the Hanafī Jurist 'Alā al-Dīn Tarābulusī, were so much influenced by Ibn Qayyim that their respective books appear to be a further elaboration of the thinking reflected in *Al-Turaq al-Hukmiyyah.*

THE BOOK ON PUBLIC FINANCE.

Abū 'Ubayd Al-Harawi

كتاب الأموال

ابو عبيد قاسم بن سلام

The author Abū 'Ubayd al-Qāsim b. Salām was born in Herat (cerea 174 A.H. (770 A.D.) where he completed his early education. He then studied in Kufa, Basra and Baghdad and excelled in Hadith, Fiqh, Arabic Language, Grammar and Literature. Returning to home country, he was appointed Qādi of Tarsūs in Cilicia where he served for about 18 years. In 213 A.H. (828 A.D.) he visited Egypt, and after sometime proceeded to Baghdad where scholars studied his books under him. In the later years of his life, he journeyed to Hijaz, performed the Hajj and died later at Makka sometime in 224 A.H.

Abū 'Ubayd was an eminent scholar of Hadith and Fiqh, and also he was most accomplished in his study of Arabic language and its style and syntax. He wrote about twenty works on these subjects, and dedicated many of them to Abdullah b. Tāhir, the Tāhirid ruler of Khurasan (207-213 A.H./828-845 A.D.) in whose opinion Abū 'Ubayd was, until then, the fourth greatest scholar of Islam (after Abdullah b. 'Abbās, al-Shu'bī, and al-Qāsim b. Ma'an in their times). Abū 'Ubayd's works on language elicited highest praise from such a distinguished literatuer as Jāhiz who observed that "None ever wrote more accurate and more useful works than him (Abū 'Ubayd)". His voluminous *"al-Gharīb al-Musannaf"* was a pioneering work on codification of ***the rare hadith*** of the Prophet (*sal'am*)

Among the early known works dealing with Public Finance, Abū 'Ubayd's book occupies chronologically the third position after *Kitāb al-kharāj* of Qadi Abū Yūsuf (d. 182 A.H.) and *Kitāb al-Kharāj* of Yahyā b. Ādam (d.203 A.H.). The first two deal mainly with Law, rather Constitutional law, governing interstate relations. Abū 'Ubayd's work is much more comprehensive in so far as the subject of public finance of an Islamic State is concerned. He begins by stressing the mutual rights and obligations of the *Imām* (the ruling leader) and the community, and their responsibilities under Islamic Polity. He discusses the institution of *Bayt al-māl* (The Public Treasury) and how the accumulated incomes therein are to be distributed.

Abū 'Ubayd refers to the main sources of the finance, of which *Bayt al-Māl* becomes the sole repository and the administration of which, both on income and expenditure side, is the responsibility of Islamic State. In *Kitāb al-Amwāl* he deals elaborately with *Ghanīma*(war-booty), the *Khums* (one-fifth of the booty earmarked for the Prophet), *Fai'* (the property that falls in the hands of the Muslims without battle), *Jiziya* (tax realised from the non-Muslim subjects) and *Kharāj* (an annual grant realised from the defeated states). He also explains which of the lands are subject to *'Ushr* and which to *Kharāj* and how to divide them among the Muslims.

In the latter part on *Sadaqāt* and *Zakāt*, the methods of collection and distribution thereof are discussed. The final chapter on *Sadaqah* pertains to the property of orphans and other relevant details.

THE BOOK OF MINISTERS AND SECRETARIES.

Al-Jahshayārī

كتاب الوزراء والكتاب

أبو عبد الله محمد المعروف بالجهشياري

The author Abu Abdullah Muhammad b. Abdūs, known as 'al-Jahshayārī', was born by about the middle of the 3rd century A.H. in Kufa. That city was a great centre of learning, and there he received good education. He cultivated skill in penmanship under his father who was a professional scribe and became Secretary to the Prime Minister Ali b. 'Isā in 301 A.H. (913/14 A.D.) during the reign of the Abbasid Caliph al-Muqtadar (295-320 A.H./908-932). Following his father's footsteps, Abu Abdullah also entered Secretarial service. In 306 A.H., he was Secretary to Ali b. Isa who was then assisting the Prime Minister Hamid b. Abbās. In Ramadan 317 A.H. (929), Jahshayārī was in charge of the *ghilāf* of Ka'ba being taken to Makka for the Hajj occasion. Not much is known about the later years of his life except that he was arrested, and released on payment of heavy fine. He died in 331 A.H (942/943). According to the author of *al-Nujūm al-Zāhirah,* Jahshayārī "was a scholar of high status and well versed in arts".

Jahshayārī was a prolific writer. Nadim has noted in AL-FIHRIST that as an author Jahshayārī began by compiling a compendium of One Hundred Stories selected from a wide range of sources - Arabic, Persian and Roman. Besides his "Book of Ministers and Secretaries", he had authored a book on poetry *(Kitab Mizān al-Shi'r)* and another one on prosody *(al-Ishtimāl 'alā Anwā' al-'Urūd).* Mas'ūdi has observed in his *Murūj al-Dhahb* that it was generally believed that Jahshayārī wrote the history of al-Muqtadir which according to a knowledgeable source covered one thousand folios.

Kitāb al-Wuzarā' wa al- Kuttāb or 'The Book of the Ministers And the Secretaries' is an important work in which the author has detailed the history of penmanship and correspondence *(al-Kitābat wa al-Inshā)* from the days of the Prophet (*sal'am*) to his own times. It is a pioneer work in this field, and has been used as the main source of information by such eminent authors as Sūlī, Nadīm, Ibn al-Athīr, Yaqūt, Ibn Khallikān and Ibn Taghri Birdī. According to Sābī, Jahshayārī had brought his account of the ministers and secretaries up to the year 296 A.H. when Abu Ahmad al-Abbās b. Hasan was the Prime Minister of Caliph al- Muktafī.

THE CLEAR EXPOSITION OF THE PRINCIPLES OF ACCOUNTABILITY.

Ibn al-Ukhuwwah

معالم القربة في أحكام الحسبة

ضياء الدين محمد المشهور بابن الأخوة

The author Diyā al-Din Muhammad b. Muhammad b. Ahmad al-Qurashi al-Shāfi'ī Al-Ash'arī, known as 'Ibn al-Ukhuwwah, was born by about the middle of the 7th century A.H. (13th A.D.) and died in Rajab 729 A.H. (1329 A.D.).

Social regulations in Islam included supervision of public safety with the all awareness provided for in Holy Quran and Hadith. This supervision and the accountability that went with it was *hisbah* which in its essence was a Muslim's obligation arising from the Quranic injunction *al-amr bi al-ma'arūf wa al-nahyi un al-munkar,* to promote good and prevent evil. *Hisbah* as 'accountability' was an essential corollary of Islamic Justice as applied to public services and public transactions. It called for supervision, inspection, and stock taking in order to ensure proper performance of public and professional services. From this obligation emerged the office of a *Sāhib al-Sūq* (Supervisor of the Market) for supervision and promotion of public morality and fair play in professional dealings and transactions in crafts, trades and markets. The *Hisbah* Department though a part of the Chief-Justice's Secretariat was headed by a separate official with the special status of 'Muhtasib' (Administrator of Accountability). He was sought to be a God fearing religious man and was invested with all powers to allow the licit and forbid the illicit. He ranked higher than the Qadi and was appointed by the Caliph himself.

The first 'Muhtasib' (replacing 'Sāhib al-Sūq') was appointed in the 3rd century A.H. during the reign of the Abbasid Caliph Māmūn.

Instructions issued to him and the procedures adopted and the cases decided by the Muhtasib led to the development of *Hisbah* literature wherein the subject was discussed and elaborated in all its dimensions. By the end of the 5th century A.H., Imam Ghazzali (d. 505 A.H./1111) devoted a section to it in *'Ihyā' 'Ulūm al-Dīn'*. As *Hisbah* became an essential feature of Islamic Polity, Māwardī (d. 589/1193) included a chapter on it in his *al-Ahkām al-Sultāniyah,* thus bringing *Hisbah* within the orbit of Constitutional Law.

The full-fledged works written on *Hisbah* were of two categories: the works of a judicial nature which defined the essence and scope of *hisbah* and the obligations arising out of it for the Muhtasib, and those of an administrative nature which dealt with technical details of the supervision for guiding and enlightening the Muhtasib. However, all the works on the subject underlined the great importance of the office of the Muhtasib and stressed his high qualifications so that he would be above any reproach whatsoever. More specifically, he was to be God-fearing and religious, noble, learned, modest, experienced, intelligent, unbiassed, rich and honest above corruption.

In the Muslim West, al-Saqtī of Malāga (Spain) wrote *Kitāb fi Abāb al-Hisbah* (The Book on Requirements for Hisbah) by about 500/1106. Later in the 6th century, Ibn 'Abdūn of Seville wrote *Risāla fi al-Qadā wa al-Hisbah* (The Treatise on Justice and Hisbah) while Ibn Bassām authored a more comprehensive work *Nihāyat al-Rutba fi Talab al-Hisbah* (Standard Achievement in Investigation of Hisbah) containing as many as 118 chapters. In the Muslim East, the first full-fledged work, with the same title as Ibn Bassām's, containing 40 chapters, was authored for Sultan Salāhuddin Ayūbī by Abd al-Rahmān b. Nasr b. Abdullah al-Shāfi'ī al-Shīzarī (d. 589/1193). Later in the 7th/13th century Ibn al-Ukhuwwah wrote *Ma'ālim al-Qurbah fi Ahkām al-Hisbah* (The Clear Exposition of Principles of Accountability). In this work, extending to seventy chapters, Ibn al-Ukhuwwah has enlarged upon al-Shizari's work incorporating considerably advanced material on the subject, including discussion of difficult cases , some of them hypothetical in nature for purpose of explanation. Written as a guide book for the Muhtasib, it provides a summary of the positive and negative injunctions contained in the standard codes of the *Sharī'ah* together with regulations for safeguarding of public morality, for ensuring the purity of the faith and for protecting the public against tickery, charlatanry, fraud and exhortation (E.I.).

THE BOOK OF ROUTES AND KINGDOMS.

Ibn Khurdādhbīh

كتاب المسالك والممالك

ابو القاسم عبيد الله بن احمد ابن خرداذبه

Not much is known about biographical details of the author, Abu al- Qāsim ‘Ubaydullah b. Ahmad (or Abdullah) b. Khurdādhbih. His father was governor of Tabaristān under Caliph Māmūn (198-218 A.H/813-833), and Abu al-Qāsim was probably born in Baghdad in 205A.H./820 A.D. (or in 211/825) and died by about 280 A.H./893 A.D. (or 300/911). He grew up in Baghdad, received good education and studied under such eminent scholars as Ishāq al-Mawsili who was also a great musicologist.

Abu al-Qāsim grew up to be a knowledgeable scholar, and during the reign of Caliph al-Mu‘tamid (256-279 A.H/870-892) he was appointed as Director of Post and Information in the province of Jibāl. Subsequently, he was promoted as Post Master General for all the provinces of the Caliphate, with his headquarter first in Baghdad and then in Sāmarrā. He gained favour of al-Mu‘tamid who made him his *nadīm*, a personal confident and boon-companion. Under the impulse of lighter side of the court life, he wrote treatises on entertainment, music and revelley. But he also authored scholarly works such as “The Book of the Principal Persian Genealogies And of the Newly Settled Population”; a historical work, *Kitāb al- Tārīkh,* which according to al-Mas‘ūdī was the best planned and most comprehensive work; and *Kitāb al- Anwā’* on traditional wisdom regarding seasons and atmospherics.

Ibn Khurdādhbih’s most outstanding contribution, based on his specialised knowledge and professional work as Post Master General, was his *Kitāb al-Masālik wa al-Mamālik*, an official compendium on caravan and trade routes and the journey halts and stages in the different regions and provinces of the Caliphate. Ibn Khurdādhbih probably did not travel himself: he relied mainly on official record and reports received from time to time. He published this work in two editions, the first one in the early thirties of the third century (c.232 A.H./846) and the second enlarged one four decades later (c.272 A.H./885). This is a pioneer work associated with postal services, and is also an important early source on the historical-cum-cultural geography of the Caliphate. The book opened up a new field of study and investigation, and works with comparable titles appeared soon thereafter.

In the introductory part, he indicates the location of the different countries/regions/cities direction-wise with reference to the Ka'ba, its four walls representing the four main directions. In the next four sections, he describes the countries lying to the East, West, North and the South (of Baghdad) respectively along with the cities, caravan routes, and the journeying stages thereof.

This is followed by a short but important section on postal service: "There are" he says "nine hundred and thirty postal stations (*Sikak al-Barīd*) in the State". Indeed, safety of travel and facilities for halting stations on the highways had enabled not only the Muslims, but also non-Muslims to carry on international trade uninterrupted. Ibn Khurdadhbih specifically mentions the Jewish and the Russian traders who were then travelling and trading from East to West and West to East. In the last section, he has recorded the peculiarities and 'wonders' of the different regions.

As already observed, Ibn Khurdadhbih had prepared his book by bringing together information from official records and reports. He had not travelled himself and followed the trade routes. This was done later by the great investigator al-Mas'ūdī who authored a book by the same name *Kitāb al-Masālik wa* al-Mamālik which though now lost must have been an authentic work of great merit; Al-Bayrūni has cited it (in his *Kitāb al-Jamāhir*) as an authority and also Ibn Abi 'Usaybi'ah has mentioned it among al-Mas'ūdi's works.

THE BEGINNING OF THE ADVANCED (MUJTAHID) AND THE END OF THE AVERAGE (MUQTASID).

Ibn Rushd

بداية المجتهد ونهاية المقتصد

القاضي أبو الوليد محمد بن أحمد المعروف بابن رشد الحفيد الأندلسي

Ibn Rushd, Abu al-Walīd, Muhammad b. Ahmad b. Rushd, famous in the West as Averroes, was the most eminent philosopher, jurisprudent, and physician who flourished in the Muslim West. He was born at Cordova in 520 A.H. (1198 A.D.) and died in Marrākush in 595 A.H. (1273 A.D.).

He hailed from a prominent family of the jurists. His grandfather also bore the same name and the *kuniya,* and to distinguish between the two, 'al-Hafīd' (grandson) was affixed to his name. In this milieu, Ibn Rushd Junior received good education and was especially trained in Law by his teacher al-Hāfiz Abu Muhammad Ibn Rizq. He learnt by heart the *Muwattā'* of Imām Mālik. He was also initiated into the Science of Hadith, but devoted himself mainly to Jurisprudence, Philosophy and Medicine.

Ibn Rushd was the greatest commentator on Aristotle, and as such he became known as 'The Commentator'. There are altogether thirty eight commentaries by Ibn Rushd on different works of Aristotle, including physics and metaphysics, in addition to short treatises devoted to particular aspects of Aristotalian philosophy.

Ibn Rushd studied medicine under Abu Ja'far Hārūn al-Tajāli, a noted figure in Seville who was well-versed in the works of ancient physicians. Ibn Rushd grew up as the most qualified and competent physician, and entered the service of Amir Abu Ya'qūb Yūsuf (1163-1184 A.D.), followed by al-Mansūr Ya'qūb Ibn Yūsuf (1184 - 1199). Al-Mansur during his stay in Seville, had honoured and attracted thirty eniment philosophers, scientists, physicians and poets, and also patronized their meetings which were attended by scholars like Ibn Tufayl, Ibn Zuhr (Avenzoar), and Ibn Rushd himself. As a great physician, Ibn Rushd authored the comprehensive *Kitāb al-Kulliyāt fi al-Tibb,* 'Colleget' or 'The Book of Universals', on general principles of medicine which is philosophical in outlook and is dialectical in expression.

Like his father and grandfather, Ibn Rushd served as Qadi and Imam of the Great Mosque of Cordova. Among the *fuqahā'* (jurisprudents), he is known as 'Abu al-Walid Ibn Rushd *al- Hafīd.* He wrote as many as sixty books on Fiqh, Qadā and Literature, most of which are well known and have been in wide circulation.

In the domain of Jurisprudence, his book *Bidāyat al- Mujtahid wa Nihāyat al-Muqtasid* (The Beginning of the Advanced and the End of the Average) is of special importance. The great merit of this work is that it is so very accurately balanced in presenting the different opinions concerning *Shari'ah laws* that, despite Ibn Rushd's philosophical views anchored in Greek thought, this book of his gained widest acceptance and popularity.

In his exposition of Islamic Jurisprudence Ibn Rushd has brought under discussion the views and arguments of the early leading *mujtahid* jurists, in the light of the foundational sources of Islamic Law, viz. the 'Kitāb', the 'Sunnah', the 'Ijmā' and the 'Qiyās'. He himself states in his introduction that his aim and object is to bring together in this book all those *Sharī'ah* laws concerning which there is agreement or disagreement among the *fuqahā'* (jurists) from the time of the *Sahāba* (Prophet's Companions) to his own times, giving arguments and reasons for disagreements. In his presentation he first explains the different methods by which the *Sharī'ah* laws are deduced, and then cites the reasons which impelled the pioneer jurists to record their own differing opinions.

AL-HIDĀYAH IN THE EXPOSITION OF AL-BIDĀYAH.

Al-Marghīnānī

الهداية في شرح البداية

برهان الدين ابو الحسن علي بن ابي بكر المرغيناني

Abu al-Hasan Burhān al-Dīn 'Ali b. Abī Bakr b. 'Abd al-Jalāl al-Farghāni, al-Marghīnānī, the great Hanafite jurist, was born at Marghīnān in the vicinity of Farghāna in 530 A.H. (1135 A.H.). He died in 593 A.H. (1197 A.D.).

He studied with Muftī Najm al-Dīn Abu Hafs 'Umar al- Nasafī, his son Abu'l Layth Ahmad b. 'Umar al-Nasafi and other eminent teachers, and excelled in Hadith, Tafsir, Fiqh and other studies. His scholarship was recognised and praised by eminent scholars such as Imam Fakhr al-Din Qādī Khān, Zahīr al-Din Muhammad b. Ahmad al-Bukhari (the author of *al- Fatāwa al-Zahīriyyah*) and others.

He authored a number of works in law and jurisprudence. In the introduction to his *Bidāyat al-Mubtādi'*, he explains the circumstances under which he composed 'al-Hidāyah'. He wanted to write a book in Fiqh, smaller in size but extensive in usefulness, comprehensive enough containing all the agreed decisions with reference to different procedures (*turuq*) and schools. "In this respect, I found the elementary brief book of al-Qudūrī as the best of the lot in preciseness and diction, and yet I saw that all the scholars were devoted to memorizing *al-Jāmi' al- Saghīr* of Imam Muhammad. I therefore synthecised the two together, following the arrangement of *al-Jāmi'* and adding only what was urgently needed , and entitled it as *Bidāyat al-Mubtadī*. I commented upon this book in another work entitled *Kifāyat al-Muntahī* running into eighty volumes. I then abridged this under the name of *al- Hidāyah* in the year 573 A.H., retaining all the necessary and useful comments and leaving out the elaborate details which were not urgently needed."

The text of al-Hidayah presents Sharī'ah laws on all aspects of life. It summarises the contents of the works of Imām Muhammad, called *'Zāhir al-Riwāyah'*, and also those of Imam Abū Yūsuf. Its subject matter illustrates *'Ibādāt*; social, political and moral obligations; the injunctions of the Quran and Sunnah; the legal restrictions upon adult prodigals for the advantage of the community to preserve the property and peace of families and the virtue of individuals. Though most of the arguments advanced corroborate with the Hanafite School of legal interpretation, it also compares and contrasts the views and counter arguments of other legal schools with all care and caution.

Eversince its publication, *al-Hidāyah* has been read, critically studied and commented upon by a large number of competent scholars. Some had raised the question about the Prophet's sayings quoted in it, and therefore this aspect was examined critically and all the *ahādīth* quoted were traced out in the recognized Hadith Collections. This was done by such eminent scholars as Shaykh Muhiyuddin Abd al-Qādir b. Muhammad al-Qarashi of Egypt (d. 775/1373) in his *al-'Ināyah bi Ma'rifat Ahādith al-Hidāyah* and by Shaykh 'Ala al-Din Abdullah b. Yusuf al-Zayla'ī in his work "*Nasb al-Rāyah li Ahādith al-Hidāyā*" which was abridged and revised by Ahmad b. 'Ali b. Hajar al-'Asqalāni (d. 852/1448) under the title *al-Dirāyah fi Muntakhab Ahādith al-Hidāyah* (c.f.*Kashf al- Zunūn* and *al-Maqaddima*). Thus, the reliability of *al-Hidāyah* and the competence and integrity of its author were amply established.

Al-Hidāyah attained great name and fame and became an indispensable source book of Sharī'ah Law according to Hanafite School of Jurisprudence. The author had prepared it during the course of thirteen years in a state of fasting and piety. It is divided into four parts which are further sub-divided into sections each known as 'Kitāb' or 'Book'. The *Hidāyah* is comprehensive in content and so very convenient in reference that with its publication the previous works on the subject became outmoded and fell into disuse. In the considered opinion of the scholarly 'Abd al-Hayy, *al-Hidāyah* has been accepted by the people because of its preciseness and comprehensiveness.

Al-Hidāyah served as the main source of reference for Hanafite Law for the succeeding generations of Muslims in Turkey, Central Asia and the Hindostan Subcontinent.*

---

* It was used by courts in the British India during the colonial period. Hamilton translated it into English abridging it in some parts and omitting some sections of the text altogether.

PRINCIPLES OF JURISPRUDENCE.

Imām al-Shāfiʻī

الرسالة

أبو عبد الله محمد بن إدريس الشافعي

Abū ʻAbdullah Muhammad b. Idrīs b. al-ʻAbbās b. ʻUthmān Ibn Shāfiʻī whose lineage joins with of the Holy Prophet in ʻAbd Manāf, was born at Ghazzah (Palestine) in 150 H. and was taken to Makka Mukarramah when he was two years old. He was brought up in the Hudhayl tribe and memorized their verses which the eminent linguist al-Asmaʻī learnt from him.

Thus, young Muhammad became fully conversant with the early Arabic society, their custom and tradition. On learning of Imam Mālik's great reputation, he borrowed a copy of *al-Muwattā*, memorized it in nine days and then travelled to Madina and obtained *ijāzah* (permission) for narrating and transmitting the text from Imam Mālik who appreciated his good memory and sound understanding of legal decisions. Imam Ahmad ibn Hanbal considered him as "the most knowledgeable of all" about the Quran, seldom in need of a *hadith* (as he was fully accomplished in it). He also said, 'I did not recognize the abrogating *hadith* from the abrogated one until I kept sitting with Shāfiʻī'. One of the greatest jurists of all times, al-Shāfiʻī died in 204 A.H. (820 A.D.).

Imam Shāfiʻī is the founder of one of the four schools of Islamic Jurisprudence. He authored a number of important works, but it is in his voluminous work *Kitāb al-Umm* (The Mother Book) that Islamic Law is extensively codified. Therein he has also taken cognizance of the conflicting views of contemporary jurists of Hijaz, Iraq, Syria, Yaman and Egypt and given their legalistic analysis in term of the basic principles.

Imam Shāfi'ī became the first jurist in Islam to enunciate the principles he employed for arriving at legal decisions. Some of the *usul* of principles of *Fiqh* (Law) were discussed by *Qadi* Abu Yusuf and his pupil al-Shaybāni, but Shāfi'ī in his creative thinking conceived the *usul* as a source of law. Thus by elaborating the new meaningful concept of the *usul* in the *Risalah,* Shāfi'ī became the Founder of the Science of Jurisprudence under Islam. To quote Khadduri: "No other jurist seems to have discussed the subject in so coherent and systematic manner, and the Risālah appears to be the first complete and well-organized survey of the *usul*, their inter-relationship, and how the detailed rules and decisions were derived from the authoritive sources. The significance of the Risālah, therefore, lies not so much in the detailed matters it discusses, although these have had their influences on Muslim jurists, as in the comprehensive view of the whole subject of usūl and in the logical and systematic method Shāfi'ī provided for legal reasoning. The originality of the book lies in its new departure in the study of jurisprudence."

A TREASURY FOR ACHIEVING THE KNOWLEDGE OF PRINCIPLES OF JURISPRUDENCE.

Al-Bazdawi

الأصول

علي بن محمد بن عبد الكريم البزدوي

The author Abu'l Hasan Ali b. Muhammad b. al-Husayn b. 'Abd al- Karīm was born at Bazdah, a fortress near Nasaf within the jurisdiction of Samarqand, in 400 A.H., and died in 428 A.H./1089. He was an eminent Hanafite jurist, exegesisist (*mufassir*) and traditionist (*muhadddith*), and was respectfully acclaimed as "*Fakhr al-Islam* al-Bazdawi".

He was a contemporary of great jurists and thinkers such as Ghazzali's illustrious teacher Imam al-Haramayn, the Shafi'ī jurist Abu Ishaq Shirazi, the Maliki jurist and traditionist Abu'l Wahid al-Baji, Saif al-Din al-Āmidi, Baihaqi and Ibn Hazm. That Bazdawi was hailed as *Fakhr al-Islam* ('Pride of Islam') among a galaxy such scholars and sevants, attests to his high stature as a jurist.

Bazdawi authored voluminous works on Law (*Fiqh*) and Jurisprudence (*Usūl al-Fiqh*) as well as on exegesis of the Quran (*Tafsīr*). Of these, *al- Mabsūt* in eleven volumes, a commentary of Imam Shaybānī's *al-Jāmi' al-Kabīr,* another commentary on *al-Jāmi' al-Saghīr,* a commentary of the Quran *Kashf al-Asrār*, in one hundred and twenty parts, and his well- known text on Islamic Jurisprudence deserve special mention. But his recognition as a celebrated jurist is based on his *Kanz al-Wusūl ilā Ma'rifat al-Usūl* ('A Treasury for Achieving the Knowledge of Jurisprudence') generally known as *Usūl al-Bazdawi*, i.e. 'Bazdawi's Principles' (of Jurisprudence).

'Bazdawi's Principles' is an important work in which the author has established the principles for deriving decisions from the verses of the Holy Quran, and from the text (*nass*) of the sayings, actions and approvals of the Prophet (*sal'am*). Comprehensive in scope but brief and meaningful in diction, it became popular, and many eminent scholars centered their attention on it and wrote commentaries and annotations. At least twelve commentaries have been listed by Haji Khalifa in his *Kashf* Bibliography. Among them the commentary by Shaykh Ala' al-Din Abd al-Aziz b. Ahmad al-Bukhārī (d. 730 A.H.), entitled *Kash al-'Asrār* was judged to be the best in the academic circles and was also used as a text book in educational institutions.

Bazdawi begins his book with a discussion of 'Knowledge' (*'Ilm*) and differentiates it into *'Ilm al-Tawhīd wa al-Sifāt* (Knowledge of Oneness of God and His Attributes) and *'Ilm al-Sharī'ah wa al-Ahkām'* (Knowledge of the Sharī'ah laws and decisions). The first has been explained as 'holding fast to the Qur'an and the Sunnah'. The second has been defined as *'Ilm al-Furū'* or *al-Fiqh* which is subdivided into (i) knowledge of the prescribed law itself; (ii) accurate knowledge of texts and their meanings and the application of 'Principles' (*usul*) to their subidiaries (*furū'*); and (iii) acting in the light of knowledge but without the knowledge being considered as an object in itself. He therefore calls *'Ilm al-Sharī'ah* as *'hikmah'* or 'Wisdom'.

Bazdawi, then deals with the *Khāss*, i.e. application of law in a particular case, and the *Ām* (application in general). Next, he discusses *'Amr* (the imperatives to do) and *Nahyi* (not to do), factual and actual, metaphors, direct and indirect, meanings of 'huruf' (prepositions), *'azimat'* (determination) and *'rukhsat'* (permission), and causes of the prescribed laws. After this, he discusses *'Sunnat'* and all that is related to it. *Ijmā'* and *'Qiyās'*, *Ijtihad* and the principles of *'Ijtihad'*, causes and effects, and the related topics are elaborated thereafter.

However, it is not the mere contents and their organization and sequence in the book but application of his advanced dialectical method integrating logic and juridical concepts that distinguishes Bazdawi's Principles as being of a pioneering nature.

Usūl al-Bazdawī represents the first successful attempt to present and systematizes the science of 'Usul al- Fiqh' on the logical dialectical pattern developed by Bazdawi in this field. According to Ibn Khaldun, the need to develop a systematic method of dialectical reasoning and argumentation was felt in the early centuries of Islam when polemical discussions in the field of religious sciences were very popular. However, no systematic methodology was developed in a scientific and logical manner to be followed by the discussants in order to avoid erroneous argumentation and illogical reasoning, Ibn Khaldun tells us, two methods were developed, the one by Bazdawi and the other by 'Amīdi. Bazdawi's method was specific to jurisprudential issues and dealt with legal argumentation and other related problems, while 'Amīdi's method was general and could be applied to any science or discipline.

SIMILARS AND PARALLELS: ANALOGUES AND PRECEDENTS.

Ibn Nujaym

كتاب الأشباه والنظائر

زين العابدين بن إبراهيم بن نجيم الحنفي

Zayn al-Dīn b. Ibrāhim b. Muhammad, better known as 'Ibn Nujaym', was born in 926 A.H. (1520) in Cairo. The completed his education there, taught at the Madrasā of Amīr Sarghitmish, and attained fame as a scholar and as a jurist. He was inclined to Sufism and remained attached to the renowned Sufi Abd al-Wahhāb al- Sha'rānī. He died in Cairo in 970 A.H. (1563).

Ibn Nujaym was one of the most illustrious jurists of the later centuries of Islam. He authored books and treatises in various branches of knowledge, but his main contribution was in the field of law and jurisprudence. He is considered to be one of the few Hanafi jurists whose legal thinking and juridical writings have left a deep impact on subsequent development of Hanafi law and jurisprudence. As a student of law, Ibn Nujaym was particularly interested in the systematic structure of Fiqh, which the he attempted in his *Al-Qawā'id al-Zayniyya.* Therein he has established more than one thousand legal rules or norms *(qawā'id)*, presumably following the example of Ibn Rajab. He also wrote *Bahr al-Rā'iq* as a commentary on *Kanz al-Daqā'iq* (up to the beginning of *'Kitāb al-Ijāra'*, to be completed later by Muhammad b. Ali al-Tūrī d.1004 A.H.). His smaller treatises and *fatāwās* (legal opinions) were collected after his death by his son Ahmad under the title *al-Rasā'il al-Dīniya fi Madhhab al-Hannafiya.*

The *Magnum Opus* of Ibn Najaym, which assigned him an abiding place in the history of legal thought, is his *al-Ashbāh wa al-Nazā'ir* (lit.

'Similars And Parallels', or 'Analogues And Precedents'). It is partly based on al-Suyuti's work of the same name. The juridical discipline of 'Analogues And Precedents' *(al- ashbāh wa al-nazā'ir)* which was developed by Muslim jurists over a long period of time aimed not only at presenting a systematic exposition of the *corpus juris* of Islam but also at discovering the underlying principles which guaranteed systematic development of the law. Although elaborate and exhaustive works on each of these disciplines were authored by great many jurists of different periods, areas and schools, Ibn Nujaym's work excels in its precision, coprehensiveness and originality in dealing with some of the important legal issues. Divided into seven *funūn,* sections of 'general rules' *(al-qawā'id al-kulliya),* the book deals with difficult details *(fawā'id)* chapter by chapter, similar and dis-similar cases *(al-Jam'a wa al-furūq),* puzzles *(al-Lughz),* subterfuges or legal devices *(hiyal),* distinctions *(al-furūq)* and finally some anecdotes.

The first section on legal maxims deals with six primary maxims and nineteen secondary ones. Ibn Nujaym not only traces the origin of the maxim but also highlights the scope of its application by citing illustrative examples from various branches of Law. He also points out the various apparent or real exceptions to the application of a maxim. In the second section, more than five hundred *fawā'id* which serve as key to solving and understanding complicated legal rules are arranged chapter-wise according to the *fiqhi* classification adopted in *Kanz al-Daqā'iq.* In the course of discussion. relevant legal maxims are cited under each chapter. In the third section on *al-Jam'a wa al-Furūq* are detailed the key principles to understand and quickly analyse the similarities and dissimilarities between corresponding and close legal concepts. In the fourth section are given legal riddles and puzzles which aim at training the student in speculative legal thinking and finding out solutions to important and complicated legal problems. The fifth section deals with such legal stratigems and contrivances as are sometimes employed by clever people in order to frustrate the objectives of the law through the devices of the law itself. The main purpose is to inform and educate the student so that later on while seving as a Judge, Mufti or in any other judicial or quasī judicial capacity, he is able to frustrate such attempts and designs. The sixth section gives legal distinctions (and is, in essence, an appendix to the material already given in the third section). The last part of the book gives some anecdotes of early jurists in order to underline the high moral conduct of a jurist/judge.

Ibn Nujaym's work is monumental in so far it represents the development of Muslim legal thought in the tenth century A.H. It has always been considered a primary source of original material on Islamic legal maxims. As such, it has had its impact on the legislative process in many Muslim countries; the celebrated civil law of the Ottoman Empire, the Mejelle, specially its first chapter, heavily drew upon *al- Ashbāh wa'l Nazā'ir* of Ibn Nujaym.

RULES ON DIFFERENCE BETWEEN LEGAL OPINIONS AND LAWS.

Al-Qarāfī

الإحكام في تمييز الفتاوى عن الأحكام

شهاب الدين القرافي

Shihāb al-Dīn, Abū al-'Abbās, Ahmad b. Idrīs b. 'Abd al-Rahmān al-Sanhāji, al-Bahnasi, known as al-Qarāfi flourished in the 7th/13th century. He was born in Egypt, died at Dayr al-Tin in Jumada-II 684 A.H. (1268 A.D.) and was buried at Qarafah (a locality near the grave of Imam Shafi'ī) in Cairo.

Al-Qarāfī was the leading Malikite Jurist of his time, and excelled in Law and Jurisprudence as well as rational sciences. He was attached to Shaikh 'Izz al-Dīn b. Abd al-Salām al- Shaf'ī under whom he received the best of advanced education. The contemporary scholar Qadi Taqi al-Din used to say: 'The Malikites and Shaf'ītes agree that the most excellent savants of our age in Egypt are three: Qarāfī in Old Egypt, Nasir al-Din al-Munīr at Alexandria, and Ibn Daqiq al-'Id in Cairo'.

Qarāfī authored a number of wooks on Law *(Fiqh)* and Jurisprudence *(Usul al-Fiqh)* of which three stand out to be the most prominent. His *al-Dhakhīrah fi al-Fiqh,* in six volumes, is a great work in Malikite Jurisprudence. In his "*Anwār al-Burūq fi Anwā' Al-Furūq*" in 4 volumes, the juridical branch Legal Distinctions which was developed by Karābisī, has received exhaustive enunciation and exposition. Therein he has detailed five hundred and forty eight rules *(qawā'id)* with illustrative examples of the relevant cases and problems. The third book, equally important since it is of a pioneering nature, is his *al- Ihkām fi Tamyīz al-Fatāwā un al-Ahkām* (Rules on Difference Between Legal Opinions and the Law).

LEGAL DISTINCTIONS IN THE BRANCHES OF HANAFITE LAW

Al Karābīsī

كتاب الفروق في فروع الحنفية

جمال الدين ابو المظفر اسعد بن محمد الكرابيسي

Abu al-Muzaffar, As'ad b. Muhammad b. al-Husain, al-Karābīsī was born in Nishapur sometime before 490 A.H. and flourished in the sixth Hijra century. He died in Baghdad in 570 A.H. (1174/75 A.D.). He belonged to the family who traded in cotton cloth (*Kirbās*) and hence his surname al-Karābīsī. He studied law and jurisprudence with distinguished scholars like Abu Mansur al-Jawālīqī (d.540 A.H./1145 A.D.), and was a junior contemporary of such well known scholars, theologians and jurists as Abu Bakr Ibn al-'Arabi, Qadi Iyād al-Yahsubi, Abdullah al-Mazīri, and Qadi Abu al-Walid Ibn Rushd.

Al-Furūq or Legal Distinctions, an important and interesting juridical discipline in the domain of Islamic Jurisprudence, originated early in the works of the great jurist Muhammad b. al-Hasan al-Shaybānī (d. 189 A.H./805 A.D.). His *al-Jāmi' al-Kabīr, Kitāb al-Āsl* and *Kitāb al-Hujjah 'alā Ahl al-Madinah* contained material which served as the foundation on which the juridical discipline of *al-Furūq* was later developed.

Independent works on *al-Furūq* were written beginning from the 3rd century, *Al-Farq fi Furū' al-Shāfi'iyah* of Abu Abdullah Muhammad b. Ali al-Hākim al-Tirmidhi (d.255 A.H.) being one of the early texts on the subject. Such works were prepared by eminent jurists belonging to different schools of law, each one delineating the legal distinctions specific to his own school. Thus, Abu al-Fadl Muhammad b. Sālih al-Karābīsī (d.232 A.h.) of the same family of

Nisapur (?) wrote his book *Al-Furūq* pertaining to the Hanafite School of Jurisprudence two centuries earlier than Abu al-Muzaffar. Abu al-Abbās Muhammad b. Muhammad al-Jurjānī al-Shafi'ī (d.482) wrote "*Kitāb al-Ma'āyāt fi al-Aql*" which became known after his name as '*Kitāb al-Furūq of al-Jurjānī*'.

The *Al-Furūq* of Abu al- Muzaffar al-Karābīsī is, however, a landmark between the earlier texts and the later works in so far as the developmental history of this juridical discipline is concerned.

Abu al-Muzaffar As'ad al-Karābīsī, by his learning and legal knowledge, enjoyed high reputation in so far as he was hailed by his contemporaries as 'al-Shaykh' and 'al-Imām', and was also given the more honorific title of 'Jamāl al-Islam'. He wrote a commentary entitled *al-Mūjiz* on the Hanafite text *al-Mukhtasar* (of Abu Hafs 'Umar b. Muhammad al-Nasafī), and also a 'Commentary on Holy Quran' (*Tafsir al-Quran al-Karim)* is ascribed to him. But the most important work which he authored and which has survived is *Kitāb al-Furūq (fi Furū' al-Hanafiyah),* i.e. Legal Distinctions in the Hanafite Law.

The book is divided into thirty-eight chapters arranged in accordance with the approved *fiqhi* classification. It deals with seven hundred seventy-nine issues of legal importance, in which the author tries to establish the distinction in respect of content, or in respect of application, or in respect of the legal position to be adopted.

Al-Karābīsī's book influenced later works in the domain of Legal Distinctions, the most important of them being *Anwār al-Burūq fi Anwā' al-Furūq* of Shihāb al-Din Abu al-Abbās Ahmad b. Idrīs al-Sanhājī better known as al-Qarāfi (d.684 A.H.) in which he has discussed five hundred and forty-eight 'distinctions'. The other work is of Abu Bakr Sulaymān al-Bakrī's *Kitāb al-I'itinā fi al-Farq wa al-Istithnā'* which deals with some six hundred such cases.

THE AGREEABLE PRINCIPLES.

Al-Shātibī

الموافقات في أصول الشريعة

أبو إسحق إبراهيم الشاطبي

Abu Ishāq Ibrāhīm b. Mūsā b. Muhammad al-Lakhmī, known as al-Shātibī, was a great *muhaddith, faqqīh* and *muffasir* and he also excelled in *Nahv* and *Lughat*. He was born in Granada (Andalus/Spain) in the early decades of the 7th century A.H. (13 A.D.), and studied with eminent teachers of Granada and Andalus, such as Abū 'Abd Allah b. al-Fakhkhār al-Alberi, al-Sharīf Abu al- Qāsim al-Sabli, Abū 'Abd Allah al-Muqri', Abū Ali Mansūr b. Muhammad al-Zawawī and others. He achieved excellence particularly in Principles of Jurisprudence and attained the position of *Ijtihād*. He was a leading Maliki jurist of Andalus and Maghrib in his times. He died in 790 A.H. (1388 A.D.).

Shātibi is considered to be the greatest exponent of the philosophy of Islamic Law. The tendancy to introduce logical argumentation into, and philosophical treatment of, legal and juridical issues initiated by Fakr al-Islam Bazdawi and his contemporaries and intensified by Fakhr al-Dīn Rāzi, was taken to its climax by Shātibī.

He authored a number of important works on jurisprudence such as *al-I'tisām, al-Majālī, al- Maqāsid al-Shāfi'ah* but the one in which his genius is reflected is his *magnum opus, al- Muwāfaqāt fi Usūl al-Sharī'ah.* It represents the most elaborate attempt by any Muslim jurist to reconstruct what we now generally call philosophy of Islamic law. Although scholars like Ghazzālī (d. 505 A.H.) and Izz al-Din al-Sulami had addressed themselves to the task of developing an elaborate philosophical exposition of Islamic Law, a science which was then known as the *Maqāsid al-Sharī'ah* (The Objectives of the

Sharī'ah), Shātibī has surpassed them all both in the breadth and depth of his presentation and in optimizing and systematizing all earlier ideas on the subject. His book not only emobdies the pre-Shātibī development of *Maqāsid al- Sharī'ah* but also represents the culmination of Muslim juridico-speculative thinking.

Al-Muwafāqāt is one of those very few books on Islamic Jurisprudence which have exerted utmost impact upon the subsequent development of that discipline. His elucidation of the five basic objectives of the principle of *Maslahat* (public weal) and his treatment of the delicate subjects of *Ijtihad* and *taqlid* have their strong echo in the writings of the post-Shātibī period. In this respect, some scholars have rightly ranked him with Shāfi'ī's *al-Risālah:* both represent a successful effort to systematize the thinking in vogue on their respective subjects; and both have provided such thought-pattern in their respective fields that seldom any subsequent writer could escape their influence.

Even in the modern juridico-legal thinking of the Muslims, the impact and prestige of *al-Muwāfaqāt* is no less than what has been in the past. Rashīd Ridā has counted Shatibi's *al-Muwāfaqāt* among such epoch-making contributions as the *Prolegomena* on Ibn Khaldun.

The eminent Mufti Muhammad Abduhu (Egypt) used to advise his students to dive deep into Shatibi's book in order to gain a deeper understanding of Islamic Law and of the philosophy of legislation in Islam. In Pakistan, Sayyid Abu'l 'Alā Maudūdī recommended the translation and publication of *al-Muwafaqāt* as this would contribute to a deeper insight into, and a correct understanding of, the real spirit of Islamic Law.

THE RULES OF SOVEREIGNTY IN THE GOVERNANCE OF AN ISLAMIC STATE.

Al-Mawardi

الأحكام السلطانية والولايات الدينية

ابو الحسن علي بن محمد بن الماوردي

The author Abu al-Hassan, Ali b. Muhammad b. Habīb, who became widely known by the *nisba* of 'al-Māwardī' (after his family's profession of selling *mā'al-ward*, rose water) was born in Basra in 364 A.H. (1058 A.D.). There he received good education, as Basra had been traditionally a great centre of learning, and then he transferred himself to Baghdad. With his superior knowledge of Law and Jurisprudence, he gained practical experience as a judge *(qādi)* in different places. Eventually, during the relign of the Abbasid Caliph al-Qā'im (422-467/1031-1075 A.D.), Māwardī was elevated to the highest position of 'Supreme Justice' of the Caliphate.

Māwardī authored a number of important books including a commentary on Holy Quran in three volumes, a comprehensive work *al-Hāwi* on Shafi'ite Law in more than twenty volumes, and a basic work on Civics entitled *Adab al-Dunyā wa al- Dīn.* Most of his works were devoted to practical problems of human affairs such as the conduct of the ruler, governance of the State and management of public affairs. He developed original ideas on these subjects in his different works such as: *Siyāsat al-Mulk* (Governance of the State), *Nasīhat al-Mulūk* (Counsel to the Rulers), *Tashil al-Nazr* about the management of governments, *Adab al-Wazīr* (The Prime Minister's Qualification), *Qānūn al-Waz*ārat (Constitution of the Ministry) etc.

In his book *al-Ahkām al-Sultāniyya fi Siyāst al-Madniyya al-Shara'iyya*, (The Rules of Sovereignty in the Governance of An Islamic State'), Māwardi deals with the basic institutions of Imāmat, Wazārat and Shūrā and such other important subjects as *Kharāj*, *Ghanima*, *Fay*, *Hudūd* and *Hisbah* (the system of justice and accountability). The work represents Māwardi's best thought on political theory and government, being the first attempt in Muslim history to evolve a comprehensive theory of the State. As such, it has left an enduring influence on the course of Muslim political thought.

Māwardi does not present his ideas merely as a philosopher on the basis of abstract reasoning. He is essentially a jurist and builds on the opinions of the earlier authorities, gives a wider scope to their opinions, and uses his own insight to apply them intelligently to the special conditions of his own times. Thus, avoiding abstract speculation, he correlates the opinions of early jurists to the historical prospective of his age though , all along, he maintains independence of thought, of ten expresses views contrary to the earlier authorities, and gives out opinions altogether original.

THE CONCISE BOOK OF INTERNATIONAL LAW.

Al-Shaybani

كتاب السير الصغير

الإمام محمد بن الحسن الشيباني

Muhammad b. al-Hasan b. Farqad al-Shaybani was born in 132 H. at Kufāh. He studied Law with Imām Abū Hanīfah and after his death in 15 A.H. (768 A.D.) with his pupil Abū Yūsuf an elderly classmate of Muhammad himself. He obtained *Ijāzah'* in Hadith from Imām Mālik, Awzāī, Thawri and other leading *muhaddithūn* of his time.

Shaybānī flourished as a great jurist in his own right. Imam Shāfi'ī had acknowledged his own deep indebtedness to Shaybani. He taught law in Kufa, and was appointed by Caliph Harun al- Rashid as Qadi of Raqqa in 180 A.H. (797 A.D.). He held that post until 187 A.H. (803 A.D.), and being relieved he went to Baghdad and lectured there for two years. In 189/80, the Caliph appointed him as Qadi of Rayy, and he accompanied the Caliph, who was proceeding to Samarqand, up to Rayy where he died while the Caliph was still there.

The earlier works on *Siyar,* such as of Awzā'i and others were concerned mainly with the subject of war and the specific issues arising out of it such as the treatment of the enemy, his person and property. For the first time, Imam Abu Hanifa enunciated general principles governing relationship between Muslims and non-Muslims, Islamic State and other States. His pupil Abu Yusuf in his works codified Abu Hanifa's opinions and also included his own as well as of other jurists. Shaybani was a younger pupil of Abu Hanifa, and a classmate and pupil of Abu Yusuf the third in line who developed International Law into a full-fledged discipline.

'Siyar' is the plural of 'sīrah' meaning 'course, procedure or life.' Early in the 2nd quarter of the 2nd century A.H. (about the year 750 A.D.) the word SIRH came to be used in the general meaning of "biography", and SIYAR (in plural form) for the *ghazawāt,* the military expeditions undertaken by the Prophet for the defence of Islam and the practices which he followed and which then became rules and laws of war and of relations with the enemy. Thus, *al-Siyar* governing the Inter-State relations, as Inter- National Law, came to be codified by the jurists of Islam.

On this subject, *al-Siyār al- Saghīr* of Shaybānī is a concise but important work which has come down to us through Sarakhsi's commentary, *al- Mabsūt.* In this work, Shaybānī has enunciated the rules of belligerency for the Muslims, e.g. that the fighters for the sake of faith and religion are not allowed to kill women, children, aged persons, invalid, paralytics, monks and hermits, and other nonbelligerents on the warring side, and that the killing of hostages is strictly forbidden.

The SIYAR postulates three institutional imperatives: first AL-AMĀN to guarantee the security of individual unbelievers as well as unbelieving communities against any belligerent acts of the Muslims; second DHIMMAH citizens; and the third MUWADA'AH or international treaty obligation.

Shaybāni wrote a number of works, some under the guidance of Abu Yusuf and others independently. He gave much time and thought to the subject of *Siyar,* and discussed it more or less in all his works. In his *Kitāb al-Asl,* a part was specially devoted to it, while his two works, Concise International Law' *(Kitāb al- Siyar al-Saghīr)* and 'Comprehensive International Law' *(Kitā al-Siyar al-Kabīr)*, specially dealt with this subject. In so far as Shaybāni consolidated the prior legal knowledge on 'law of nations' in general and codified the legal knowledge coming from Imam Abu Hanifa and Qadi Abu Yusuf in particular, he is to be regarded as the founder of the discipline of 'Inter-National Law'.

Shaybāni's works deal with every aspect of the Siyar Law, and also more elaborately than any of the previous works ones. The text of his

Kitab al-Siyar al-Kabīr has survived to the extent that it is cited in Sarkhasi's commentary (Sharah) on it, the original having been lost. But *Kitab al-Siyar al-Saghir* is complete and text is preserved as an appendix to Shaibani's'Kitāb al-Asl' or 'Kitāb al-Mubsūt'.* It is most authentic as it is of direct 'obvious transmission' (*Zāhir al- rewāyāh*) having been dictated by Qadi Abu Yusuf. As it embodys essentially the doctrine of Imam Abu Hanifa, it is also known as 'Siyar of Abu Hanifa'.

---

* Majid Khadduri has erred in his observation that "Neither Shaybani's *Siyar al-Saghir* nor Awzā'is *Siyar* has reached us" (Majid Khadduri: *The Islamic Law of Nations, Shaybani's Siyar,* The Hopkins Press Baltimore, Maryland. 1966, p. 41).

AL-SIRA (BIOGRAPHY) OF THE HOLY PROPHET.

Ibn Hishām

السيرة النبوية

إبن هشام. جلال الدين أبو محمد عبد الملك

Jamāl al-Din Abu Muhammad 'Abd al-Malik b. Hishām al-Himyari al-Basri was born in Egypt where his family had migrated from Basra. He flourished in Egypt and lived the last years of his life at Fustāt where he died on 13 Rabi-II, 218 A.H. (8 May, 833) or in 213 A.H. (828 A.D.). Ibn Hishām particularly excelled in his knowledge of Hadith and history and was a trustworthy author. He was also well-versed in the knowledge of genealogy, grammar and ancient history. His *Kitab al-Tijān* (Book of Crowns) on South Arabian antiquities has survived.

Ibn Hishām attained fame by 'AL-SIRA,' Biography of the Holy Prophet'(*sal'am*). The work is based on earlier sources, mainly on the *Sira* of Ibn Ishāq of which the text is lost but passages are preserved in other works. Ibn Hishām made Ibn Ishāq's *Sira* as the basis for his own work. The text of the *Sīrā* of Ibn Ishāq (Muhammad b. Ishāq al-Muttalibī who died by about 150-53 A.H.) was transmitted to Ibn Hishām by Ziyād b. Abdullah al-Bakkā'ī.

Ibn Ishāq had concentrated mainly on the *Maghāzi* wars of the Prophet. Ibn Hishām presented that material more critically. He not only screened and streamlined Ibn Ishāq's work, but also reorganized and supplemented it with important information on all aspects of Prophet's life. However he omitted such passages of Ibn Ishāq as were not directly relevant to the Holy Prophet's biography, as explained by him in his introduction:

"I will begin this book with the account of Ismā'īl son of Ibrāhīm and his progeny who were the ancestors of the 'Messanger of God' (*Rasūlullah*) omitting the account of other descendents of Ismā'il for purpose of brevity, and bring the narration to the 'biographical Account of the Messanger of God' (*Hadīth sīrat Rasūlullah*). I will leave out from Ibn Ishāq's book that which does not concern 'Rasūlullāh' and about which nothing has been revealed in the Quran, and which is also not directly relevant in the context of the present book, there being neither any explanation nor any evidence about it -- in order to be brief: and also the verses which no one knowledgeable about poetry has known, such other things as some people consider it blame worthy to recount, and that which is not confirmed by al- Bakkā'ī (will be omitted from Ibn Ishaq's Book). Excepting this matter, all else (that is relevant) will be explored and recorded, if Allah wills, in the light of the tradition and knowledge concerning it. Indeed true knowledge belongs to Him."

With this clear objective in view, Ibn Hishām has produced a streamlined edition of Ibn Ishāq's book by retaining all its contents which are relevant to the biography of the Prophet (*sal'am*). He has made the work more useful by himself supplying additional information wherever feasible. For the reader, he clearly differentiates between what Ibn Ishaq has transmitted (قال ابن اسحق) and what he himself has supplemented.(قال ابن هشام).

It is to be noted that the previous works were concerned mainly with the subject of *Maghāzī* (the holy wars) of the Prophet (*sal'am*) and, as such, were classed as 'Maghāzi books'. Ibn Hishām's book became the first definite work on *the Sīrah* as he specifically meant it to be so. In his very first opening sentence he said: "This is the Book of Sīrah of Rasūlullāh" هذا كتاب سيرة رسول الله.

KITĀB 'AL-TĀRĪKH'.

Khalīfa b. Khayyāt

كتاب التاريخ

خليفة بن خيّاط

AL-TĀRĪKH' of Ibn Khayyāt is probably the earliest extant general history of Islam which has preserved information even on the events of the distant provinces of the Caliphate, such as North Africa and Sind, which is not available in any other source. It is annalistic in arrangement and presents information chronologically, year by year until 231 A.H. (845/46 A.D.). This is the earliest and complete on historical text in which the *Khabar-cum-Isnād* (chain reporting) methodology has been employed in reporting and recording historical events on the analogy of 'reporting and recording of the Hadith.'

Abū 'Amr Khalīfah b. Khayyāt al-Laythī al- 'Usfurī hailed from a learned family of Basra. He was born by about 160 A.H. and died aged eighty in 240 A.H. (854 A.D.). His grandfather Abū Hubayrah was also an eminent *muhaddith* (scholar of the Hadith) from whom the *hadith* was narrated by such prominent *mahuddithūn* as 'Amr b. Mansūr, Wakī' b. al- Jarrāh, and Abu'l-Walid al-Tiyālsi and others.

Ibn Khayyāt was also a highly qualified *muhaddith*, and he has been recognized as the most respected and reliable authority. He had such eminent pupils as Bukhari, Abdullah b. Ahmad, Ahmad b. Hanbal and Baqī b. Makhlad.

Ibn Khayyāt was an eminent author. His four works, including THE HISTORY, have been referred to by Ibn al-Nadim in his *Al- Fihrist.* Of these, *the tabaqāt* has survived (in a unique manuscript of the al-Zahiriyyah Library, Damascus) has been published (ed. Suhail Zakkār, Damascus, 1966). The second one is his *Al-Tarikh* which is not only the earliest work on history, but being based on *'Hadith* methodology' it is also important from the point of authenticity and reliability.

This work, though referred to in other sources, was considered to have been lost, until a unique manuscript of it (written in Spain in the *maghribi* character in 477/1084) was traced in Morocco. Its first edition was published in Baghdad in 1386/1967 under the auspices of the Iraqi Academy (Majma' al-'Ilmi al'Irāqi).

HISTORY OF THE CONQUEST OF SIND TRANSLATED.

Ali Kufi

فتحنامهٔ سند

علي بن حامد بن ابي بكر كوفي

During the reign of Sultan Nāsiruddin Qabācha the ruler of Sind and the S.W. Punjab (602-625A.H./1205-1228 A.D.), an eminent literary scholar named Ali b. Hāmid b. Abu Bakr Kufi, came across an Arabic work on the early history of the Arab conquest of Sind, the manuscript of which had remained preserved with an illustrious family of the *qādis* of Aror and Bakhar in Sind. They were the direct descendants of Uthmān b. Abi al-'Ās al-Thaqafī, and thus belonged to the stock of Banū Thaqīf whose members had played an important role in the conquest of Sind. In view of 'the recognized importance of this work,' Ali Kufi translated it into Persian in 613 A.H. (1216) 'for purpose of wider publicity and recognition. 'History of the Conquest of Sind' (*Fathnāmah-i-Sind**) is the translated version of the original Arabic, which has not survived.

The opening chapters, which are copious enough, deal with the two Pre-Muslim dynasties, viz. the Budhist Rai Dynasty and the Brahman Dynasty. This part is an important contribution, either by the *qādis* of Bakhar-Aror or an earlier author, in so far it has preserved the early history of Sind during the 6th and 7th centuries A.D. No comparable early written historical record exists of any other part of the Subcontinent.

---

* Ali Kufi had, at the end of his translation, conceived two elaborate titles decorated with the name of his patron for his work, but actually did not put any finalised title before his 'Preface' to the work. The title *'Fathnamah-i-Sind'* is suggested by the actual references and expressions occuring in the text (Ed. N.A. Baloch, Islamabad, 1402, 1982).

Next follows on account of the naval expeditions sent in 15 A.H. against the port of Daybal and other ports, and of the overland advance of the Muslim armies (as a result of the great conflict with the Sassanid Persia) and the conquest of Makran, Kaikānān and Khuzdār (the central Baluchistan) during the 7th century A.D. (15-90 A.H.). Lastly, the main body of the text contains an elaborate account of Muhammad b. Qasim's compaigns and conquests during a period of about 3-1/2 years (92-96 A.H./ 712-715 A.D.) beginning with Makran and Sind, and extending through Multan to the border of Kashmir, the Rajputana regions adjoining Sind (mainly the Bikaner, Jesalmer and Jadhpur-Mawar countries), the northern Kaira kingdom of Gujerat, and the whole of Kathiawār and Kachch. This part is based on detailed report of the compaigns in general and on the eye witness accounts of the different battles in particular. Accordingly, it becomes the repository of the most important contemporary record not found in any other source.

Internal evidence shows that most of the authentic historical content in *Fathnāma* is derived from the historical works of Madā'īnī (135-225 A.H./752-839) which were composed in the 3rd/9th century (al-Nadīm: *Fihrist*). There is another category of information drawn from local sources which might have been supplemented later by the first ancestors of the *qādis* of Aror and Bakhar. Even if it be so, Fathnāmah would rank as the very first books extant in the field of Indo-Muslim history. *It may even be regarded as the first truly historical work about historical events, which took place during a known historical period, ever compiled in the South- Asian Subcontinent.*

In so far as they reflect the literary genius of Ali Kufi and lend lustre to his prose style, these may be assigned the merit of having made Fathnāmah a unique book of Persian prose in the early 7th century A.H., probably the earliest one of a substantial size produced in the South-Asian Subcontinent.

THE ‘NĀSIRITE’ DYNASTIES.

Minhāj-Sirāj Juzjānī

طبقات ناصري

مِنهاج الدّین عثمان بن سراج الدّین جوزجانی

The author Abū ‘Amr Uthmān ‘Minhāj al-Din’ was son of Muhammad ‘Siraj al-Din’ and hence his popular name ‘Minhaj-i-Siraj’ (Minhaj of Sirāj). He was born in the Ghurid capital Firuzkoh in 589 A.H. (1193 C.E.), and his mother being the foster sister and classmate of princess Māh Malik, the daughter of Sultan Ghiyath al-Din of Ghūr, young Uthmān spent his childhood in comport in the *harem* of the princess. Thus, he was brought up well and received good education in Firuzkoh where he grew up as a young scholar 17 years of age. In 607 A.H., he was still in Firūzkoh, but by that time the Ghurid power had been eclipsed by the Khwaazmshāhs who in turn were soon to be attacked by the Mongols. Therefore, he left Firuzkoh and eventually headed for Hindostan reaching Uch the capital of Sultan Nāsiruddin Qabācha the ruler of Sind and Multan in 624 A.H. He was put in charge of the Firūzi College and also appointed Qadi of the forces of the Sultan’s son. But he had hardly settled down when Qabāchā abandoned the capital which was besieged (625 A.H.) and conquered by Sultan Iltutmish of Delhi. Minhāj who was now favored by Sultan Iltutmish, joined his court and reached Delhi in Ramadan 625 (August 1228). During the next two decades (except for a brief interval of 639-642 A.H.), he held important posts. The Sultan appointed him Qadi, Khatīb and Imam of Gawaliar and its dependencies (630 A.H.), Rector of the Nāsiria College, Delhi (635 and 643 A.H.), and Chief Justice of Hindostan (639 A.H.). During the long reign of Sultan Nāsiruddin Mahmūd Shah (644-664 A.H./1246-4266), the venerable. Minhajuddin received all honours and all favours (except for a precaious period of about 2 years, 651-652

A.H.): he was bestowed the title *Sadr-i- Jahān* and held the high office of the Chief Justice of the realm.

It was during the reign of Sultan Nāsiruddin Mahmūd Shah, that Minhajuddin wrote his important historical work and named it after Sultan Nāsiruddin as "Tarīkh Tabaqāt-i-Nāsiri" and also dedicated it to him.

This was the first *comprehensive general history* written in the Persian language. The learned author, however, conceived and executed it in the best form of early Islamic/Arabic tradition. Following Tabari, he planned it as a university history from the beginning of the creation to his own times. In his own works:

"This frail one desired, therefore, that this meagre History should be filled up from first to last, from beginning to end, with an account of the whole of Mamāliks and Sultans of Islam, both of Arab and of 'Ajam."

He entitled it as "Tabaqāt", the term that had been used by Ibn Sa'ad in writing about the successive generations of the Prophet's companions, and then by other authors who wrote about poets, men of letters and physicians. In this work, Minhājuddin has offered, in simple direct style, a consistent chronological account of the different dynasties of each of the Eastern Islamic realms (in Asia, leaving out the Western realms of Africa and Spain), with overlapping links between the accounts of the proceeding and the succeeding lines of rulers, thus eliminating any gap or confusion. He closed his narration with the events of 658 A.H. (1200 A.D.) when he was in the 70th year of his age.

The work is divided into twenty three 'books' or chapters, some further subdivided into sections, the contents of which may be summarised as under:

Book I. Account of the early Prophets and Patriarchs, and of the last Prophet Muhammad (sal'am).

Book II. History of the first four Khalifas; of the descendants of Ali, and of the ten Mubashshar.

Book III. The Ummayyad Caliphs.

Book V. early kings of Persia, the Peshdādians, the Kaiānians, the Ashkānians, the Sasānians, and the Akāsira from Naushirwān to Yazdjird.

Book VI. Kings of Yaman, from Harisu-r-Rāi to Bādān, who accepted Islam.

Book VII. The Tāhirids from Tāhir Zul-Yamīnain to Muhammad b. Tahir, who was conquered by Ya'qūb b. Laith in A.H. 259 (A.D. 872).

Book VIII. The Saffarides from Ya'qūb b. Laith to the death of 'Amr 6. Laith in A.H. 289(A.D. 901).

Book IX. The Sāmānides from their origin to A.H. 389 (A.D. 998) when 'Abd al-Malik b. Nūh was sent as a captive to Uzjand.

Book X. The Buwaihids, from beginning to Abu'l Fawāris Sharaf al-Daula.

Book XI. The Ghaznivides, from Subuktigīn to the death of Khusraw Malik in A.H. 589 (A.D. 1201).

Book XII. The Saljuqs of Persia from their origin to the death of Sultan Sanjar in A.H. 552 (A.D. 1157); the Saljuks of Rum and 'Iraq, from their origin to the time of Ruk al-din Kilij Araslān; and an account of Tughril to his death, and the conquest of Iraq by Takash, King of Khwarāzm.

Book XIII. The Sanjari Kings; (1) The Atabak of Iraq and Azarbaijān (2) The Atabaks of Fārs, (3) The Kings of Nasihāpur.

Book XIV. The Kings of Nimruz and Sijistan from Tahir b. Muhammad to Tājud din Niāltigīn Khwarazmi who was slain by the Mongols in A.H. 625 (A.D. 1227).

Book XV. The Kurdiya Kings: The Atabaks of Syria, Nur al-din Zangi and al-Malik al-Salih; and the Ayyubites of Egypt.

Book XVI. The Khwarazmians, from their origin to the death of Jalal al-din Mankbarni, in A.H. 629 (A.D. 1231).

Book XVII. The Shansabāniya Sultans of Ghūr.

Book XVIII. The Shansabāniya Kings of Bāmiān and Tukharistan.

Book XIX. The Shansabaniya Sultans of Ghaznin, from Saifuddin Sūri to Qutbuddin Aibak, who expelled Tajuddin Yalduz, in A.H. 603 (A.D. 1206).

Book XX. The Mu'izziya Sultans of Hindostan, comprising the history of Qutbuddin Aibak, and of his son Aram Shah; of Nasiruddin Qabācha of Uch, and the four Khilji princes of Lakhnauti or Gaur until in A.H. 634 (A.D. 1226).

Book XXI. The Shamsiya Sultans of Hindostan, whose capital was Delhi, from Shamsuddin Iltutmish to Nasiruddin Mahmud, the seventh king of the dynasty who reigned Delhi, and the author completed the present history.

Book XXII. Account of the most eminent nobles, viceroy's governors, etc., who flourished under the Shamsiya dynasty, from A.H. 625 (A.D. 122&) to the author's own time.

Book XXIII. The war between Sultan Sanjar Saljuki and the tribes of Kara Khita; of the conquest of Turkistan, by Muhammad Khwarazm Shah, and the defeat and death of Gur Khan, the Kara Khitaian in A.H. 607 (A.D. 1210); and the incursions of the Mongols, Changiz Khan and his descendants.

Minhājuddin wrote in year 658 A.H. when he was in the 70th years of his life, that he would continue to record the events further if he were alive and had the opportunity to do so, but no more events were recorded thereafter and the narration remained closed with the 658 A.H. In view of some of his references to later times, the author would appear to have died, most probably, in the beginning of the reign of

Sultan Ghiyasuddin Balban who came to the throne in 664 A.H. (1266).

The author's indisputable scholarship and sound judgment being the most eminent Judge of his time, makes *Tabaqāt* a work of unique merit. His personal integrity is attested by Abdul Haqq learned author of *Akhbār al-Akhyār* who says that the author of the *Tabaqāt-i-Nāsirī* was a saint, and one of the most learned and excellent man of his time, and when he became Kāzī of Hindōstan that office assumed integrity and rectitude.

Among modern writers, Elliot and Dowson have observed that "the *Tabakat-i-Nasiri* is held in very high esteem both in India and Europe. Firishta and others refer to it as an excellent work of high authority. Anquetil du Perron calls it a "Precious work," and Elphinstone mentions it as a work of the highest celebrity. Stewart in his History of Bengal, follows it very closely, and considers it "a very valuable book."*

* The parts of the text dealing with India have been edited by Captain Nassau Lees in the Bibliotheca Indica and translated into English by Major Henry Feorge Reverty: 'A General History of the Muhammadan Dynasties of Asia, including Hindustan from 194 to 658 and irruption of the infidel Mughals into Islam' (2 vols. London, 1881).

WASHINGS OF GOLD AND MINES OF DIAMONDS.

Al-Mas'ūdī

مروج الذهب ومعادن الجوهر

أبو الحسن علي بن الحسين المسعودي

Abu al-Hasan Ali b. al-Husayn al-Mas'ūdī was born by about 283 A.H. (896 A.D.), and flourished in the 4th century A.H. He grew up in the great capital city of Baghdad where he had received good education that motivated him to undertake long journeys in pursuit of knowledge. Thus, he became a great traveller-cum-researcher and visited Persia, Sind (in 902 A.H.), the countries along the western coastline of India from Cambay to Knonkan and further on to Ceylon (303- 304 A.H.); thereafter Madagascar, Adherbījān, Jurjan and Syria, and lastly Egypt where he settled down at Fustāt and died there in Jumada-II 345 A.H. (September, 956).

As a scholar and investigator, Mas'ūdī imbibed a spirit of scientific inquiry, and observed and evaluated the different phenomena, physical and cultural, critically. His studies covered such varied fields of knowledge as history, geography, cosmology, meteorology, astronomy, law, philosophy and comparative religion. He recorded his observations and ideas meticulously in a large number of works of which about thirty six have come under reference though complete texts of only two have survived. These are *Murūj al-Dhahb wa Ma'ādin al-Jauhar* ('Washings of Gold and Mines of Diamond')[1] and *Kitāb*

(1) The title has been translated and widely used as "Meadows of Gold And Mines of Precious Stones." George Sarton was the first to observe that the translation of *muruj* as *meadows* "did not seem to fit the sense or the parallelism". Gold was not obtained in meadows, just as diamonds were obtained in mines: the gold was gathered by man, in the long past, usually by the technique of '*washing*' the rich river sands, or as it was naturally *washed* down the streams and river beds.

al-Tanbīh wa al- Ishrāf (Book of Attention And Supervention). The *Murūj* was completed in 366 A.H. /947 A.D. and the *Tanbīh* in 345 A.H./956 A.D. The stupendous, and probably the most valuable of all his works, was *Akhbār al- Zamān wa Mun Abādahu al-Hadathān* (Chronociles of the Age And of the Bygone Races) which he had composed in thirty volumes.

Mas'ūdī's statements, ideas, inferences and conclusions regarding an immense variety of subjects in his MURŪJ and TANBĪH amply testify to his being a great historian, great geographer and a great student of human culture and civilization. Though these works, particularly the *Murūj,* have been studied by eminent scholars and scientists for centuries, beginning with Ibn Khaldun in the 8th century to George Sarton and others in our own times, who have fully recognized Mas'ūdī's originality and versatile genius, there is still considerable content in the two works the implications of which are yet to be determined in order to fully assess Mas'ūdī's contribution in the context of world history and civilization. But as amply testified by his exposition in these works, Mas'ūdī is to be regarded as the founder of two important disciplines, History of Civilization and Human Geography. Moreover his concept of 'history' was that of a 'universal history', history of the whole creation.

The *Muruj* is the first universal history that was ever written. 'It is universal' in the unique sense that not only it attempts to cover the history of the human kind but of the then known whole universe, both terrestrial and celestial. It is both horizontal and vertical in scope, from horizon to horizon and from the beginning of the creation to his own times. It opens up with a discussion of the creation of the earth wherein Mas'ūdī has made important observations which amount to a theory of evolution.

Masū'dī has classified all the then known peoples inhabiting the earth on racial, linguistic and cultural bases into seven main groups: 1. Persians; 2. Chaldaeans. Arabs and those related to them; 3. Greeks, Slavs and Franks; 4. Libyans and Egyptians; 5 Turks; 6. Indians; and 7. Chinese. The classification of races and world cultures made by modern anthropologists is basically of a similar pattern.

Mas‘ūdī's accounts of the chronology of Kings of the Franks or of the genealogy of the Sassasian monarchs, and his accounts of the Slavs or of the Indians and their rulers, constitute original historical record of great value. As a historian, Mas‘ūdī has been called (by Max Meyerhof) ‘Pliney of the Arabs’ a comparison which may hold good so far as Mas‘ūdī's racial origin is concerned, but in his achievements of a universal nature he stands shoulders high above Pliney and other ancient predecessors. Ibn Khaldun, who used Mas‘ūdī's two works in his own *Muqaddimah* and *The History* (‘Ibar), has paid rich compliments to him as being among those few great historians who can be "recognized as authorities" who had replaced the works of their predecessors by their own advanced contributions. According to Ibn Khaldun, Mas‘ūdī's works have been ‘a basic source’ on which the later historians have relied.

Ibn Khaldun has also complimented Mas‘ūdī as being the one who for the first time saw a close relationship between history and geography *(Muqaddimah,* Bulaq ed., I/27). According to Mas‘ūdī, there is a positive connection between man and environment. Thus, racial and cultural characteristic of different peoples have developed as a result of their different geographical habitats, and the differing climatic and environmental factors have conditioned their physical features as well as cultural behaviour. In the *Muruj,* he explains the Arabian characteristics in terms of their open air beduien life, and so also the distinctive characteristics of the indigenous dwellers in the other climes. He has underlined the concept of man's adaptation to environment by pointing out that, in the long past, one stock of the Turkish race had migrated from their original habitat in the north into the frontier regions of India where local climate and conditions influenced their physique and their way of life so that "they are like the Indians in complexion and not like the Turks".[(2)] Also the Zanj and the Abyssinians in Africa have scorched faces and curly hair because of "the excessive heat and dry vapours".[(3)] The phenomenon of adaptation (an important phase in evolution) is referred to in his important observation

(2) *Muruj,* Paris ed. with French trans., Vol. I pp. 124-27, 243-45 & 289.

(3) *Tanbīh,* p. 24.

that animals and plants adapt the natural form and colour of the environment in which they dwell and grow.(4)

Mas'ūdī has also made important observations in the domain of physical geography. He has explained the role of the cycle of erosion by observing that the water and the land-mass factors are not constant on the earth's surface but "a perpetual revolution takes place" due to the rivers which are always shifting. He has made significant observations on the shape and size of the different seas. He surmised that the Indian Ocean was linked up with the Atlantic by a narrow channel south of Africa. This observation had led the Muslim navigators, Ibn Mājid as well as his predecessors, to see the possibility of circumnavigation of South Africa. Mas'ūdī had visualised the sphericity of the earth and made important observations on its shape, size and movement. Indeed, he established a scientific basis for a study of geography. Also he is to be regarded as the pioneer who, by elaborating some of the important concepts, laid the foundations of Human Geography.

---

(4) *Tanabīh*, p. 29 and *Muruj* I/336.

HISTORY OF MAKKA AND OF ITS MONUMENTS.

Al-Azraqī

أخبار مكة

أبو الوليد أحمد الأزرقي

With speedy expansion of knowledge in the Islamic society during the 2nd century A.H., the dimension of historical writings expanded much beyond the story of events and occurrences, and history of cities came to be written. Azraqī's history of the holy city of Makka is one of the earliest scholarly works on this subject.

Descended from Azraq, a 'companion' whom the Prophet had settled in Makka, the author Muhammad b. Abdullah b. Ahmad b. Muhammad b. al- Walīd b. 'Uqba b. al-Azraq al-Ghassānī, Abu al-Walīd al-Azraqī, had the family background and the information available to him which qualified him to write a detailed history of the holy sanctuary of the Ka'ba and of the city in which in it was located. The work was entitled *Kitāb Akhbār Makkah wa ma jā' fīhā min al-Āthār* (History of Makka And of Its Monuments).

Abu al-Walid al-Azraqī flourished in the 3rd century of the Hijra and died by about 254 A.H./868 A.D. The quality of authorship of this work and his use of all possible sources of information show that he was well informed and that he had made a special study of the subject. Before him, Azraqi's grandfather Ahmad had intended to write the history of Makka and the Ka'ba. He had collected considerable information from knowledgeable scholars of his times and also from the people of Makka, but it was not compiled by him into book form. Availability of this material subsequently inspired his grandson Azraqī to write a comprehensive work on the subject.

Azraqi considerably enlarged upon the material left by his grandfather. He studied the important Islamic sources of Hadith and Tafsir (transmitted on the authority of Ibn 'Abbās) and also extended his inquiries into the pre-Islamic past of the city and the Ka'ba making full use of the more reliable information recorded by Ibn Ishāq as well as of the lore transmitted by Ibn al-Kalbī and Wahab b. Munabbih. He himself supplied the detailed typographical description to make the work as complete as possible.

Azraqi transmitted the text of his book through his pupil Abu Muhammad Ishāq b. Ahmad al-Khuzā'ī (d. 308/921) who later transmitted it to his grand-nephew Abu al-Hasan Muhammad al- Khuzā'ī, both of whom made some additions – the former mainly on the renovations of the Ka'ba made during the years 281-84 A.H. (894 - 7 A.D.).

Azraqi's book has remained the foundational source of information on the history of the Ka'ba and the city of Makka for the scholars dealing with the subject. Besides, this work gave impetus to the writing of HISTORY OF CITIES, which was a significant development in the domain of Historiography.

THE MUQADDIMA* (PROLEGOMENON).

Ibn Khaldun

المقدمة

ابو زيد ولي الدين عبدالرحمن ابن خلدون

Ibn Khaldun's ancestor Khalī, also called Khaldūn, who had settled in Seville in Spain originally hailed from Hadrmawt in Yaman. Later the family migrated to Tunis, where Ibn Khaldūn was born on the 1st of Ramadan 732 A.H. (27 May 1332 A.D.). Because of this family background, Ibn Khaldun was *al-Ishbili* (Sivillian),but as a historian, he was also particular to underline his original *nisba* i.e., *al-Hadramī* which appears in his own handwriting (below, last line).

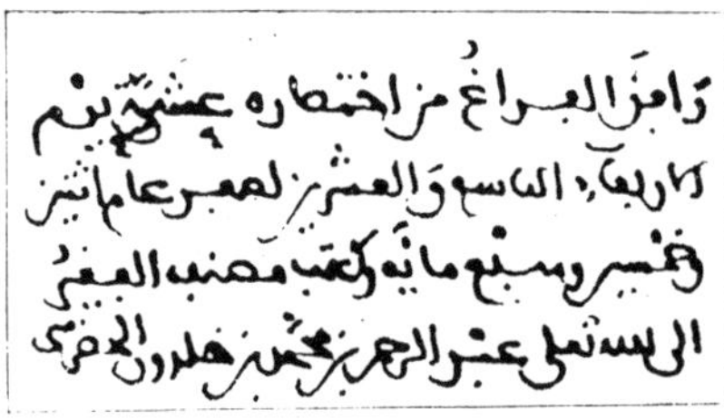
وكان الفراغ من اختصاره عشية يوم
الاربعاء التاسع والعشرين لمحرم عام اثنين
وخمسين وسبعمائة وكتب مصنفه الفقير
الى الله تعالى عبدالرحمن بن محمد بن خلدون الحضرمي

In Ibn Khaldun's Qwn Hand
with his full name.
[Acknowledgement. al-Zirkili: AL-A'LĀM]

Ibn Khaldun was brought up and educated in Tunis. He studied Holy Quran, Arabic, Hadith, Fiqh and Philosophy. At the age of 17,

* The 1st edition of the Muqaddimah was published by Etienna Quatrmiere (3 vols. Notices etextraits, Paris 1858). There are many other editions: (Cairo (456 p) and Beirut 588 p. and reprinted 1879, 1886, 1900. English Trans. by F. Rosenthal. Urdu Trans. by M. Abdur Rahman of Allahabad.

he migrated to Fez and then to Granada and Talmisān in Spain. There he held high positions before he returned to Tunis. He then went to Egypt and was honoured and appointed to the high position of the Chief Malikite Judge. He died in Tunis in 832 A.H. (1406 A.D.).

Ibn Khaldun had acquired a broad liberal education and was a widely read man of his times besides his rich life experience of the most satisfying as well as challenging situations. He was strong in Jurisprudence, Logic, Literature and Philosophy. During the period 752-65 A.H. (1351-64) he authored a commentary on Busiri's *Burda,* a treatise on logic, another one on arithmetic, digests of some works of Ibn Rushd, and a commentary on a peom of Ibn al-Khatīb. These earlier works show his bent of mind as an educator and as a man of letters. Professionally he had been a jurisprudent and a judge, a minister and a plenipotentiary. However, it was by his authorship of the Muqaddima that Ibn Khaldun was destined to gain world wide fame. In this great work, he simultaneously became the founder of the Science of History and of the Science of Sociology.

It was by about 1374 A.D. that he withdrew to the 'Qala'āt Ibn Salāma (Tā'ūghzut, in the Mina mountains of the province of Orān) and remained there four years working on his history entitled *Kitāb al-'Ibar* etc., meaning "Instructive Examples And Composition about Origin And Elaboration of the History of the Arabs, Persians and Berbers And Their Great Contemporary Rulers". This compilation in itself is one of the monuments of Arabic literature. It begins with a preface and introduction explaining the value of historical work in general, the plan of this particular work and its main sources, the methods to be followed, and errors to be avoided.

Formally, 'Maqaddima' is an introduction to *Kitāb al-Ibar,* but it transcends its ordinary meaning, being a monumental 'Introduction' to the very Discipline of History. It is "presented as an encyclopedic synthesis of the methodological and cultural knowledge necessary to enable the historian to produce a truly scientific work". (E.I.). To start with, Ibn Khaldun was mainly concerned with epistemplogy, but as he meditated "on the method and the matter of history, he was led, in full consciousness of what he was doing, to create what he refers to as his new science *('ilm mustanbat al-Nash'a,* which itself turned out to contain more or less implicitly the starting points of several avenues of research leading to the philosophy of history, sociology, economics and yet other disciplines" (E.I.).

Maqaddima deals with the description and discussion of human society in its various aspects (such as nomadic and sedentary life, means of livelihood, sciences and arts, social causes and results). It is divided into six sections, the contents of which are briefly as follows:-

(i) On civilization, geography and anthropology, communications with the invisible world ensured by seers and prophets: psychology of divination etc.

(ii) Discussion of nomadic culture and its contrast with sedentary culture. Sociological and historical cultures and consequences of the conflict arising continually from the fundamental opposition.

(iii) Dynasties, kingdom, caliphate, order of dignitories in a Sultanate. Principles of government and administration, and various institutions.

(iv) Observations concerning life in villages and towns.

(v) Means of livelihood, professions, arts and trades, business, agriculture, exportation, building, carpentry, weaving, tailoring, obstetrics, medicine, secretarial work, singing etc.

(vi) Various kinds of sciences, psychology of learning and teaching, classification of sciences.

AN OPEN DENUNCIATION OF ADVERSE CRITICS OF THE HISTORIANS.

Al-Sakhāwī

الإعلان بالتوبيخ لمن ذم أهل التاريخ

شمس الدين محمد بن عبد الرحمن السخاوي

Shams al-dīn Muhammad b. 'Abd Al-Rahmān al- Sakhāwī, whose family originally belonged to the village of Sakhā in Egypt, was born in Cairo in 831 A.H. (1427) and died in Median in 902 A.H. (1497). He was a widely travelled scholar of great repute and excelled in the knowledge of Hadith, Tafsir, History and Literature. He authored about two hundred works on these subject.

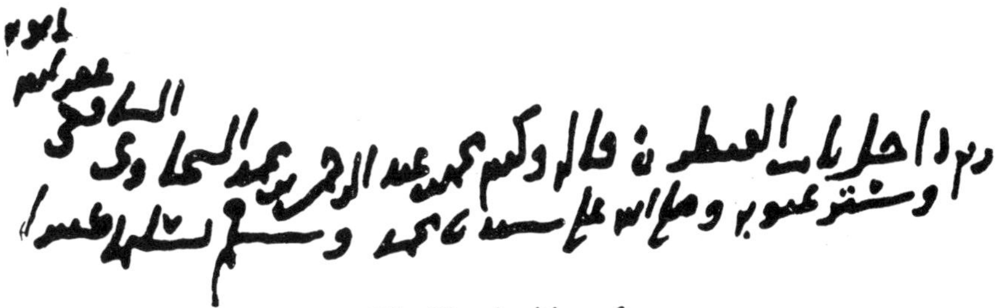

The Handwriting of
Muhammad b. Abd al-Rahman al-Sakhawi
[Acknowledgment: AL-A'LAM of al-Zirkili]

It was in 831 A.H. (1427) that he wrote an important book, unique in its theme, in defense of historians and history entitled *al- I'lān bi al-Taubīkh li-man Dhamma Ahl al- Tārīkh* ('An Open Denunciation of Adverse Critics of the Historians'). It is an advanced work on historiography, much more comprehensive than any earlier work on the subject. According to Rosenthal: "In the *I'lān*, the author has erected a worthy monument to Arabic historiography." However, as no other comparative work is to be found in any other language prior to 'The I'lan', it becomes a worthy monument to the Science of Historiography. The Muslim scholars took to history as a Quranic subject, and produced a variety of historical literature not then available in any other language and culture; eventually they created a highly developed discipline *'Ilm al-Tarikh,* 'The Science of History'.

A number of eminent scholars recorded their opinions on history and its objectives and methodology, while others wrote on *'Ilm al-Tarikh* or Historiography itself. Besides Sakhāwi, two other authors who wrote specifically on historiography and whose works have come to light were Muhammad b. Ibrahim al-'Ijī who composed his *Tuhfat al- Faqīr ilā Sāhib al-Sārir* ('The Gift of the Humble For the Master of the Throne') in 783 A.H./ 1381- 82, and Muhy al-Din Muhammad b. Sulaymān al-Kāfiyājī who wrote his treatise *al-Mukhtasar fi 'Ilm al-Tārīkh* ('A Brief Compendium on Historiography') in 867 A.H.(1463).

Sakhāwi's work which represents a more complete and systematic treatment of Historiography covers the following thirteen main topics on the subject.

(i) A linguistic definition of the word *ta'rikh*

(ii) A definition of *ta'rikh* as a technical term.

(iii) The object of history

(iv) The usefulness of history

(v) The goal of occupied with history

(vi) The legal classification of history

(vii) The evidence in favour of history

(viii) The blameworthiness of the critics of history

(ix) The qualifications required of the historians

(x) The introduction of the Muslim Era

(xi) The works composed on history

(xii) An alphabetical list of historians

(xiii) The chief representatives of personality criticism.

THE LAW OF THE LANGUAGE

Ibn Fāris the Linguist

الصاحبي في فقه اللغة وسنن العرب في كلامها

أبو الحسين احمد بن فارس اللغوي

Abu al-Husayn Ahmad b. Fāris b. Zakariyā b. Muhammad b. Habīb became known, in view of his expertise, as 'Lexicographer/Linguist' (al- Lughawī). For the title of his book incorporating the concept of 'Law of the Language' he may be regarded as 'Father of Linguistics'. He studied in Qazwin, gained prominence in Hamadān and died at Rayy in 395 A.H. (1004/1005).

Ibn Fāris was not only a great scholar but also a great teacher of his times. To his illustrious pupil, al-Sāhib Ismāil b. 'Abbād, Prime Minister of the Buwayhid ruler Fakhr al-Dawlah (734-50 A.H./1334-49 A.D.), he dedicated the present work which he named after him as 'AL-SĀHIBĪ'.

Ibn Fāris was a of poet of merit and could also write in fine prose style. He was grammarian, philologist and linguist par excellence. His studies had also extended to Seerat, Jurisprudence, Quranic Exegesis and Poetry. Forty seven of his monographs and treatises as well as voluminous works authored on these subjects are known through references in different sources.

The main contribution of Ibn Fāris consists in his important works in the cognate areas of etymology, philology, lexicography and linguistics, such as (i) The Book on the Principles of Language *(Kitāb Maqāyīs al-Lughah),* (ii) The Book of Generalities/Synthesis in Language *(Kitāb al-Mujmal fi al- Lughah),* and (iii) 'Al-Sāhibī in the Law of the Language and the Usages of the Arabs in Their Speech' *(Al-Sāhibī fi Fiqh al-Lughah wa Sunan al-Arab fi Kalamihā*).

Ibn Fāris completed AL-SĀHIBĪ in or before 382 A.H. (992 A.D.), the year in which he dedicated it to the learned Prime Minister Ismāil Sāhib b. 'Abbād who was himself well versed in Lexicography. AL-SAHIBI is his advanced work in which Ibn Fāris "goes beyond the purely grammatical lexicographical framework in the study of Arabic language, to reach the level of linguistic speculation" (E.I.). In fact, he envisaged truly linguistic concepts and initiated linguistic discussion.

As the title of his work indicates, Ibn Fāris became the first to establish a clear distinction between 'language' and 'speech', thus laying the foundation of what he called 'The Law of the Language' *(Fiqh al-Lughah),* i.e. The Science of Language. In his introduction he refers to it as *Ilm* (Science) which he correlates with 'The Principle' *(al-Asl)* in order to differentiate it from what is subsidiary or derivative *(al-Fara')* such as the figures of speech–noun, adjective etc. He then defines the Science in terms of 'The Principle' (and with reference to the Arabic Language) as under:

"The Principle is to be defined as the substance of the Language and its origin and development, with reference to its customary usage as recognized by the Arabs, and its artistic modes of expression by way of reality or metaphor."

Besides dealing with the different aspects of Linguistics, Ibn Fāris has also brought under discussion subjects dealing with etymology *(al-Nahv)* and syntax *(al-Sarf),* the high literary style of expression *(al-Balāgha)* and literary cticisim *(al-Naqd).* He quotes and critically examines the views of his ...... such as the 'lab (d. 291 A.H.) and Ibn Qutaiba (d. 276).

This work of Ibn Fāris influenced later developments in Linguistics. It was under the direct impact of this book, that Abu Mansur al-Tha'ālibī (d. 350 - 429 A.H.) wrote and entitled his book as *'Fiqh al-Lughah wa Sirr al-Arabiyah'.* Later still, al-Suyuti (1849 - 911 A.H.) in his *al-Muzhir* not only quoted the definition of the science of Linguistis given by Ibn Fāris, but also summarized from *al- Sāhibi* in the later chapters of *al-Muzhir.*

INTRODUCTION TO THE CLASSES OF NATIONS.

Ibn Sā'id

كتاب التعريف بطبقات الأمم

أبو القاسم صاعد بن أحمد ابن صاعد القرطبي

Abu al-Qāsim Sā'id b. Ahmad b. Abd al-Rahmān b. Sā'id al-Qurtubī, also known as Qadi Sā'id, was an eminent historian and astronomer. Born of a Cordovan family at Almeria in 420 A.H. (1209), he served as *qadi* (judge) of Toledo where he died in 462 A.H. (1070).

Qadi Sā'id was deeply interested in astronomy and wrote a book entitled *Islāh Harakāt al-Nujūm* (Correction of Motions of Stars). He was a keen observer, and the observations made by him and other Muslim and Jewish astronomers working with him were of great value to Zaraqālī for the compilation of his new Tables. But Qadi Sā'id was essentially a historian, and wrote a book on the biographies of learned men, a history of Islam and a history of Andalusia. In this domain, his main interest lay in studying the different peoples. He wrote about peoples professing different faiths and sects *(Maqālāt ahl al-Milal wa al-Nihal)* and a comprehensive work on the Arab and the Non-Arab peoples *(Jawāmi' Akhbār al-Umam min al-Arab wa al- 'Ajam).*

It was in 1067/68 A.D. that he wrote his more important work *Kitāb al-Ta'rīf bi Tabaqāt al-Umam* (Introduction to the Classes of Nations'). In this work, Ibn Sā'id has classified different peoples in terms of their contribution to science and learning. According to him, eight nations have contributed the most to the progress of science: Indians, Persians, Chaldaeans, Greek, Latin (including Oriental Christians), Egyptians, Muslims and Hebrews. His accounts of Greeks and Muslims are far more elaborate than those of other peoples.

Much use was made of Ibn Sā'id's work by Ibn al-Qifṭī and Ibn Abī 'Usaybi'ah in the 1st half, and by Barhebraeus in the 2nd half of the 13th century A.D.

---

* The text was edited by Louis Cheikho with notes and tables (Beirut, 1912). It was several times printed in Cairo. A revised edition of the text with English translation prepared by M. Sabir Khan was published from Leiden.

THE INDICA OR ALBAYRUNI'S INDIA.

Al-Bayruni

كتاب ما للهند من مقولة مقبولة في العقل أو مرذولة

ابو ريحان محمد بن احمد البيروني

Abu al-Rayhān Muhammad b. Ahmad al-Bayruni was born in the outer part *(bayrūn)* of Kāth, the capital of Khwarazm ('Madinah Khwārazm') on Thursday, the 3rd of Dhu al-Hijjah, 362 A.H. (973 A.D.) and died in Ghazni in 443 A.H.* Known by the honorific title of *'al-Ustadh'* ('The Master') he was an intellectual giant of his times. He remained in pursuit of knowledge for all his life, and even while on the death bed he inquired from a friend who had come to see him, about the number of rotations which a particular planet made.

Bayruni conducted advanced researches and wrote original standard works in different areas of knowledge - such as mathematics, astronomy, astrology, physics, pharmacology, cosmology, mineralogy, geography, history, chronology and cultural anthropology. The number of books he wrote on these subjects would count up to 180. He excelled in his knowledge of classical languages as well as vernaculars of Central Asia, wrote both in Arabic and Persian, translated from Sanskrit and also composed verse in it.

Bayruni studied in Kāth and was already an accomplished scholar, scientist and author when under the changed political events in his native country, grave otherwise but fortutious for him, he got the long awaited opportunity to conduct his researches on 'Indian' subjects under the liberal patronage of Sultan Mahmud of Ghazni. In 407 A.H.

* In absence of a clear contemporary evidence, the year 443 A.H. can be validly inferred from the more relevant references on record (Cf. *Ghurrat al-Zijāt or Karan Tilaka,* Arabic text, ed. N.A Baloch, Sind University, Pakistan, Oct., 1973, Preface).

(1016-17), when Bayruni was serving as a trusted courtier and advisor to Prince Abu al- 'Abbās al-Mamūn of Khwārazm, the army rebelled and assassinated the Prince who was a brother-in-law of Sultan Mahmud. Thereupon, the Sultan occupied Khwārazm, punished the rebels, and patronized the learned men of the Mamunid Court including Bayruni. For long, Bayruni had been in search of original source books on Hindu astronomy and he now saw it clearly that for his Indian studies Ghazni was his future destination. The Sultan's favour and patronage offered a welcome opportunity to him to accompany the Sultan to Ghazni. There he conducted his researches without any interference and to his entire satisfaction.

From Ghazni, Bayruni continued on his field studies, undertook journeys into the interior of the Subcontinent and travelled as far as Multan and possibly more southwards to Sind. Sometime during the years 411-414 A.H. (1020 - 1924 A.D.) he visited and stayed at Fort Nandanā (Jhelum district) and conducted his memorable experiment whereby he determined more precisely the length of one degree of the arc of the meridian circle, and calculated the radius and the circumference of the Earth – his figures coming very close to the modern ones. He made oral inquiries, studied the source materials, obtained Sanskrit texts and collected all information he possibly could during a period of about 12 years (408-420/1017-1029), and wrote as many as 28 works on the Indian subjects. His extensive studies and expositions had developed a full- fledged discipline of 'Indology'.

The most celebrated of his works on this subject is the INDICA or ALBERUNI'S INDIA. These are brief and convenient titles improvised by modern scholars, the latter one by Edward Sachau. Bayruni himself gave his book a much more expressive and versified title. It would seem that in a delightful moment of having seen the book completed, he couched its title in verse as if symbolizing the local Sanskrit tradition in which the texts were usually composed in verse:

Kitaāb māli al-Hind min maqūlah maqbūlatun fi al-aql ano mardhūlah.

Translated literally it would mean:

> "The Book is Based on the Indians' own Tradition Acceptable to Reason, or Prone to Rejection".

Bayruni had collected the needed information both from oral and written sources, and he authored this book at Ghazni during the course of 5 months (30 April - 30 September) in the year 1030 A.D.

The INDICA is comprehensive in exposition of the cultural achievements of the *Indians*, predominantly though not exclusively of the Hindus. Historically, it happens to be the first book on record, demonstrating 'complete, objective and scientific description of a culture'. Thus, Bayruni became 'Father of the Science of Cultural/Social Anthropology'. Edward C. Sachau, the producer of "Alberunis India" (an English version of Bayruni's original text) observed in 1888 as follows. "In general, it is the method of our author not to speak himself, but to let the Hindus speak, giving extensive quotations from their classical authors. He presents a picture of Indial civilization as painted by the Hindus themselves" (Preface p. xxiv). "As far as the present state of research allows one to judge, the work of Alberuni has not been continued" (Preface, p. xiii). Indeed, in its scheme and exposition of the Indian culture in all its essential dimensions, the INDICA stands unsurpassed to this day.

THE CHOICEST CHRONICLES.

Ibn Qutaybā

عُيُونُ الأَخبار

ابو محمّد عبد الله بن مسلم بن قتيبة الدينوري

Abu Muhammad Abdullah b. Muslim, Ibn Qutaybā was born in Kufa in 213 A.H. (828 A.D.). He studied under great teachers such as Abū Hātim Sijistānī, a master of grammar and philology, al-'Abbās al-Riyāshi, the pupil of al-'Asma'ī, and Ibrahim al- Hanzalī, the disciple of Imam Ahmad ibn Hanbal. Thus, sound religious learning as well as classical literary tradition of the pioneers of the 2nd century A.H. were transmitted to him, and he grew up to be a scholar of varied accomplishments.

Ibn Qutaybā's attainments were noticed by Prime Minister Abu al-Hasan 'Ubaydullah b. Khāqān who appointed him as Chief Judge of Dīnawar where he stayed for long, and hence was known as 'al-Dīnawarī'. Subsequently, he held another appointment as 'Inspector of Mazālim' in Basra, but finally during the last 20 years of his life he devoted himself entirely to scholarly pursuits, teaching and transmitting his works in Baghdad until his death in 276 A.H. (889 A.D.).

Ibn Qutaybā was a first rate scholar and a prolific writer. He authored a number of books, more than sixty according to al-Nu'awi (of which atleast two dozen are extant) which deal with varied subjects such as Quranic Study, Tafsir, Hadith, Theology, Dialectics, Law and Jurisprudence, Grammar, Philology, History, Political-cum-Religio-cultural ideas, and such scientific subjects as Secretarial Requirements,Seasonal Calendar, Agriculture and Botany. What specifically distinguished him in the galaxy of contemporary scholars were his attainments and scholarly contributions in *adab*, literature, poetry, and general culture.

A unique genre of *adab* began developing from the 2nd century Hijra onwards as a result of varied scholarly interests. It was rooted in the background of informative and entertaining oral Arab tradition, and flourished further in the scholarly circles of Basra and Kufa due to the continued importance of oral communication and functional knowledge. 'knowledge is that which can be readily communicated' *(ma hūzira be-hī)* was the dictum laid down by scholarly al-Mubarrad (d. 285 A.H.) in his book *al- Kāmil.* He meant the knowledge in an all-inclusive sense, all information acquired by a scholar from different sources and on different subjects along with his ability to communicate orally and effectively. Accomplishment in this art led the scholars to author books. As developed in its different dimensions, *adab* was inclusive of what is known as *belles-letters* or polite literature, but it transcended both in its scope and objectives, being a combination of the best of poetry, eloquent ideas, literary ancedotes, grammatical-cum-philological points, historical allusions, genealogical citations, cultural concepts–often replete with wit and humor. It was demonstrated in genial conversation or presented in stylistics writing.

In the introduction to his poetical anthology *Kitāb al-Shi'r wa al-Shua'rā* and in his *Ma'āni al-Shi'r,* Ibn Qutaybā came up with an objective appreciation of poetry, and became the first to give due credit to contemporary poets for their innovative compositions. He urged the poets of his day to compose with fresh new ideas. Thus, the recognized superiority of classical models of the *mu'allaqā* came to be questioned for the first time. In his *Kitāb al- Ma'āni* he supplemented the historical content with considerable information on other subjects so that it become a compendium of general knowledge. In his introduction to *Adab al- Kātib* (Qualification of Secretary) Ibn Qutaybā delineated the political-cum-cultural perspective (for the would be Secretary) in such a scholarly manner that it become a master piece of Arabic literature. According to Ibn Khaldūn, it had been traditionally well recognized that *Adab al-Kātib* of Ibn Qutaybā, *Kitāb al-Kāmil of al-Mubarrad, Kitab al- Bayān wa al-Tabyīn* of al-Jāhiz (d. 255 A.H.) and *Kitāb al-Nawādir* of Abu 'Ali al-Qāli (d. 356 A.H.) were the four pillars of *al-adab.*

And yet, a book of much wider scope and varied content that Ibn Qutaybā authored was *'Uyūn al-Akhbār* (The Choicest Chronicles) which became more popular than any other work. He composed *'Uyūn al-Akhbār* in ten 'Books' (Parts) under the following heads; (1) Book of the Ruler, (2) Book of Warfare, (3) Book of Leadership, (4) Book of Dispositions and Ill Conduct, (5) Book of Knowledge and Exposition, (6) Book of Asceticism *(al-Zuhd),* (7) Book of Friends/Brothers, (8) Book of Wants, (9) Book of Food, and (10) Book of Women Folk. He has explained the purpose and plan of the book in his introduction elaborately and figuratively, his main objective being to inform, educate and entertain in a pleasing and persuasive manner.'It is a dinning tables laid up with a variety of tasty dishes to satiate the appetite of the diners'.

In Ibn Qutaybā's literary works, and more so in *'Uyūn al- Akhbār,* the genre of *Adab* came up of age, attained maturity and established its own identity in writing. In this genre, Ibn Qutaybā unfolded a future orientated humanism. Preceding Ibn Qutaybā, the more significant contribution in *adab* was made by Jāhiz (d. 255) whose artistic prose style, with a sharp edge and power to impress, was somewhat terse and difficult. In contrast, Ibn Qutaybā presented the genre of *adab* in an easy, facile. placid and pleasing style. The great literary figure and linguist Ibn Durayd (d. 321 A.H.) was all admiration for the most pleasing and entertaining qualities of *'Uyūn al-Akhbār* which he placed above all other works in this domain.

THE BOOK ON POETIC INNOVATION.

Ibn Al-Mu'tazz

كتاب البديع

ابن المعتز

Abdullah b. Muhammad b. al-Mutawakkil was born as a prince in the house of the Abbasid Caliphs in 247 A.H. (861 A.D.), the year in which his grandfather Caliph al-Mutawakkil was killed. His uncle al-Muntasir ascended the throne for a short while (861-2 A.D.) and was followed by his father Muhammad entitled *al-Mu'tazz Billāh* (866-9), and hence the son became known as 'Ibn al-Mu'tazz'. Young Abdullah received best of education that was then available for the princes, but he was hardly 8 years old when his Caliph father was imprisoned for life (869 A.D.). The period of next forty years (869-809 A.H.) was of great instability, during which four rulers were put on throne and removed one after another by the powerful military guard. During this whole period of turmoil, Abdullah remained devoted to scholarly pursuits. He developed fine literary taste as well as poetic talents par excellence, and also authored a number of books. When Caliph al-Muktafī died in 295 A.H./908 A.D., the prince scholar Abdullah, having remained devoted to intellectual pursuits for long, allowed himself to be pulled into power struggle by the courtiers forgetting that he had never been a party to power struggle before. The ill luck only favuored him to be but a 'One Day Caliph:' he occupied the throne against his cousin al- Muqtadir only to be deposed and killed the next day (17 December, 1908). Though Ibn al-Mu'tazz's romance with power politics was short-lived, his place in literary history remained secure as a result of his achievements as an innovative poet and a pioneer in poetics. Contemporary poets mourned his death and composed moving elegies.

Of the books authored by Ibn al-Mu'tazz, names of about a dozen are known. These pertain mainly to polite literature and poetry. He also wrote a book on music *(al-Jāmi' fi al-Ghinā')*. Being well versed in the historical development and tradition of Arabic poetry, he authored two books on the subject, 'Compositions of Kings' *(Ash'ār al- Mulūk)* and 'Generations of Poets' *(Tabaqāt al- Shua'rā')*. He wrote in simple and refreshing prose style, and excelled in the art of poetry for his use of similitudes *(tashbīhāt)* and figures of speech in an innovative way. His own compositions were later collected and edited into *Diwan* (two parts) by his friend Abu Bakr al-Sūfī.

New trends in poetry had appeared after the close of the Umayyid period and the ushering in of the Abbasid era. Poets also received public recognition in 'Poets' Hall' in the Mosque of Baghdad in which the first entry of a poet with public applause (as of Abu Tammām) became a memorable occasion. The new trends became conspicuous in the compositions of Abu Tammām (d. 231/845) and his pupil Buhtarī (d. 284/845). Both were well acquainted with the verses of carrier poets, both pre-Islamic and post-Islamic, and compiled selective anthologies. Abu Tammām's tasteful anthology, the famous *Hamāsa*, not only covered a vast convass of the much admired traditional verse, but also reflected his own poetic insight.

Poet in Hamāsā than in his own verse. But while these'modern' 'neo-classical' poets retained the format and features of traditional verse in their compositions, they simultaneously made conspicuous deviations by introducing innovations of their own. Buhtarī in the erotic prelude *(nasīb/tashbīb)* of his earlier *qasīdās* had named the traditional 'Hind' as his beloved, but in his later compositions he named his real lady love 'Alwā of Aleppo. The innovations of the 'new style poets' included abstract ideas, far-fetched metaphors, new similitudes *(tashbīhāt)* and rhetoric figures, artful imagery and collocations, and unfamiliar subtleties and poetic conceits. These innovations which became conspicuous in the compositions of Abu Tammām and Buhtarī continued to crystalize in the compositions of Ibn al-Mu'tazz and his compatriots, and reached their climax later in the poetry of Mutanabbī (354/965).

Men of letters questioned these innovations, which then became controversial. Mixed judgments continued to be pronounced on their merits and demerits even by the later day critics. Thus, eminent Tabrezi observed that Abu Tammām was better poet in his compilation of the Hamāsā than in his own poetry. (Even a modern scholar, H. Ritter, as if to fall in line, proceeded to confirm that "Abu Tammām's *qasīdās* contain, side by side with brilliant conceits which have established the poet's name, much that is unpleasant"). The eminent critic Tha'ālibī (d. 429/1037-38) even said about the great Mutanabbi that "he strings pearls and bricks together".

After Abu Tammām and Bukhtari, Ibn al-Mu'tazz was the leading poet among the innovators. Like his predecessors, he had studied the earlier poetic tradition and compiled anthologies. He himself was a versatile poet of great talent. However, being scholarly, he was much concerned about ambivalence in mixed opinions about the innovative trends *(badi')* expressed in poetry. With his good knowledge of rehtorical figures and other embellishments occurring not only in the compositions of earlier poets but also in Quran and Hadith, he could see that what was being questioned as 'innovation' was a natural development implicit in the previous perspective. To substantiate this, he wrote two works on the subject, *al-fusūl al-Hisār* and *Kitāb al-Badī'*. He showed great originality of ideas particularly in *Kitāb al-Badī'* which became, in effect, the first important work on Poetics in Islamic literature.

THE BOOK OF MUSICAL MODES.

Al-Urmawī

كتاب الأدوار أو الرسالة الشرفية

صفي الدين عبد المؤمن الأرموي البغدادي

Safī al-Din Abu al-Mafākhir ‘Abd al-Mu‘min b. Yusuf b. Fākhir al-Urmawī al-Baghdadi was born in Baghdād in the early years of the 6th/13th century. The family originally belonged to Urmia, a town in Adharbāijān. Safi al-Din received good education, and specially excelled in music, calligraphy and correspondence (inshā’). Eventually he attained high positions as official scribe, librarian, and court minstrel and boon companion of Caliph Al-Musta‘sim (1243-58 A.D.). He received a pension of 5,000 golden pieces a year. Safī al-Dīn was in Baghdād when it was sacked by Hūlāgū in 656/1258. When the city was given over to the Mongol holders for slaughter and pillage, his music reputation helped Safi al-Din and he gained access to Hūlāgū and ‘so charmed the conqueror by his performances on the *‘ūd* that Hūlāgū ordered that Safī al-Dīn, his family and property should be spared in general devestation’. Hūlāgū took him into service and his pension was doubled to 10,000 pieces of gold, which was paid out of the revenues of Baghdād. He then became tutor to the sons of the wazīr Shams al-Dīn Muhammad b. Muhammad al-Juwaynī, who with his brother ‘Atā Malik, the author of the *Tārīkh-i Jahān Gushā*’, appointed the famous musician to head the Correspondence Bureau *(Dīwān-i Inshā)* in Baghdād.

Safī al-Dīn’s two pupils, Bahā’ al-Dīn Muhammad and Sharaf al-Dīn Hārūn, the sons of the wazīr were extremely kind to him. Baha al-Din on being appointed as governor took Safī al-Dīn with himself to Isfahān in 1265 A.D. On the death of Bahā’ al-Din (1279) and the fall of the family of Al-Juwayni (1284), the great musician fell on evil days, was imprisoned for a debt of 300 pieces of gold and died in a debtor's prison in 693 A.H. (1284).

For his great skill in music, he was excelled by none since the days of Ishāq al-Mausilī, the boon companion of Harun al- Rashid. He was the inventor of two stringed instruments, the *mughni* (an arch-lute) and the *nuzha* (a new type of psaltery).

After Farabi, Safi al-Din was the greatest of music theorists. He was the pioneer of a school which propagated the "Systematist Theory". Safī al-Dīn authored two important works on the theory of music - *Kitāb al-Adwār* (Book of Musical Modes) and *al-Risālat al-Sharafiyya* (The Sharafiya Treatise). Both were used as text books, and remained authority among music theorists for centuries.

Kitab al-Adwār, better known to the theorists, was probably written in 1252 A.D. It is divided into fifteen sections (fusūl) dealing with

1. the notes (anghām),
2. the frets (dasātīn),
3. the lute ('ud),
4. the intervals (ab'ād),
5. the composition (ta'līf),
6. the modes (adwār),
7. the two stringted pandores (tanābīr),
8. the lute of five strings,
9. the popular modes (adwār),
10. the related notes
11. the scales (tabaqāt),
12. the accordatur (istihāb),
13. the rythm (īqā'),
14. the influence (ta'thir) of notes
15. the performance.

The other book *al-Risālat al-Sharafīya fi al-Nisāb al-Ta'līfīya* (The Sharafiya Treatise on Musical Conformities in Compostion) was written by about 666/1267 and dedicated to the Wazir's son Sharaf al-Dīn Hārūn (d. 678/1279). The book is divided into five Discourses (maqālāt) with the usual sections (fusūl). These deal with the bases of sound *(saut),* intervals *(ab'ād),* as well as the six 'finger scales' *(mawājib).* According to Farmer, it is a more finished work than 'The Adwar'.

Regarding Safī al-Din's stature as a music theorist, Farmer has observed that in the East, Safi al-Din was 'looked upon as fountain head in the subject, whilst the European West has penned fulsome praise of his abilities. Kiesewetter called him 'the Zarlino of the Orient', Sir Hubert Parry considered the Systematist Scale to be 'the most perfect ever devised', for, as Riemann says, it gives consonances purer than our scale can afford us. Even Helmholtz considered that the theory of Safi al-Din was 'noteworthy in the history of the development of music'.

FARTHEST PERCEPTION IN THE COMPREHENSION OF HEAVENS.

Qutb Al-Din Al-Shīrāzī

نهاية الادراك في دراية الافلاك والهيئة

محمود بن مسعود الشهير بقطب الدين الشيرازي

The author Qutb al-Dīn Mahmūd b. Diyā' al- Dīn Mas'ūd b. al-Muslih belonged originally to a family of Gāzarūn that had settled in Shiraz where he was born in 634 A.H. (1236). His father was a prominent physician and a devoted disciple of Shihāb al-Din Maqtūl al-Suhrawardī (539 - 632 A.H.). Young Mahmud received education and studied medicine under his father, and also became his Sufi disciple.

At fourteen years of age, when his father died, Qutb al-Dīn was assigned his father's position as a physician in the Muzaffari Hospital of Shiraz. He served there for ten years where after he took to higher studies, visited Marāgha where he attached himself to Nāsir al- Din al-Tusi andstudied the works of Ibn Sina under him and also acquired greater understanding of astronomy. He then went to Nishapur and from there to Isfahān where he would appear to have been favoured by the governor Bahā' al-Dīn Muhammad al-Juwayni (to whom he later dedicated his work *Nihāyat al-'Idrāk).* From there he went to Baghdad where he met the great Sufi Muhammad b. al-Sukrān (d. 667 A.H.). He journeyed onwards to al-Rūm, visited Qoniya and met Maulana Jalāl al-Dīn Rūmī (d. 672 A.H.). Here he stayed for some-time, lectured and also served as a *Qadi* under Prince Ahmad Nikodar, the ruler of al-Rum (680-683 A.H.), who sent him as an ambassador to Egypt in (81 A.H.).Eventually, he returned to Tabriz where he devoted the last 6 years of his life to study and writing.He died in 710 A.H. (1131 A.D.).

With all the weight of his knowledge, Qutāb al-Dīn preferred to be a man of lively temperament who would engage in jests, play chess and also music on the rebāb. He was a highly knowledgeable scholar and wrote important works on different subjects such as Qurānic Exegesis, Theology, Medicine, Philosophy, Grammer, Metaphysics, Astronomy and Rhetorics. In *Tafsīr,* he composed a voluminous commentary "*Fath al-Mannān fi Tafsīr al-Quran*" in forty volumes; in Tibb he wrote 'The Comprehensive' (Kulliyāt) entitling it as *al- Tuhfat al-Sa'diyah,* and a 'Commentary on the Principles of Canon of Ibn Sina' *(Sharh Kulliyāt al-Qānūn);* and in philosophy he authored *Durrat al-Tāj* (The Pearl of Crown). He was the foremost exponent of al-Suhrawardī's 'Theosophy of the Orient' (*Hikmat al-Ishrāq*) and wrote commentary on it entitled *Sharh Hikmat al-Ishrāq.*

Qutb al-Din authored two works on astronomy, first *Nihayāt al-Idrāk fi Dirāyat al- Aflāk* and the other *al-Tuhfat al- Shāhiyya fi al-Hay'at.* He dedicated his 'Nihāyat' to the governor of Isfahān Bahā' al-Din Muhammad al-Juwayini (d. 678 A.H.), which would indicate that he wrote this book before the year 678 A.H. (1279). Qutb al-Din was much influenced by Tūsī's *Afkār al-Tadkhira al-Nasīriya* which work he follows in his astronomical expositions.

He, however, expresses his own ideas which are not to be found in Tusi's works. He also brings under discussion the viewpoints of other earlier scientists including Ibn al-Haytham. Thus, his work is more eleborate and comprehensive than that of Tūsī. He wrote a separate commentary on Tusi's TADHKIRA entitled *Sharh al-Tadhkirh al-Nasīriyah.* After writing *Nihāyat al-Idrāk,* he saw the need for a further elaboration of the subject and wrote, by way of Commentary on it, *Fi Harakāt al-Daharja wa al-Nisba bayn al-Mustavī wa al-Munhanī* (On the motion of the rolling and the relation between the straight and the curved).

SELECTION OF AGE FROM THE WONDERS OF EARTH AND OCEAN.

Al-Dimashqī

نخبة الدهر في عجائب البر والبحر

شمس الدين أبو عبد الله الأنصاري الدمشقي

The author, Shams al-Din Abu Abdullah al-Ansari was born by the middle of the 6th century A.H. (13th A.D.) in a suburb of Damascus and grew up there, and hence came to be called 'al-Dimishqi'. He died at Safad in 727 A.H. (1327). As a man of learning and piety, and also as an able exponent of Islam, he was known and respected as *al-Shaykh* and *al-Imam.*

Shaykh Shams al-Din was deeply interested in Philosophy and Sufism, attempting to seek abiding values in life in relationto higher human destination. His compass of knowledge and information was vast, extending from higher academic disciplines to the more practical domains and he authored encyclopaedic works in these two areas of knowledge. His book written in the time-honored and interesting format of MAQĀMĀT entitled *al-Māqāmāt* al-Falsafiyya wa al-Tarjm*āt al-Sūfiyya* ('Discourses Philosophical And Presentations Sufistic') contains fifty 'Māqāmat' or 'Discoures' on physical, mathematical, theological and other subjects which are pronounced by *Abu al-Qasim al- Tawwāb* ('the Penitent') on the authority of Abu Abdullah *al-Awwāb* ('the Repentent').

The other better known work is *Nukhbat al-Dahr fi Ajā'jb al-Barr wa al-Bahr* ('Selection of Age from the Wonders of Earth and Ocean') a cosmographic encyclopaedia, which being vast in scope provides general information and yet there is much in it that is not found in other sources. It is divided into 9 chapters dealing with geography, mineralogy, rivers, water resources, islands, occeans, Asian countries,

African countries, genealogies, festivals, and calanders of nations. The work concludes with an important section on human race, the perfection of 'human being' and his place and role in the creation.

THE BOOK ON SHAPE OF THE EARTH.

Ibn Hawkal

كتاب صورة الأرض

ابو القاسم محمّد بن على ابن حوقل

The author Abu al-Qāsim Ibn Hawqal was born in Nasībīn in Al-Jazīra (in Upper Iraq) by the turn of the 3rd century A.H. As a youth, he became interested in geographical works particularly those which dealt with caravan routes, such as of Ibn Khurdādhbeh, Jaihānī and Qadāmā, but he could not find a satisfying comprehensive text on the subject.[1] He also used to meet agents of merchants to seek information from them.[2] Thus young Ibn Hawqal was motivated early enough to acquire more of geographical information, to know more about other countries and their products and peoples, and to have a first hand knowledge of the caravan routes that linked them. He decided to achieve this by travel and trade.

Some details of his journeys are known from the references recorded by him in *K.Sūrat al-Ard.* He embarked upon his first journey from *Dar al-Salām* (Baghdad) on 8 Ramadan 331 A.H.(943 A.D.). He visited North African countries and Spain during 336-340 A.H. (947-951); Egypt, Armenia and Ādharabijān during 344 A.H.; Sind and Multan during 345-350 A.H.; al-Jazīra, Iraq, Khuzistān and Fars during 350-358 A.H. (961-969 A.D.); and Sicily in 362 A.H. (973 A.D.[3] It may be presumed that some time later he returned to Bagh-

---

(1) This is stated in the introduction of the work (p. 3, Kramer's ed.).

(2) This statement comes much later in the text (p.339, Kramer's ed.).

(3) These details are from E.I. where the date of the commencement of the first journey is given as '7 Rajab 331'. Kramer's edition of the text has '7 days past of Ramadan 331'.

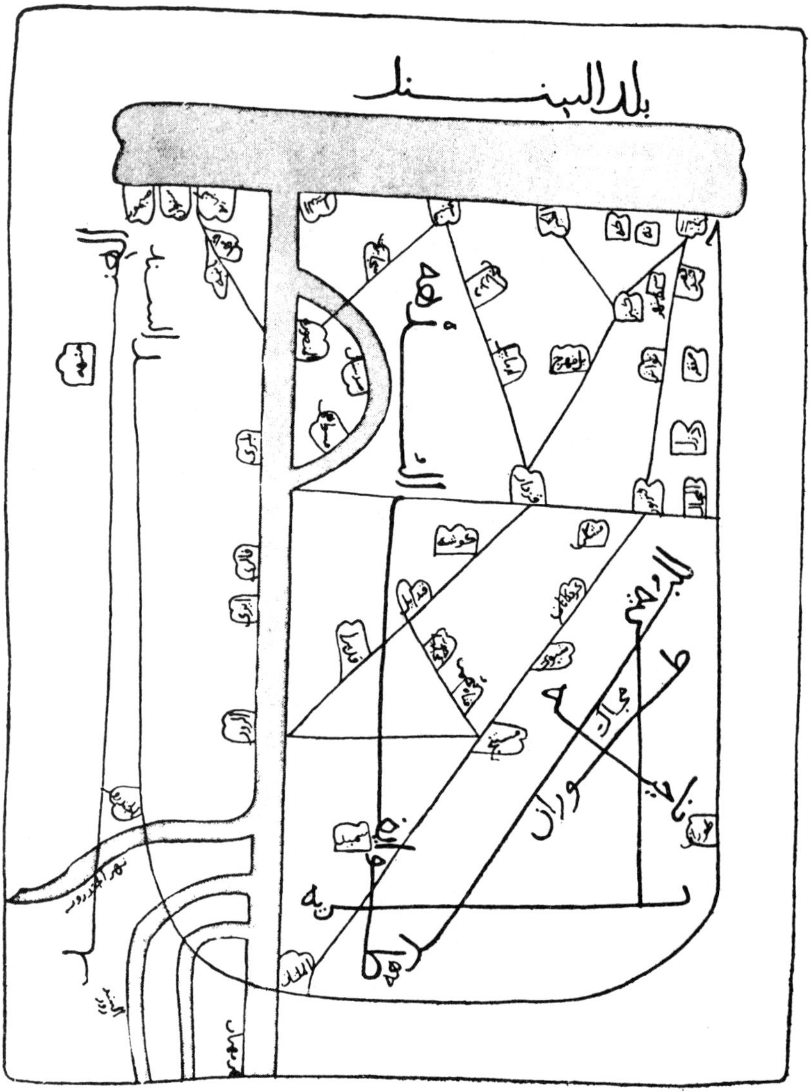

Ibn Hawkal's
MAP OF AL-SIND

dad and compiled his information in stages, and thus issued two editions of his work. In 378 A.H., he published the third and the last edition of it, and possibly he died sometime after (?) 380 A.H. (990 A.D.).

Ibn Hawqal wrote a separate work on Sicily which is lost. However from the very out set, his main objective was to gain a wider acquaintance of the different Islamic lands and the trade routes which linked them. On this, he prepared the first edition of his work *before* the year 356 A.H. in which the Hamdānid ruler Sayf al-Dawla, to whom it is dedicated, died. He entitled it as *Kitāb Masālik al-Mamālik* i.e. "Book on Routes of Kingdom".

However, as the orbit of his journeys had extended reaching as far as the Indus Valley in the East and Spain in the West, he intended o produce a global work on geography. This decision might have been influenced by his meeting with another researcher on geography, Abu Ishāq al-Istakhari al-Fārisi who had drawn up a map of Sind and Fars, while Ibn Hawqal had drawn the maps of Adharbijan and al-Jazira. They both exchanged views on their maps. Al-Istakhari is said to have asked him to correct his maps, but he thereby gave Ibn Hawkal the idea of writing a more comprehensive work.(4)

As his information and data accumulated at different stages, he made use of it in the three successive editions of his work. In order to update geographical knowledge to his own times, he also incorporated Istakhari's work into his own, often quoting it verbatim and also modifying its statements in the lights of his own understandings and information. After the first edition which was made before 356 A.H., the second appeared in 367/977 and the third one "a definitive and complete version in about 378/988" (E.I.).

(4) *Kitab Masalik al-Mamalik*, ed. De. Goeje, was published from Leiden in 1973. The more complete edition entitled *'Kitāb Sūrat al-Ard'* ed. J.M. Kramers, was published by Brill during 1938-39.

AL-REHLA: THE TRAVEL.

Ibn Battuta

تحفة النظار في غرائب الأمصار وعجائب الأسفار

ابن بطوطة

Shams al-Din, Abū Abdullah, Muhammad b. Abdullah al-Lawātī al-Tanjī better known as *IBN BATTŪTA*, the first great globe trotter in history, was born in a family of Berber origin (and hence called '*al-lawātī*') at Tanjah (Tanjier, in Morocco) on 27 Rajab 703 A.H. (25 February 1304). He grew up in Tanjah, received good education in the Maliki curriculum and stayed in his home town till he was 22 years old. During this period, he read and heard about other countries, had an awareness of the different regions and the peoples inhabiting them, and developed a strong urge and inquisitiveness to see the vast world around him. He commenced his first journey with the intention of performing the pilgrimage, but then the lure of the unknown possessed him and he merged himself into distant horizons, only to reappear and disappear again.

Leaving Tanjah on 2 Rajab 725 (13 June 1325), he returned to his home country for the first time after 25 years by the end of Sha'bān 750 A.H. (November 1349). During the first phase of this long period he made Makka - Madina as the central destination to which he would return for pilgrimage. Chronologically, his intineraries were as under (E.I.): 725- 726/1325-1326 - Tanjah, North Africa, Egypt, Syria, Makka-Madina; 726- 727/1326-1327- Makka, Iraq, Khuzistan, Fars, Jibal, Tabrez, Baghdad, Sāmarrā, Mosul, Baghdad; 727-730/1327-1330 - Stay in Arabia for three pilgrimages; 730-31-732/1330-1332 Yemen, Aden, Zayla, Mogadeshu coastal ports of East Africa, Uman, Makka Madina (pilgrimage); 732-33 A.H. - Egypt, Syria, Asia Minor, Tartar country (of the Golden Hordes), Constantinople, Tartar country, Transoxiana, Afghanistan, Sind (arriving on 01 Muharram

734/2 September 1333), Delhi (stay for 10 years 734 Safar 743); 743 – Muharram 748/1342 - 1347 - Delhi, Malabar, Maldives (stay for 1 - 1/2 years), Ceylon, Maldives (2nd time), Bengal, Assam, Sumatara, Chinese port of Zaytūn (Ts'uan-Chou), Sumatara, Malabar; Muharram 748-Dhu'l Hijjah 748 (1347-48) - Uman, Iraq (Baghdad, Syria, Egypt, Arabia (pilgrimage); 748/49 Sha'ban 750 (1348 November 1349) - Arabia, Egypt, Alexandria (Safar 750 A.H.), Tunis, Sardina, Algeria, Fās (Morocco).

After having travelled for 25 years he was still unsatiated and made two more journies, one to Granada in the north and the other to Niger in the South. (i) 750-751/1350-51: from Fās to Granādā (Andalus) and back to Morocco, (ii) Muharram 753 Dhu'l Qa'dah 754/February 1352 December 1353: from Sijlimāsā (Morocco) across Sahārā to Niger and back to Sijilmāsā.

On return to the home country, he came to the State Capital of Fās (instead of Ṭanjah where probably his parents had already died) which was ruled by the enlightened Sultan Abū 'Inān of the Banū Marīn dynasty. Being impressed by Ibn Battuta's narrations of his travels, the Sultan deputed an able scholar Abū Abdullah Mohammad Ibn Juziyy to take dictation of the narrations and compile and edit the whole material into a book. Ibn Battuta agreed to the wish of the Sultan, and more so as Ibn Juziyy had become known to him after they had met in Granada. The internal evidence shows that Ibn Juziyy proved to be a good editor and carried out the assignment satisfactorily (*namaqhā wa harrarhā*). What he says in his introduction amply confirms his scholarly approach to his assignment:

> 'I have conveyed the purport of Shaykh Abū Abdullah (Ibn Battutah) in words which convey the meaning intended by him which clarify the aspects on which he relied. And usually I have retained the words according to their usage without interfering with original or derived meanings. I have produced in writing all stories and reports faithfully without discussing their veracity or going into further investigation'.(1)

Ibn Juziyy tried to record, as far as possible, in Ibn Battuta's own words. Wherever he himself supplied an annotation, he made it clear by his words "*Qāl Ibn Juziyy*" ('This is said by Ibn juziyy'). Ibn Hajar whose bilographical note on Ibn Battuta is the earliest, has noted that a contemporary scholar Ibn Marzūq had absolved Ibn Juziyy/Ibn Battutah of having manipulated any spurious accounts.(2)

Some of his accounts of the East, though true, were so strange and astounding to his listeners in the Far West (Maghrib) that they thought as if he was lying. For instance, Ibn Battuta had said about Sultan Muhammad b. Tughluq of India that on occasions when he set out from Delhi he would sanction subsistence for six months for every individual (child and adult) in the city, and that on his return people would often go out of the city to receive him and circle (dance?) around him so that, by way of reward, coins would be showered on them by means of catapults. Now there was nothing extraordinary about this statement and yet this was the very story quoted by Ibn Khaldun (who was a contemporary of Ibn Battuta) to point out that such stories made the people think that Ibn Battutah was lying.

With all his lapses, Ibn Battutah's intellectual honesty is attested by the fact that if he had forgotten something while dictating he would readily admit "I have forgotten it" (*qad ansaytu-hu*). In his introduction, Ibn Juziyy compliments Ibn Batuttah for his maturity, insight and understanding as a *reliable* and *truthful* traveller (*al-Shaykh al-faqqīh al-Sālih al-Thiqah al- Sadūq*).

It would appear that before dictating to Ibn Juziyy, Ibn Battuta had with him somewhat detailed and regularly kept notes of the later period of his travels from Malabar back home (circa 744/45 - 750 A.H.), while he had re-written from memory the accounts of the earlier period (the first twenty years, 725 - 744/45 A.H.) of which he had kept a regular record but it was lost when his boat was attacked by pirates in the Indian Ocean. Even though he had recalled much from his memory after a lapse of years and decades, there are preserved enough details in terms of proper nouns of persons and places of Per-

---

(1) Ibn Juziyy's *Introduction* to the *Rehla*.

(2) Ibn Hajar al-Asqalani : *al-Durar al-Kaminah* Haderabad, Deccan, Vol.III, p.481.

sian, Turkish, Indian and Chinese origin in his different accounts which attest to his memory being a prodigious one. Ibn Juziyy completed the whole account as dictated by Ibn Battuta on 3 Dhu'l Hijjah 756 A.H. (9 December 1357) which he edited and published soon thereafter entitling it as *Tuhfat al-nazzār fi Gharā'ib al-Amsār wa'Ajā'ib al- Asfār.*

In Ibn Battuta's epitome of his journies, the genre of *al- rihla* or *adab al-rihla* ('Travel Literature') reached its climax. 'Travel' had emphasised that human beings be engaged in positive fruitful *action* in their lives on earth. Holy Quran enjoined on the believer to travel around on earth in order (i) to realise how arrogant peoples who had deviated from the path of the truth had come to a sad end, (ii) and to be able to understand 'the origin of the creation' (*kayf kān bada' al-khalq*). The Prophet (*sala'm*) had set an example by his *hijra*, and thereafter Muslims from all walks of life were on the move negotiating distant lands. Firstly were the researchers who travelled far and wide specially in pursuit of knowledge - religious, geographical, historical, socio-cultural etc. To this class belonged such eminent researches as Imām Bukhārī, Istakhārī, Ibn Hawqal, Ya'qūbī, Maqdisī, Mas'ūdī, Barūni, Idrīsī and Yaqūt Hamavī. Later, a number of believers who proceeded on pilgrimage to Arabia either wrote full accounts of their journey or wrote some sort of memoirs. Andalusian Pilgrim Ibn Jubayr's *RIHLAH* (578-581 A.H.) is the best model of the 'Pilgrimage Journey'. Others travelled for trade and commerce, and to this class belonged Sulayman, Abu Zaid (both of the Sirāf port) and others whose purport in their voyages was mainly commercial. Then there were those who undertook their journies on official assignments: Ahmad b. Fadlān was sent on a fact finding mission to Bulgaria by the Abbasid Caliph Muqtadir in 309 A.H./921-22. There were still others who travelled primarily due to their personal urge and interest, in order to see, enjoy and learn. To this class belonged Ibn Battutah. Before him, Abū Dulaf Mas'ar Ibn Muhalhil, a literary man and poet, had travelled through Persia, Turkistan, India and China, and Abū Hamid of Granada had travelled through North Africa along the Mediterrian up to Bulgaria.

Ibn Battutah excelled all of them. It has been observed that by the sheer vastness of his travels and the immensity of the written account of them, Ibn Battutah imparted a 'new dimension' to the genre of *rihla* as being 'a description of the known world'. He took to travelling when he was 22 years old and finally settled down when he was above fifty. His journies were more numerous and lengthy, covering great many regions and extending over the three continents of Africa, Asia and Europe. He had travelled about 75000 miles.

Initially Ibn Battuta had left his home with a set purpose to perform the pilgrimage. Having done this, he took to travelling as a hobby. If he had any objective before him, it was that of *travelling*, to see and know more and more about different climes and cultures. Without being tied up to any set purposes for having undertaken his journies, his narration of them is spontaneous, genuine and natural. And yet, he has left in his account rich material on geography, history, anthropology and general culture.

Ibn Battutah died quietly in the city of Marrākush (in Morocco) in the year 770 A.H./1368-69 (or in 779 A.H./1377).

THE SURVIVING MONUMENTS OF THE BYGONE TIMES.

Al-Bayruni

الآثار الباقية من القرون الخالية

أبو الريحان محمد بن أحمد البيروني

Among all the works which Bayruni wrote in the prime of his youth, this book which he entitled as *al-Āthār al- Bāqiyah min al-Qurūn al-Khāliya,* ('The Surviving Monuments of the Bygone Times) is the most original one. It attests to his capacity for research and his erudition in exploring the frontiers of ancient history and its cultures and chronologies.

Bayruni was born, as recorded by him, on Thursday the 3rd of Dhu al-Hijjah 362 A.H. (4 September, 973 A.D.) in Kāth, the capital city of his native country of Khwārazm, in a family that was possibly linked with the royal quarters. This might explain how young Bayruni was brought up under the patronage and tuturoship of Abu Nasr Mansur b. Ali b. Iraq whom Bayruni calls "a freedman of Amir al- Mo'minīn". He expresses his gratitude to the 'House of Iraq' in general and to Mansur in particular:

> The house of Iraq nourished me and brought me up
> Of them, Mansur having established me well.

He probably came under the tutorship of Abu Nasr Mansur as a young lad and completed his entire education under him. Mansur was an eminent astronomer and mathematician of his times and Bayruni specialized under him in these disciplines. Bayruni acknowledges him as his teacher and describes Abu Nasr Mansur's method of calculating the apogee as the more advanced one.

It was due to the high quality of the tuition that young Bayruni had received that on completion of his education, he plunged into independent scientific research. He made his probably first astronomical observation in Kāth by about 380 A.H. when he was hardly 18 years old. For seven years (380 - 387 A.H.), he remained engaged in intensive studies and research in Kāth and conducted astronomical observations. During this period, he would appear to have established contacts with other scientists so that in the year 387 A.H. he made a luner observation in Kāth in cooperation with Abu al-Wafā al-Būzanjānī in Baghdad, in order to determine logitudinal difference between the two capital cities.

Thereafter he left Khwārizm. possibly due to the unsettled political conditions (culminating eventually in dynastic change) which were not propitious enough for him to pursue his studies and conduct research with single mindness. For sven years he had collected considerable information and scientific data which still remained to be compiled. His contacts with scholarly circles outside offered prospects to complete his works. Leaving Kāth early in 387 A.H., he travelled to Ray and from there to Jilān where the ruling Ispahbad, Marzubān b. Rustam received him well, and here (387/88 A.H.) he completed his book *Kitāb Maqālid 'Ilm al-Hay'ah* etc. on astronomy and dedicated it to the Ispahbad.

From Jilān he moved to Jurjān where the Ispahbad's superior, the enlightened Shams al-Ma'ālī Qābūs b. Washmgīr had come to the helm of affairs in that country for the second time (388-403). For the next 5 years (388/89-394 A.H.) that Bayruni stayed at Jurjān under the patronage of the munificent Shams al- Ma'ali, he conducted field researches in geodesy, made astronomical observations, and completed some of his works of which *Kitāb Tajrī al-Shu'ā'āt wa al- Anwār* (on LIGHT) was the first one that he dedicated to this prince. It was in (the later part of) 490 A.H. that he commenced writing AL-ĀTHAR which on completion (390/91) he dedicated to Shams al-Ma'āli. By this time, Bayruni had authored about ten books of which AL-ĀTHAR was the most scholarly and important one. Judging from its precious details on customs, calendars and chronologies as also the ancient societies brought to light and analysed by Bayruni with great understanding, it becomes obvious that he had collected its elaborate data painstakingly, over long years, beginning from his early scholarly pursuits in Khwārazm. He used the written record that became available to him but more so the oral tradition that was transmitted to him by reliable authorities.

The modern orientalist, C. Edward Sachau, performed an unparalled feat of scholarship in producing an English version of this highly scientific and technical work of Bayruni long back in 1879 (which was later followed by his edition of the original text in 1897). Probably keeping in view the more substantive part of the work, he entitled his English version as "The Chronology of Ancient Nations", with a sub-heading akin to the original as "Vestiges of the Past". However, there is much more in this work than any such title would suggest. The data, details and the references given are unique, and remain to be understood, explained and elaborated. Beside the chronological data, the book contains important information on history, religion, custom and culture of a number of ancient societies. As rightly observed by Sachau "The work of generations will be required to do full justice to Albiruni".

Defending his own appreciation of Bayruni (which is guarded enough not to amount to a 'universal recogniation', his book is declared to be "a standard work" but only "in Oriental literature". Sachau has paid Bayruni a unique complement in one particular context: "Many critics do not seem to have noticed that Albiruni, a *Muslim*, is the first of all the scholars we know who has composed a scientific system of the Jewish Chronology".

So far as the originality of AL-ĀTHĀR is concerned, observations of the learned Edward Sachau who had dived deep into it may appropriately be quoted. According to him: "The work of Albiruni has the character of a primary source" and "that as a whole, it will scarcely ever be superseded". "Even competent scholars will find it no easy matter to follow our author through all the mazes of his elaborate scientific calculations. Containing, as it does, all the technical and historical details of the various systems for the computation of time, invented and used by the Persians, Sogdians, Chorasnians, Jews,

Syrians, Hareranians, and Arabs, together with Greek traditions, it offers an equal interest to all those who study the antiquity and history of the Zoroastrain and Jewish, Christian and Muhammadan religions".

THE BOOK OF PLANTS.

Abu Hanifa al-Dīnawarī

كتاب النبات

أبو حنيفة أحمد بن داؤد الدينوري

Abu Hanifa Ahmad b. Dāwūd was born at Dīnawar in Eastern Iraq by the turn of the 2nd century A.H. (c.200-210 A.H.). He had his early education in Dīnawar and persued his higher studies with some of the renowned teachers of Basra and Kufa. He acquired sound general education, and studied philology, history and philosophy on the one hand, and botony, mathematics, and astronomy on the other. He was a pious man devoted to prayer, and wrote a commentry of Holy Quran in thirteen volumes. Also he authored important works on such diverse subjects as Astronomical Geography *(Kitāb al-Qibla wa la-Zawāl),* Climatics and Meteorology *(Kitāb al-'Anwā'*), Botony *(Kitāb al-Nabāt)* Arithmetic and Algebra. He also wrote a historical work *al-Akhbār al- Tiwāl,* as noted by *al-Nadīm* in his *K. al- Fihrist,* which as indicated by its title was a *comprehensive* work on the subject. A work by the same name which has survived and is ascribed to him, does not appear to be the original *al-Akhbār al- Tiwāl* of Abu Hanifa, because of its meagre content and poor presentation.

Abu Hanifa's *Kitab al-Nabāt* (The Book of Plants) is a monumental work on the knowledge of plants up to the author's times–a landmark in the history of Botony. He brought together in this work all information on plants that was previously available and supplemented it considerably from his own observations and collection. It represents an integrated philological, historical, and botanical approach to the study of plants, and is marked by thoroughness in the description of each specimen. Because of its comprehensive approach and authenticity of information, the book has remained a standard work of reference over centuries for not only botonists but also for lexiographers, pharmacists and students of agriculture. The introduction dealing with botonical and agricultural generalities has a special importance of its own.

The 'Book of Plants' in its original complete text is lost, but considerable part of the text has survived. Because of its importance and popularity, it was quoted in numerous later works and on the basis of these quotations which are considerable the text has been reconstructed by modern researchers and the book has been largely revived in the following prints:

Vol. I. Containing the last part of the monograph section and the letters *alif* to *zāy* of the alphabetical section (ed. Bernhard Lewin, *Uppasala Universitets Arsskrift,* 1953: 10). Published by Harrassowitz, W. Germany, 1953.

Vol. II. Edited by M. Hamidullah and published by the French Institute, Cairo.

Vol. III. Ed. Bernhard Lewin, published by Franz Steiner, Wiesbaden, W. Germany, 1974.

Vol. IV. Ed. M. Hamidullah, under publication by the Hamdard Foundation of Pakistan, Karachi.

THE COMPREHENSIVE BOOK ON ANIMAL LIFE.

Al-Damīrī

حياة الحيوان الكبرى

ابو البقا كمال الدين محمد بن موسى الدميري

Abu'l Baqā Kamāl al-Dīn Muhammad b. Mūsā b. 'Īsā b. 'Ali al-Damīrī was born in Cairo 742 A.H. (1341). He studied with the great Shafai'ī jurist al- Subkī and other eminent teachers, and excelled in his knowledge of Jurisprudence, Hadith, Quranic Exegesis, Philosophy and Literature. He was a devout believer and a scholar of repute, took to the teaching profession and lectured at Al-Azhar and other important institutions. As a Sufi he lived a simple life in piety and devotion. He died in 808 A.H. (1405 A.D.) and was buried in the Sufi graveyard by the side of Jāmi' of Sa'īd al-Su'adā.

As an eminent Shafa'ite jurist, he wrote *'al-Najm al- Wahhāj fi Sharh al-Minhāj* in four volumes being a commentary on *Minhāj al-Tālibīn,* a manual of Shafi'ite Law by al-Nuwayri. In *Hadith,* he wrote a five volume commentary *AL-DĪBĀJĀ* on the *SUNAN* of *IBN MĀJĀ*. This work remained in his handwritten draft, and al-Damiri died before publishing a fair edition of it.

Outside the orbit of religious studies, Damiri authored his *Kitab Hayāt al-Hayawān al-Kubrā* (The Comprehensive Book on Animal Life) which is a voluminous para-zoological encyclopedia dealing with great many animals in alphabetical order. There are 1069 articles one on each animal but due to duplication the number of animals dealt with is somewhat less than 1069. Also the articles vary in length, some as large as full treatises and others limited to a few lines. Under each article, information is generally given in this order: (1) *name* of the animal and *its* loxicographical and grammatical pecularities: (2)

description of the animal; (3) traditions concerning the animals; (4) legal questions licit or illicit use of each animal, for food or other purposes; (5) proverbs relating to each animal; (6) medical and other properties of different parts of the animal, their secretions and exertions; (7) interpretation of dreams concerning the animal.

Al-Damīrī's work enjoyed much popularity, being circulated in three recensions, the large one *(al-Kubrā)*, the middle one *(al-Wusṭā)* and the small one *(al-Sughrā)*. He himself made a digest of it and entitled it as. حاوي الحسان من حياة الحيوان*

---

* The largest text of the *Hayat* was first printed in Cairo, Bulaq 1958-59, then again in 1867-8 and 1887-99. English translation by the retired lieutenant colonel A.S.C. Jayakar (Vol. I., Vol. 2 Part 1, a total of 1498 pl, Bombay 1906-8). Of this Vol. 2 was left incomplete and the translation extends to about three-quarters of the total, some digressions having been omitted.

THE BOOK OF OPTICS.

Ibn Al-Haytham

كتاب المناظر

أبو علي الحسن إبن الهيثم

Ibn al-Haytham, known to the West as 'Alhazen', was born in Basra where he studied mathematics and other sciences. He flourished in Egypt under al-Hākim (996-1220 A.D.), and died in Cairo in 430 A.H. (1039 A.D.) or soon after. He was the first great physicist and the greatest investigator of optics in the history of Science. He is known to have written two hundred works on mathematics, physics, astronomy and medicine.

Although Ibn al-Haytham made major contributions in mathematics, it was specially in the realm of physics that he made his outstanding contributions. He was an accurate observer and experimenter as well as theoretician. As a physician, he wrote commentaries on Aristotle and Galen. He wrote a number of treatises on Geometry which he also used extensively in his study of Optics. Thus, his name is preserved in what is known as the 'Problem of Alhazen' which arose in connection with his work on optics and which had great influence on subsequent developments. Prior to his death, he issued a collection of problems similar to the Data of Euclid.

Ibn al-Haytham wrote numerous works on Optics and the related subjects such as atmospheric phenomenon. His major opus on the subject is *Kitāb al-Manāzir* (Optical Thesaurus), which had great influence on Western Science (R. Bacon & Kepler). The work demonstrates the great advance made in applying experimental method in scientific research. In this work, Ibn al-Haytham reveals his competence in medicine as well as physics. He begins by studying the anatomy and physiology of the eye. He traces the functioning of the eye from the optic nerve originating in the brain to the eye itself, whose various parts - such as the conjunctive iris. cornea and lens - he describes in a masterly fashion, pointing out the role of each in vision. He also shows the inter- relation between the various parts of the eye and how the eye acts as a unitary organ and dioptric system during the process of vision. Ibn al- Haytham, like Ibn Sina and several other Muslim scientists, did not hold that rays issue from the eye but believed that during the process of vision rays of light reach the eye from the object which is seen.*

He was the first to refute the optical doctrines of Euclid and Ptolemy, according to which the eye received images of various objects by sending visual rays to certain points. In his Optics, Ibn Al-Haytham proved that the process is actually the reverse and thus laid the foundations of modern Optics. His formula was that it is not a ray that leaves the eye and meets the object that gives rise to vision, but rather that the form of the perceived object passes into the eye and is transmitted by the lens. Thus, he gave a much more sound theory of vision than all his predecessors regarding the lens system of the eye itself to be the sensitive part. He established the fundamental basis which eventually led to the discovery of magnifying lenses in Italy.

Geometry was used extensively by Ibn al-Haitham in his study of optics. His work on optics which gives one of the earliest scientific accounts of atmospheric refraction, contains a geometrical solution to the problem of finding the focal point of a concave mirror; that a ray from a given point must be incident in order to be reflected to another given point. Ibn al- Haytham also discovered some original geometrical theorems such as the theorem of the radical axis. He was also able to solve a number of advanced questions in geometrical optics; for example, he solved the case of an aplanatic surface for reflection through his mastery of mathematics. His sound mathematical knowledge enabled him to propound revolutionary doctrines on such subjects as the halo and the rainbow, eclipses and shadows, and on spherical and parabolic mirrors. His tables of corresponding angles of incidence and refraction, light passing from one medium to another

* S.H. Nasr, al-Mihrijan, pp. 139-142.

show how he nearly discovered the law of the ratio of sines for any given pair of media, later attributed to Snell. He investigated twilight relating it to atmospheric refraction by estimating the sun's height to be 19 degrees below the horizon at the commencement of the phenomenon in the mornings or at its termination in the evenings. The figures generally accepted now is 18 degrees. Ibn Al-Haytham estimated the height of the homogeneous atmosphere on this basis to be about 55 miles, a rather close approximation. He understood the laws of the formation of images in spherical and parabolic mirrors. He was also familiar with the reasons for spherical aberration and of magnification produced by lenses.

BOOK OF THE BALANCE OF WISDOM.

Al-Khāzinī

ميزان الحكمة

ابو الفتح عبد الرحمن المنصور الخازني

Abul-Fath ‘Abd al-Rahmān al-Mansūr al-Khāzinī, physicist and astronomer, flourished in Merv in the 6th/12th century. He received good education, specialized in physical science and astronomy, and continued his investigations and researches in mechanics and hydrostatics in the tradition of earlier scientists. He was a pious Muslim, of simple living and austere morality. He also used to teach and guide students, and enjoyed the patronage of the Seljuq Sultan Sanjar (511-52 A.H./1117-57 A.D.). The Sultan once sent him one thousand dinars but he took only ten and returned the rest saying: ‘three *dinars* are enough for me for the year, because I have none also in the house except a cat’. He died by about 550 A.H. (c.1155 A.D.).

Of Khāzinī’s important works on astronomy and physics were a treatise on advanced astronomical instruments denoted by him as *‘ajība’ (al-ālāt al-‘ajība al-rasadiyya)*, and Astronomical Tables which he dedicated to Sultan Sanjar. The latter “were utilized, either directly or indirectly, by the Byzantine scholars george Chrysococcos and Theodore Meliteniotes” in the 14th century (J.Vernet, E.I.).

In 515/1121, he completed his *Kitāb Mizān al-Hikma* (Book of the Balance of Wisdom). It is a basic work on the Hydrotatic balance and its varieties, a crowning achievement in the long process of earlier methods and models over the centuries. Simultaneously it is one of the most remarkable books on mechanics, hydrostatics and physics. It contains table of specific gravity of many liquids and solids (based on al-Bayruni’s) and also a history of the subject. Khāzinī

صورة ميزان الحكمة المعروف بالجامع
Figure of the Balance of Wisdom, called the Comprehensive.

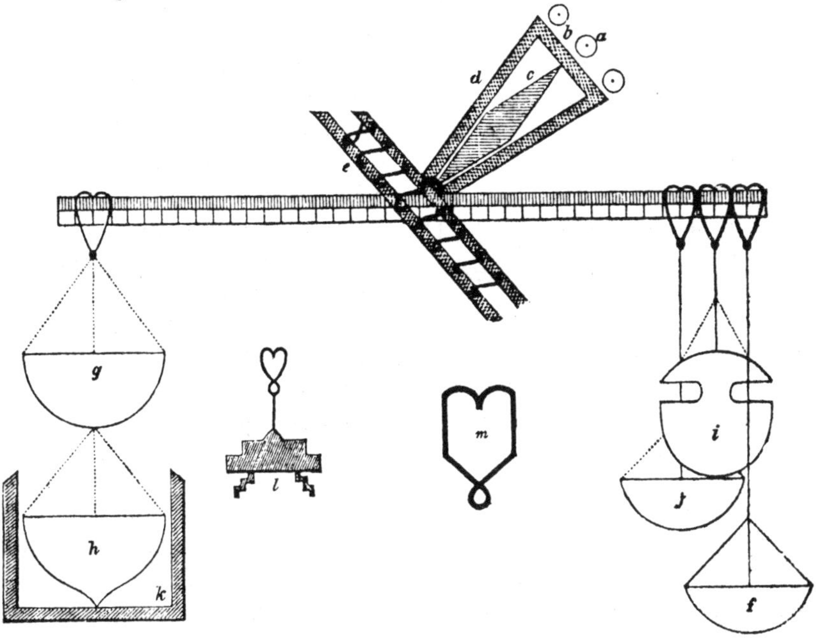

above, on the left :
النصف الايسر للجواهر Left Half, for Substances.
along the beam, on the left :
الشعيرات الظاهرة Plain Round-point Numbers.

above, on the right :
النصف الايمن للصنجات Right Half, for Counterpoises.
along the beam, on the right :
الشعيرات الخافية Hidden[34] Round-point Numbers.

under the beam, on the right :
تثبت المراكز عليه فى هذا الجانب The Specific Gravities are marked on this Side of the Beam.

a. المعلاق Means of Suspension.
b. العريضة Front-piece.
c. اللسان Tongue.
d. [m3]الفياران Two Checks [of the Front-piece].
e, and under the beam on the left :
العريضة واللسان[n5] بعد غير محكمين اذا الاحكام ياتى بعد الامتحان فى موضعه The Front-piece and the Tongue as disconnected [from the

f. الطرفية الهوائية Air-bowl for the End.
g. الطرفية الهوائية الثانية Second Air-bowl for the End.
h. كفة الماء الثالثة Third [or] Water-bowl.
i. المجنحة الرابعة Fourth [or] Winged Bowl.
j. المتنقلة الخامسة Fifth [or] Movable Bowl.

From Khanikoff's Essay on
BOOK OF THE BALANCE OF WISDOM
(Journal of the American Oriental Society, vol.vi, 1859)

advanced the theory of gravity as universal force directed toward the centre of the universe - that is, the centre of the earth. He discusses and explains gravity of air, observations on capillarity, use of areometer to measure densities and the temperature of liquids, theory of the lever, and application of the balance to levelling and to the measuring of time.

Khāzinī's hydrostatic balance (*Mīzān*) was superior in its accuracy to any that had been constructed before him. He defind weight as 'the force inherent in solid bodies which causes them to move, of their own accord, in a straight line towards the centre of the earth and towards this center alone; this force, in turn, depends upon the density of the body'. It was within Khāzinī's knowledge that temperature influences density. He also worked out table of specific weights of alloys and density of water when nearer to the centre of Earth.

The book (published in Hyderabad Deccan, 1359/1940) contains eight *Maqālās* (discourses) which are divided into *abwāb* (chapters) and subdivided into *fasls* (sections). Besides his description of the balance and his indebtedness to Bayruni, Khāzini elaborates some important earlier concepts. Thus he discusses a series of theorems deriving from the classical works of Archimedes, Euclid and Menelaus; describes the areometer of Pappus; uses frequently the works of predecessors such as Thabit b. Qurrā, Abū Sahl al-Kūhī, al-Asfizārī, al-Rāzī, 'Umar Khayyām, and above all, of Bayrūnī, whose picnometer is described; touches upon traditional problems like the determining of the law of alloys or the well-known one of the chess-board (calculation of a geometrical pregression); and explains the use of proportions (E.I). The book contains information on air and its weight, and tells us that air has a weight and an elevating power like liquids. It also shows that Archimedes' law is true on liquids and gases.

THE BOOK OF SECRETS.

Abu Bakr al-Rāzī

كتاب الأسرار

أبو بكر بن زكريّا الرّازي

Abu Bakr Muhammad b. Zakariyā al-Rāzī was born in Rayy (in North Persia, then Tabaristan) on the first day of Sha'bān in the year 251 A.H. (27 August, 865 A.D.). He completed his education there, and for some years he remained keenly interested in music, singing and composing poetry. Thereafter he centered his attention on philosophy, medicine and alchemy. As the most promising young physician, he first headed the Hospital of Ray. Then he went to Baghdad when he was in his thirties, and was appointed as Chief Physician of the Muqtadiri Hospital. Rāzī attained great name and fame as physician, philosopher and scientist, and died in Baghdad on the 5th of Sha'bān 313 A.H. (26 October, 925 A.D.).

Abu Bakr al-Rāzī's complete philosophical works are lost, but the fragments which have survived show that he favoured Plato to Aristotle. Rāzī was the first great clinical physician in the history of Medicine, well known both in the East and the West (as 'Rhazes'). As an authority on Medicine, he was second only to Ibn Sina though he excelled him in his scientific observations.

Rāzī authored about 232 works, a number of them on Medicine such as: (1) *Kitāb al-Hāwī fi al-Tibb* ('The Continents') which is an enormous encyclopaedia of medicine documenting his own original observations and also containing extracts from Greek and Indian sources; (2) *Kitāb al- Mansūri*, another important work based on Razī's own clinical observations which was known and studied in the West as *Liber medicinalis ad Almanasorem;* (3) *Kitāb Taqsīm al-'Ilal* ('The Book on Categorization of the Causes of Diseases) which was translated into Latin as "Liber divisionum"; (4) *Kitāb al-Fakhri, (Liber pretiosus);* (5) *Kitab al-Jadri wa al-Hasba,* 'The Treatise on Smallpox and Measles' which became famous as "*Liber de pestilentia*" in Europe. He also wrote some other important treatises such as 'Medicines for Heart', Rheumatism *(al- Niqris),* Colic *(al-Qulanj),* and *The Diet (al-Aghdhiya).*

Razi was the first scientist responsible for the transformation of 'Alchemy' into 'Chemistry.' Historically, he is the 'Father of the Science of Chemistry.' His two books, *Kitāb al-Asrār* (The Book mistakenly called *Kitāb Sirr al-Asrār*) or 'The Book of the Secrets' of Secrets) and *al-Madkhal al-Ta'līmī* (Prodaedeutic Introduction), though using the language of 'Alchemy are, in essence, texts of Chemistry. This is particularly true of 'The Book of Secrets' which is the major opus of Razī on the subject.

The tradition of studying ALCHEMY had become well grounded following the works of Jābir b. Hayyān (d. 200 A.H./815 A.C.),and this tradition was being carried on assiduously until al-Razī's own times. With the 'Book of Secrets' which was also translated into Latin as *Liber Secretorum bubacaris,* came the transition from ALCHEMY to CHEMISTRY. This is to be attributed to Razi's scientific bent of mind. He "negated the symbolic dimension of alchemy and transformed it into chemistry." This viewpoint has been ably elaborated as under. "Even if late Muslim alchemical sources considered Rhazes as belonging to the Jabirian tradition of alchemy, a study of his works reveals that he belongs to quite another school. The symbolic and metaphysical dimensions of Jābir are no longer to be seen in Rhazes' writings. He is describing chemical and medical properties of substances, and he is in fact credited with major discoveries in this domain including that of alcohol and of certain acids. Rhazes was writing about chemical processes albeit in an alchemical language and that he himself had little interest in the alchemical world-view that existed before him and continued to survive long after this work had seen the light of day." Thus Razi's *Kitāb al- Asrār* "is a text of chemistry which has preserved the alchemical language. It describes the chemical processes and experiments which Rhazes himself performed and which can be identified in their modern equivalent forms of distillation, calculation, crystallization etc.. Rhazes in this and other works gives also a description of a large number of chemical apparatuses, such as beakers, flasks, phials, casseroles, naptha lamps, smelting furnaces, shears, tongues, alembics, pestles, mortars and many others that have in part survived to the present day".*

After having passed through numerous editorial hands, *Kitāb al-Asrār* was rendered into Latin by Gerard of Cremona (1178 A.D.) and became a chief source of knowledge on the subject in Europe. It was quoted by Roger Becon under the title De Spiritibus et corporibus.

---

* Nasr, Seyyed Hossein: Science And Civilization of Islam, Suhaim Academy, Lahore 1983, pp. 268-69.

THE KEY TO ARITHMETIC.

Al-Kāshī

مفتاح الحساب

غياث الدين جمشيد بن مسعود الكاشي

The author, Ghiyāth al-Din Jamshed b. Jamshed b. Mas'ūd b. Mahmūd was a distinguished astronomer and Mathematician who flourished during the first half of the 9th/15 century. Not much is known about his early life but his *nisbah,* Kāshī or Kāshāni, would indicate that he belonged to the city of Kāshān where he was born sometime during the second half of the 8th/14th century and where he also completed his education. He commenced his researches in astronomy by observing the moon eclipse which was visible in Kāshān on the 14th of Dhu'l Hijja 808 A.H. (2, June, 1406 A.D.).

The period of about next thirty years was most productive for him in his advanced work in astronomy and mathematics. In 816 A.H. (1413 A.D.) he completed his *Zīj-i-Khāzānī* improving upon *Ziz-i Ilkhānī* of Nasir al-din Tusi. In 819 A.H. (1419 A.D.), he wrote a treatise on astronomical instruments. The same year he was invited by Sultan Ulugh Beg to his court in Samarqand where he settled down for the rest of his life. Qādīzāda al-Rūmi, the Sultan's chief astronomer, was assisted by al-Kāshāni in the construction of the Sultan's Samarqand Observatory and in the establishment of Ulugh Beg's Tables. He would appear to have died in Samarqand by about 832 A.H./429 A.D.

Kāshi also made original contributions in the field of Mathematics. He not only invented the decimal fraction, the approximate method for calculating problems which have no exact solution, the iterative algorism. and made a remarkably accurate calculation of π, but he must also be considered the first person to have invented a calculating machine. He was the first to solve the binomial theorem known by the name of Newton. In 725 A.H. (1423 A.D.), he completed his first important work in Mathematics, *al-Risāla al-Muhītiyya* or 'The All-Embracing Treatise' "in which he established the value of π with extra-ordinary exactitude, so that 2π = 6, 16, 59, 28, 1, 34, 51, 46, 14, 50 in sexagonal notation, and 6, 2831853071795865 in decimal notation. Allied to the algorithmic methods of this work is the determination of sine 1 worked out by an iterative method. Kāshī employed the equation: sine d=3 sine d-4 sine 3d" (E.I.) which was used in the western world by Viete (1540 - 1613) about two centuries later.

His second work, *Miftāh al-Hisāb* or 'The Key to Arithmetic,' which he dedicated to Sultan Ulugh Beg's Library in 830 A.H.(1427 A.D.), is the most important work on the science of numbers. The book comprises 5 sections each of which is sub-divided into a number of chapters. It embodies fundamental mathematical information which serves an extensive range of users such as calculators, clerks, merchants, land surveyors, architects and astronomers. Arithmetic, algebraic and geometric methods to the solution of various problems are given. In it he "expounds the arithmetical operations, teaches the method of extracting roots by the system which today is called after Riffini-Horner" (E.I.). Outstanding among the wealth of mathematical information comprised in this work are the extraction of roots and what is known as the "Binomial Theorem" and "Pascal's Triangle." The coefficients of the binomial expansion are given by Kāshī up to the 9th power, long before Blaise Pascal (1623 - 1662).

Kāshi's work has been extensively commented upon and analysed more recently by modern mathematicians such as P. Lackey ('Die Rechenkunst bei Gamsid b. Mas'ud al-Kāsi, mit Rūckblicken fūr die alter Geschichte des Rechnens', Abhandlungen fur die kunde des Morgenlandes, XXXI, 1951). An extensive commentary on this work along with its translation into Russian by Rosenfeld, Segal and Yuschkewitsch, Moscow, 1956; and A. Qorbānī, *Kashāni-nāma*, Tehran, 1350, A.H. Solar, part three).

THE BOOK OF FIGURE OF THE SECTOR.

Nasīr Al-Dīn Al-Tūsī

كتاب شكل القطاع

نصير الدين محمد بن محمد الطوسي

Muhammad b. Muhammad b. al-Hasan, Abu Ja'far, Nasīr al-Din al-Tūsī was born in Tus in 597 A.H. (1201 A.D), studied mathematics with Kamāl al-Dīn Ibn Yunus and gained fame as mathematician and astronomer. He began his career in the service of some of the local princes, but when Hulāqū conquered Persia, he entered his service as astrologer and astronomer, gained the Mongol ruler's confidence and was able to induce him to establish the Marāgha Observatory. Here Tūsī assembled a huge collection of four hundred thousand books taken from the libraries of Baghdad, Jazira and Syria. As Director of Observatory, he attracted mathematicians and astronomers to Marāgha, fixed adequate stipends for them and revived the study of astronomy and mathematics. He spent most of his later years in Marāghā, and went to Kazimayn near Baghdad in old age and died there in 672 A.H. (1274 A.D.).

Tusi was the leading figure of his times in the study of arts, sciences, mathematics and philosophy. He was a prolific writers in both Arabic and Persian. In philosophy, he wrote two works centering on the study of Ibn Sina's *AL-ISHĀRĀT,* and a critical commentary on Fakhr al-Din al-Razi's *Al-Muhassal. Akhlāq-i- Nāsirī* was his important work in Ethics. He made significant contribution in the domain of Mathematics and Astronomy, and wrote commentaries on the whole cycle of Greek mathematical texts from Euclid to Ptolemy. He criticised Ptolemy and even proposed a new Planetary model. In astronomy, he wrote a number of works, of which *al-Tadhkira fi al-*

Hay'at was an advanced work on the subject.

He wrote a treatise entitled *Jawāmi' al-Hisāb bi al-Naht wa al-Turāb* on summaries of Arithmetic through 'Board and Dust'. The 'dustboard method' still survives as a 'folk' practice in certain regions along with other popular methods of calculation such as the *siyāq* system which was fairly prevalent in the Iran.

Kitāb Shakl al-Qattā', 'The Book of Figure of the Sector', represents Tusi's most outstanding contribution to mathematics, as it comprises the development of Trigonometry as an independent discipline. It is the first book on Trigonometry in history which comprises all the six cases for a right-angled spherical triangle independent of Menelaus's theorem. Tusi has also presented in it the fundamental theorem of Sines, namely:

$$a/\sin A = b/\sin B = c/\sin C$$

a, b and c being the sides of the triangle facing the angles A, B and C respectively.

THE BOOK OF ALGEBRA

Al-Khwārazmī

كتاب المختصر في حساب الجبر والمقابلة

أبو جعفر محمد بن موسى الخوارزمي

Very little biographical information is available about the great mathematician, astronomer and geographer Abu Ja'far Muhammad b. Mūsā al-Khwārazmī. As his *nisbah* 'Khwārazmī' would indicate, either his family originally belonged to Khwārazm or he himself was born there. He completed his higher studies in Baghdad where he qualified himself in mathematics and sciences and was appointed by Caliph Māmūn (192-218 A.H./813-33 A.D.) in the 'Academy of Higher Knowledge or Science' *(Bait al- Hikmah)* which was established earlier by Caliph Haroon al-Rashid. Khwārazmī served as a leading scientist and mathematician in the Academy and enjoyed full confidence of Caliph Māmūn. He continued his researches at least for 35 years (813-847) and was still alive in the year 847 A.D., and died sometime thereafter.

Besides Khwārazmī's renowned ALGEBRA, the following of his other works have survived (either in original texts or in translations). (i) Khwārazmī's Arithmetic in translation of John of Seville *(Liber al-ghaorismi de practica arismetrice)* which explains the four basic operations of adding, subtracting, multiplying and dividing. (ii) Another work which has survived in its Toledan translation *Algorisimi de numeror indoreum* had a profound effect upon academic institutions of the West, and bestowed upon western languages such terms as *algorithm* in English (from the name of Khwārazmī himself) and *gnarismo* in Spanish, as well as the word *cipher*(from the Arabic *Sifr* or Zero). (iii) *Zīj al-Sindhind*, the astronomical tables, "which had a great influence on the birth of western science" (E.I.). The works which have survived in original, besides ALGEBRA, are *Kitāb Sūrat al-Ard* (Book on the Shape of the Earth) and *Istikhiraj Tarikh al-Yahud* on the 'Derivation of the Jewish Calender'. Among those which are lost, were the two works on the astrolabe, a book on history *(Kitab al-Tarikh)* and a book on sun-dials *(Kitab al-Rukhama)*.

Khwarazmi's works on arithmetic, algebra, astronomy and geography were translated into Latin and exercised powerful influence on early academic advancement in Europe.

The most original and the one that had greatest impact is his book on Algebra, *Al-Kitab al-Mukhtasr Fi Hisab al-Jabr wa al-Muqabala*. This title has been translated variously as: (i) Restoring and balancing, (ii) transposing and simplifying, (iii) transposition and reduction, (iv) restoration and reduction, (v) restoration and completion, and (vi) the Science of Equation. Baha al-Din al-'Amili explained in his *Khulasat al-Hisab* as under:

> The member which is affected by a minus sign will be increased and the same added to the other member, this being algebra; the honomgeneous and equal terms will then be cancelled, this being Al- Muqabala.

Of the two terms, *al-gabr* may convey the concept of 'restoration' or 'completion', while *al-muqabata* that of 'comparison' or reduction.

The title would suggest that the book was either a digest of what was a more comprehensive work on the subject, or it represented a brief exposition of the theories which in Khwarazmi's conception were too elaborate and complicated to be expounded in this introductory work. Here he tried to simplify so that others could grasp the basic concepts. As pointed out by Khwarazmi himself in his introduction, Caliph Mamun had expressely asked him to give a brief exposition of the new subject so the *its essentials could be easily understood* by all. It may be surmized that he was to summerise what was already available on the subject, but this would be a mere conjecture. For, neither Khwarazmi says so, nor does he mention any other works on Algebra which already existed and which were available to him. Before Khwarazmi, there were, at best, some diverse traditions in the growth of rudiments of algebric ideas -- such as the Babylonian, the Greek, the Indian and the Dipphantine, but as pointed by Aydin Sayili[1] there was no continued tradition in an uninterrupted histori-cal process, which may be supposed to have culminated into Al-Khwārazmī's algebra. There is definitely no evidence to prove that the mathematicians of the Islamic era inherited Algebra ready-made from the past.

No doubt Khwārazmī's knowledge of the subject transcended the brief presentation of it in this book. In his discussion of the first and the second degree equations Khwārazmī firmly established the 'Science of Algebra' as an important branch of Mathematics. Its early translation "introduced into Europe a science completely unknown till then, and with it, a terminology which was still capable of growth but already completely developed".[2] Also Khwārazmī's algebra is regarded as the foundation and cornerstone of the sciences. Khwārazmī is truly 'the founding father of algebra'. His predecessors, includ-ing Diophantos of Alexandria had not realised the innovative concept of this entirely new discipline in computation. "Al-Khwārazmī is the first to teach algebra in an elementary form and for its own sake, Diophantos is primarily concerned with the theory of numbers."[3] On the authority of his own work, Khwārazmī stands out as the found-ing Father of Algebra. It was his book which motivated scholars in the domain of Islam and in Europe to study and advance this branch of Mathematics further.

---

(1) In his introduction to the new edition of Rosen's translation of Al- Khwārazmī's Algebra, published under the Great Books Project of the Pakistan Hijra Council, Islamabad, 1989.

(2) J. Vernet, in E.I.

(3) Solomon Gandz, 'The Source of Khwārazmī's Algebra, Osiris (Bruges, Belgium, The Saint Catherin Press Ltd., 1936), Vol. I, p.264.

THE ENCOMPASSER OF PREMISES AND CONCLUSIONS.

Al-Marrākushī

جامع المبادي والغايات

أبو علي الحسن بن علي المراكشي

Sharf al-Din, Abu 'Ali al-Hasan b. 'Ali b. 'Umar al-Marrākushī (also known as 'Abu'l Hasan 'Ali') was born by about the turn of the 6th century A.H. (12th A.D.). Not much is known of his early educational and professional career, but he flourished as an eminent astronomer, mathematician and geographer and died by about 660 A.h. (1262 A.D.).[1] His achievements were significant as may be seen from references to his works on these subjects.

Marrākushī wrote astronomical treatises such as *Talkhīs al-A'amāl fi Ru'yat al-Hilāl* (A Summary of Practical Measures in Sighting the New Moon), *Ālāt al-Taqvīm* (Instruments for Calender), and Influence of Planetary Conjunctions And Eclipses.

His complete work which has survived[2] and attests to his stature as a scientist and mathematician is his *Jāmi' al-mabādī wa al-Ghāyāt fi 'Ilm al-Mīqāt*** (The Encompasser of Premises And Conclusions in Ascertaining the Time And the Season) which he probably completed in 627/28 A.h. (1229/1230 A.D.). This voluminous work, is an original contribution of al-Marrākushi, on Mathematical Geography including trigonometry, gnonomics and related questions. The part dealing with gnonomics contains studies of dials traced on horizontal,

1. So Brocklemann, I/866.
2. Two manuscripts of it are so far known to exist, the one in the Chester Bettay Collection (No. 4487) and the other in the Tope Kapu (III/762).

cylindrical, conical, and other surfaces, for every latitude. Marrākushi's practical knowledge of astronomical instruments and methods is of a high standard.

Bibliographer Haji Khalīfā (No. 572) has noted *Jāmi' al-Mabādī wa al-Ghāyat* as the greatest work ever written on the subject. According to George Sarton al-Marrākushī's work is "The most important contribution to mathematical geography - not only in Islam but anywhere".

CANON MEDICINAE.

Ibn Sīnā

القانون في الطب

أبو علي الحسين بن عبد الله بن سينا

Abū' Ali al-Husayn b. Abdullah b. Sīnā, the famous 'Avicenna' of Medieval Europe, was born in Afshāna in 370 A.H. (980 A.D.). He received his education in the nearby metropolitan Bukhara, the renowned capital of the great Sāmānids. Ibn Sīnā lived a full active life not only as a scholar but also as a busy medical practitioner and even as a political advisor and vazeir to his patron princes. He spent the last 14 years of his productive life in Isphahān and died in Hamadān in 428 A.H. (1037 A.D.)

Ibn Sīnā continued to write even under trying circumstances: he wrote while in prison and also while on horse back. According to one estimate, as many as 276 works are attributed to him, and according to another 241 are ascribed to him of which 131 are authentic and 110 doubtful. He grew up to be a scholar of encyclopaedic knowledge and was recognized as "*al-Shaykh al- Ra'īs*", 'the presiding' philosopher and physician of his times. Indeed he is to be recognized as one of the greatest philosophers and physicians of all times.

Ibn Sīnā's 'Canon Medicinae', *Al-Qānūn fi al- Tubb,* is an immense encyclopaedia of medical knowledge, a codification of the whole of ancient and contemporary theory and practice of medicine, and also embracing anatomy, physiology, pathology and pharmacopoeia. Ibn Sīnā elaborated, classified and codified the subject in a scientific manner so that the Canon is "a clear and ordered" 'Summa' of all the medical knowledge of Ibn Sīnā's times augmented from his own observations" (Goichon: E.I).

The *Qānūn fi al-Tibb* is divided into five books (parts):

- The first gives General Principles of Medicine (*Kulliyāt* in Arabic and 'Colliget' in Latin) which includes philosophy of medicine, generalities of human body, anatomy, physiology, hygiene and treatment of diseases and therapeutics.
- The second pertains to materia medica and pharmacology, herbs and simple drugs.
- The third deals with special pathology, with disorders of particular internal and external organs of the body.
- The fourth is concerned with illnesses which affect the body in general and are not limited to a single organ or limb, such as fevers, critical drugs, tumours, wounds, ulcers, fractures, toxicology. It opens with Ibn Sīnā's famous treatise on fevers, while the later part deals with symptoms, diagnosis and prognosis.
- The fifth deals with compound medicines and pharmacopoeia.

Besides making extensive use of all the medical experience and knowledge of both Islamic and non-Islamic sources available to him, Ibn Sīnā also made many independent observations of his own, including the discovery of meningitis, the manner of spread of epidemics, the contagous nature of tuberculosis, etc. He has given good clear description of ankylostomiasis, dracunculus medinensis, pathisis, mediastinitis, measles, smallpox etc. He also made many discoveries in what is called psychosomatic medicine today. *Qānūn* of Ibn Sīnā as well as al-*Hāwī* of Rāzī and some other works of medicine of Islamic era have still much to reveal in terms of theory and practice when these are studied meticulously and exhaustively.

'The Canon' became the first original and greatest medical work, and the unique one to have influenced, more than any other single work, the very history of medicine. In the West it was used as an all important text book for a long time. Because of its formal perfection as well as its intrinsic value, the Canon superseded the ancient works of Galen, and also of Rāzī's *Hāwī* and 'Alī Ibn Abbās's *Maliki,* and remained supreme for six centuries (Sarton, I/709). It was translated into Latin by Gherardo Gremonese and many partial editions of this translations were printed before 1500 A.D. (Melano, 1473; Padua, 1476; Venice, 1480; Hebrew Trans, Naples, 1491-92).

COMMENTARY ON ANATOMY IN IBN SĪNĀ'S QĀNŪN.

Ibn Al-Nafīs

كتاب شرح تشريح القانون

علاء الدين علي بن أبي الحزم القرشي المعروف بابن النفيس

The author, 'Alā' al-Dīn Ali b. Abu al-Hazm al-Qarshi, known as 'Ibn al-Nafīs, was born in Damascus during the first decade of the 6th century A.H. The family had originated from the village of 'Qarsh' in Transoxiana and hence his *nisba* 'al-Qarshi'.

He studied medicine in Damascus at the Nūrī Hospital. His more renowned teacher was Muhadhab al-Din Al-Dakhwār (1169 - 1230 A.D.), the great medical doctor and Chief Physician of Syria and Egypt. After completing his studies, he moved to Cairo where he practiced medicine and was first associated with the Nāsiri hospital. Thereafter, when the Mansūrī Hospital was established in 1285 A.D. by the Mamluk monarch Mansūr Qalāwūn (1279-90 A.D.), Ibn al-Nafīs was appointed as Chief Physician and he held that post until his death in 687 A.I. (1288 A.D.). He left his books and his property as a trust to the Mansuri Hospital.

Besides medicine in which he was unrivalled in his times, Ibn al-Nafīs was also an eminent teacher of Law in which he lectured at Jāmi' Masrūriyya in Cairo. Inclusion of his name in the book *Tabaqāt al-Shāfi'yya al-Kubrā* (The Great Classes of the Shafi'ī Scholars) of Taj al-Din al-Subkī (d. 1370/772), indicates his eminence as a religious scholar. He was also well versed in *Sīra,* Tradition, Philosophy, Logic, Grammar and Rhetoric. He wrote a treatise on the *Sira* of the Holy Prophet, a commentary on Ibn Sīnā's "Hidāya" in logic, and the philosophical romance "Fādil ibn Nātiq" on the analogy of "Hayy Ibn Yaqzān" of Ibn Tufayl.

Ibn al-Nafīs authored a number of works on medicine. His *Kitāb al-Shāmil fi al-Tibb,* which he wrote in his thirties, contains an important section on surgical techniques and throws new light on Ibn al-Nafīs as a surgeon; also it defines the role of a surgeon giving a detailed description of the duties of surgeons and the relationship among patients, surgeons and nurses. *Kitāb al-Muhadhab fi Tibb al-'Ain* (The Well-Composed Book on Ophthalmology) and *Kitab al-Mukhtār min al- Aghdhiya* (The Choice of Diets) are his other important works in the domain of his profession.

Ibn Nafīs was reputed to have recorded his own experiences, observations, and deductions rather than using references. He explained his method in these words: "In determining the use of each organ we shall rely necessarily on verified examinations and straight forward research, disregarding whether our opinions will agree or disagree with those of our predecessors".

Ibn Nafīs worte two works on the great CANON of Ibn Sīnā, *'Kitāb Mūjiz al- Qānūn'* ('The Digest of the Canon') and *Sharh Tashrīh al-Qānūn* (Commentary on Anatomy in Qānūn) which he wrote in 20 volumes. In his COMMENTARY which he wrote by about the middle of the 6th/12 century, he presented, for the first time, a clear conception of pulmonary circulation of the blood (long before William Harvey in 1659 A.D). However this great discovery of Ibn Nafīs remained confined to the text of his Commentary until it was re-discovered and relieved from the text in 1924 by Dr. Muhyi al-Din al-Tatāwi. Ibn al-Nafis also presented his explanation of general anatomy and physiology independently with no direct relation to Ibn Sīnā's *Qanūn.* From his studies, experience and observation of human bodies (involved in accidents) Ibn Nafīs concluded that 'the thick blood coming from the liver is purified in the R. Vena Cave, and travels through the pulsating pulmonary artery to the lungs slowly but surely assisted by the pulmonary action, and the thickness of the pulmonary artery. The blood after reaching the lungs divides into (a) a soft part which passes through the pores of the pulmonary artery interchanging with the pulmonary air (reaching via trachea), entering into the pulmonary vein passing through its thin walls. As to (b) the second part of the blood - the thick part - this remains to nourish the lung tissue.'

In his own words (Meyerhof's tr.): "We say, however, Allāh knows better: As the production of the [vital] spirit is one of the functions of the heart, and as this spirit consists of much- refined blood with a large admixture of airy substance, it is necessary that the heart should contain both refined blood and air so that the spirit may be generated out of the substance produced by their mixture; this takes place where the spirit is generated, viz. in the left cavity of the heart. It is, moreover, indispensable for the heart of man and of such animals as have lungs like him, to possess another cavity in which the blood is refined in order to become apt for the mixture with the air; for, if air is mixed with thick blood, it is not possible to form a homogeneous substance out of them. This cavity is the right cavity of the heart. The blood, after it has been refined in this cavity must be transmitted to the left cavity where the [vital] spirit is generated. But there is no passage between these two cavities; for the substance of the heart is solid in this region and has neither a visible passage, as was thought by some persons, nor an invisible one which could have permitted the transmission of blood, as was alleged by Galen. The pores of the heart there are closed and its substance is thick. Therefore, the blood, after having been refined, must rise in the arterious vein to the lung in order to expand in its volume and to be mixed with air so that its finest part may be clarified and may reach the venous artery in which it is transmitted to the left cavity of the heart. Thus, after having been mixed with the air and having attained the aptitude to generate the [vital] spirit. That part [of the blood] which is less refined, is used by the lung for its nutrition.

For this reason the arterious vein has solid substance with two layers in order to make more refined that (the blood) which transsudes from it. The venous artery, on the other hand, has thin substance in order to facilitate the reception of the transsuded [blood] from the vein in question. And for the same reason there exist perceptible passages (or pores, manāfidh) between the two [blood- vessels]."

THE BOOK OF CONCESSIONS* TO THE WOULD-BE AUTHORS (ON MEDICINE).

Abu al-Qāsim al-Zahrāwī

التصريف لمن عجز عن التأليف

أبو القاسم خلف بن العباس الزهراوي

Abu al-Qāsim Khalaf b. 'Abbās al-Zahrāwī was born in the Zahrā suburb of Cordova by the middle of the 4th century A.H. He excelled in his knowledge of meidcine and became a pioneer in surgery in so far as the invention and use of sophisticated surgical instruments and the methodology of operation were concerned. He was the greatest surgeon of his times and one of the greatest of all times. He died in 427 A.H. (1036 A.D.). Of the works authored by Al-Zahāwī, the one on 'Measures and Doxes' *(al-Akyāl wa al-Auzān)* and the other *'The Tasrīf'* are important.

Kitab al-Tasrīf li mun Ajiza un al- Ta'līf (The Book of Concessions or Concessio') is a medical encyclopaedia which has remained guide for surgeons over the centuries. The name of 'Abu al-Qāsim' was well known in the medical profession not only in the Muslim East but also in the West in his Latinised form as 'Albucasis'. The *Kitāb al-Tasrīf,* which he wrote in thirty parts, was widely disseminated in the West through its Latin translation by Gerard of Cremona, and exercised great influence on Italian and French surgeons and laid the foundation of surgery in Europe.

---

* In its early translation, it was known as *Concessio*. Actually it means that the book *facilitates* or *explains*. Thus, Meyerhof translates it as 'Book of Explanation'.

Surgical Instruments from al-Zahrāwī

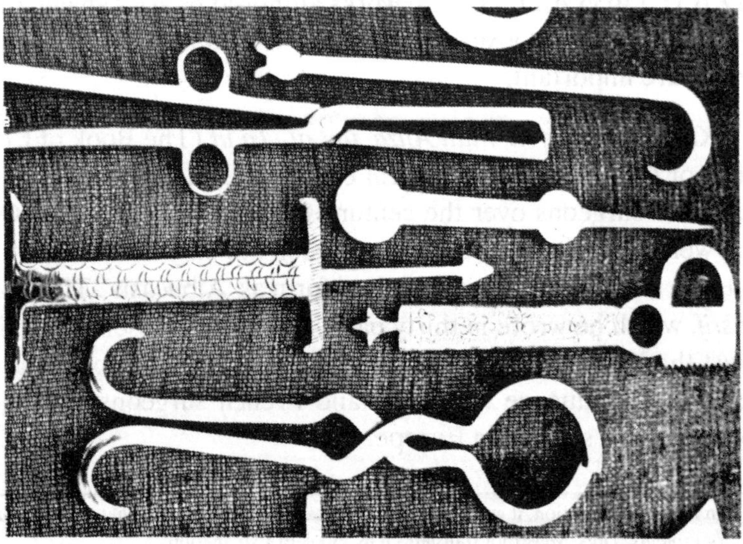

Islamic Surgical Instruments
[S.Hossein Nasr: Islamic Science]

'The Tasrīf' gives the most systematic treatment of surgery, the text being accompanied with illustrations of the instruments used by Zahrāwī. The surgical portion of the text consists of three parts: the first on cauterization advised by prophetic tradition and suggested by Zahrāwī for apoplexy; the second on operations performed with a scalpel and also operations of the eye as well as oral surgery; and the third on various forms of bone fractures and dislocations, as well as on child delivery. The best section in *al- Tasrīf* is allotted to surgery, containing many chapters one of which is entirely occupied with the manifold uses of the cautery. Operations are described in an attractive style, especially those concerning lithotomy, stone-crushing and amputations. Fractures and dislocations are described in chapter III. The paralysis resulting from fracture of a dorsal vertebra is minutely stated. Some chapters deal with midwifery and delivery of a dead foetus together with description of the required instruments. It contains the first description in medical history of Walcher's position. The book is fully decorated with numerous illustrations, most of the instruments being of his own invention. Abu al- Qasim seems to have given the first account of haemophilia. The book ends, as it begins, with his favourite watchword "Caution". "Avoid perilous practices, as I have already warned you, so shall you have the more praise and profit if God wills..."

THE TREATISE ON SMALLPOX AND MEASLES.

Al-Rāzī

كتاب الجدري والحصبة

أبوبكر محمد بن زكريا الرازي

Abū Bakr Muhammad b. Zakariyā al-Rāzī was born in Rayy in 251 A.H. (865 A.D.), and was also educated there. As a youth he migrated to Baghdad, flourished there as an authority on Medicine, Philosophy and Chemistry, and died in the year 313 A.H. (925 A.D.).

Rāzī was the first great clinical physician in the history of Medicine. He authored a number of important works in Medicine such as (1) *Kitāb al-Hāwi al-Tibb* (The Continents) which is an enormous encyclopedia of medicine documenting his own original observations and also containing extracts from Greek and Hindu sources. (2) *Kitāb al-Mansūrī*, another important work based on Rāzī's own clinical observations, which was known and studied in the West as *Liber medicinalis ad Almanasorem*. (3) *Kitāb Taqsīm al-'Ilal* ('The Book on Categorization of the Causes of Diseases) which was translated into Latin as "*Liber divisionum*". (4) *Kitāb al-Fakhrī (Liber pretiosus)*. Also Rāzī wrote different important treatises such as 'Medicines for Heart', Rheumatism (*al-nigris*), Colic (*al-Qūlanj*), and Diet (*al-Aghdhiya*). Of this class, the more celebrated was his *Kitāb al-Jadrī wa al-Hasba, 'The Treatise on Smallpox and Measles'* which became famous as "*Liber de pestilentia*" in Europe.[1]

---

1. *Nasr, al-Mehrajan, p. 177.*

'The Treatise on Smallpox and Measlesis, indeed, an ornament to Islamic medicine, and the earliest of its kind. It gives the first clear account of these two diseases in the history of Medicine. An extract will convey to the reader something of the observing spirit of the original.

'The outbreak of smallpox is preceded by continuous fever, aching in the back, itching in the nose and shivering during sleep. The main symptoms of its presence are: backache with fever, stinging pain in the whole body, congestion of the face, sometimes shrinking, violent redness of the cheeks and eyes, a sense of pressure in the body, creeping of the flesh, pain in the throat and breast accompanied by difficulty of respiration and coughing, dryness of the mouth, thick salivation, hoarseness of the voice, headache and pressure in the head, excitement, anxiety, nausea and unrest. Excitement, nausea and unrest are more pronounced in measles than in smallpox while the aching in the back is more severe in smallpox than in measles'.[2]

---

2. Kamal, Dr. Hassan. Encyclopaedia of Islamic Medicine.

THE WELL ARRANGED BOOK ON OPHTHALMOLOGY.

Ibn Al-Nafīs

الكتاب المهذب في طب العين

علاء الدين علي بن ابي الحزم القرشي المعروف بابن النفيس

As already noted under his other important work *Sharh Tashrīh al-Qanūn* (Commentary on Anatomy in Ibn Sīnā's Canon), Ibn Nafīs who flourished in the 7th/13th century was a versatile genius being a jurist, philosopher, physician, historian and a man of letters at the same time. However, his fame as a physician eclipsed his other attainments. In the medical profession also his remarkable 'Commentary on Anatomy Canon'eclipsed his equally important achievements in other areas of medicine and therapy, particularly his remarkable contribution in ophthalmology.

Development of Opthalmology as a an independent discipline in medicine and clinical surgery was achieved by eminent Muslim physicians under the Abbasids beginning from the 9th century. The earlier Greek Ophthalmology was rudimentary as confirmed by Hunayn's translated work "The Book of the Ten Discourses on the Eye" based on Greek sources. From the 10th century A.D. onwards considerable advanced development in ophthalmology with clinical information on operative and medicamentary treatment of the eye diseases, is reflected in works on general medicine particularly in such encyclopaedic ones as *K. al-Tibb al-Mansūrī* and *Al-Hāwī fi al-Tibb* of Muhammad b. Zakariyā al-Rāzī (d. 925 A.D.), *Qanūn fi al-Tibb* of Ibn Sīnā, and *Kitāb al- Tasrīf* of the great Andalusian surgeon Abu al-Qāsim al- Zahrāwī.

Beginning from the 5th/11th century, and possibly earlier, special treatises were authored on eye-diseases. Some forty of such works which have survived through the centuries are known. The two earliest ones written in the first half of the 5th/11th century are by Mawsilī and 'Ali b. 'Isā. The former, Abu al-Qāsim 'Ammār b. 'Ali al-Mawsilī, who used to practice in Cairo, wrote an original treatise on ocular therapy entitled *Kitāb al-Muntakhab fi 'Ilāj Amrād al-'Ain* ('The Choice Book on the Eye Diseases'). The Christian physician Ali b. Isa of Baghdad wrote *Thadhkirat al-Kahhālīn* ('The Memoir of Oculists') which remained a popular work on the subject. These two and such other treatises were, however, superseded in due course of time by the more comprehensive and in-depth studies based on clinical observations and operative and medicamentary treatment. Thus, in the 6th/12th century, Muhammad al-Ghāfiqī of Cordova authored a voluminous work on eye diseases. In the 7th/13th century, eminent physicians of Egypt and Syria produced advanced works on Ophthalmology. In Cairo, the Chief physician to the Ayyubid Sultan al-Malik al-Salih (1240 - 1249 AD) wrote *Natījat al-Fikr fi 'Ilāj Amrād al- Basar* ('The Result of Reflection in the Treatment of Eye-Diseases'). In Syria, Khalifa ibn Abi al-Mahāsin of Aleppo wrote a very voluminous work entitled *Kitāb al-Kāfī fi al- Kuhl* ('The Sufficient Book in Oculary') while Salāh al-Din b. Yusuf the physician of Hamā authored *Nūr al- 'Uyūn wa Jāmi' al-Funūn* ('The Light of the Eyes And The Synthesis of Techniques'.)

It was, however, in the scientific and systematic work of Ibn Nafīs, who was born in Damascus in 1210 and died in Cairo 1288 A.D., that a hitherto subsidiary medical branch of Oculary or The Eye Diseases, was raised to an independent and fullfledged status of Ophthalmology. Ibn Nafīs appropriately entitled his book as *al-Kitāb al-Muhadhdhab fi Tibb al-'Ain* – it having been planned as a systematic work on *Tibb al-'Ain,* transcending the limited concept of diseases of the eye, and embracing the wholistic view of 'The Tibb of the Eye', i.e. Ophthalmology as it is understood today.

In "The Well-Arranged Book on Ophthalmology" Ibn Nafīs for the first time brought systematically under study all the main aspects of Ophthalmology, viz. anatomy, physiology and pathology of the eye as well as the related materia medica, therapy and hygiene. Ibn Nafīs discusses the trachoma and its treatment in greater detail and depth than Ali b. Isa, and his description of "all kinds of instruments is more detailed than in any other work on eye diseases".*

* Max Mayerhof. *Studies in Medieval Arabic Medicine,* ed. Penelope Johanstone, London, 1984.

THE COMPREHENSIVE IN THE SIMPLES, OF DRUGS AND DIETS.

Ibn al-Baytār

كتاب الأغذية

ابن البيطار

Diyā' al-Dīn Abū Muhammad Abdullah b. Ahmad b. Muhammad al-Mālaqī known as Ibn al-Baytār', was born in Malāgā in Spain by the end of the 6th century A.H., and died in Damascus in 646 A.H. (1248 A.D.). He pursued his higher studies in Seville and specialized in botany and pharmacology under eminent teachers in whose company and supervision he collected plants in the surrounding region. For further research, he then travelled widely and visited the 'Maghrib' (Morocco, Algeria and Tunis), the Greek and the Roman territories, and the Asia Minor and Syria in the 'Mashriq' (Z.A),* lecturing and discussing all the time. In Damascus, he made further investigations and more collections of plants along with his student Ibn Abi Usaybi'ah. He thus became an accomplished botobnist and pharmacologist of his times. Ibn Abi Usaybi'ah praises him as the greatest authority on the knowledge of drugs, and as the most intelligent, generous, and kindly person and colleague.

From Syria he returned to Egypt and was appointed Chief Botonist, the administrative head of all the botanists in the kingdom (*Ra'īs alā sā'ir al-'ashshābīn*) by the Ayyubid monarch al-Malik al-Kāmil (615-635 A.H./1218-1238 A.D.). Thereafter, al-Malik al-Sālih (637-647 A.H/1240-1249 A.D.) also confirmed him in this high position.

---

* Z.A : al-Zirkli's *A'alām*

During his tenure of office, Ibn al-Baytār made several scientific expeditious from Cairo and collected valuable data which enabled him to author two important books. The first one was *Kitāb al-Mughnī fi al-Adwiya al-Mufrada* in which he listed the simples appropriate for each illness. He dedicated it to al-Malik al-Sālih. The other was AL-JAMI'. Besides these two works, he wrote a commentary on Discordies, a work entitled *Mizān al-Tabīb*, a treatise (*Risāla*) on diets and drugs, a monograph on the lemon and a critique of Ibn Jazala's work.

The most celebrated of his works is *al-Jāmi' li-Mufardāt al-Adwiya wa al-Aghdhiya* ('The Comprehensive in the Simples, of Drugs and Diets') which he completed in 646 A.h./1242 A.C. and dedicated to al-Malik al-Sālih. In this work, Ibn al-Baytār listed, in alphabetical order, more than 1400 simples (of animal, vegetable and compound medicines), of which about 300 were listed by him for the first time. He based this work "on his own observations and also on over 150 authorities", inclusive of such early works as of Dioscordies and Galen and also of the later authorities such as al-Razi, Ibn Sina, al-Idrisi and al-Ghāfiqi.

AL-JĀMI' acquired wide publicity both in the East and the West, and was translated into Latin, Turkish, German and French. The work influenced later authors, such as the King of Yaman al-Ashraf Yūsuf b. Rasūl al-Ghassāni (d. 695/1296) who authored a more comprehensive work on the subject and Dāwūd al-Antākī who made a Turkish translation of it three centuries later.

THE BOOK OF PRACTICAL TREATMENTS AND PRECAUTIONERY MEASURES.

Ibn Zuhr

التيسير في المداواة والتدبير

ابن زهر

Abū Marwān 'Abd al-Malik was born in a distinguished family of physicians of Seville in Spain by about 484-7 A.H. (1092-95 A.D). His father Abu 'Alā Zuhr (after whom the son was called 'Ibn Zuhr') was an eminent religious scholar, *muhaddith* and literatuer as well as a renowned practicing physician of his time who, later, in Europe, became known as Aboali/Abuleli/Ebilule or Abulelizor/Albuleizor. He authored a number of important medical works, propounded original ideas and held independent views. He laid down in his *Tadhkirah* (A Practitioners' Guide) that physicians must try to treat their patients first by medicines of lowest possible potential. "How often have doctors helped on the causes of death!" – he exclaimed.

Abd al-Malik received sound general and professional education from his father and distinguished himself as a competent physician while he was still young. Sultan 'Abd al-Mo'min (524-558 A.h./1130-1163) of the Muwahhidūn dynasty of N. Africa and Spain recognized his merit and appointed him as Vezeir. The contemporary jurist, physician and philosopher Ibn Rushd became his close friend, and both consulted one another. Ibn Zuhr educated his own son Abu Bakr Muhammad who also grew up as an accomplished scholar and a practicing physician. Ibn Zuhr whose works were studied in Europe, became known there as Abhomeron or Avenzoar. He died at Seville in the year 557 A.H. (1161 A.D).

Six medical works are known to have been authored by Ibn Zuhr of which two have survived: the one is *Kitāb al- Iqtisād* (The Book of Moderation?) and the other *Kitāb al-Taysīr fi al- Mudāwāt wa al-Tadbīr* (The Book of Practical Treatments And Precautionery Measures). His other works, equally important, were: Kitāb al-Jāmi' (on formulery), *Kitāb al-Aghadhiya* (on food and diet), *Maqālah fi 'Ilal al-Kulā* (on kidney diseases), *Risālā fi 'Illatay al-baras wa al-bahaq* (Communication to a fellow doctor in Seville on the two diseases, white leprosy and pityriasis) and *Kitāb al-Zīnah* (on purgative) written for his son Abu Bakr.

In Zuhr's high stature as a physician may be judged form the fact that he wrote AL-TAYSĪR at the request of his friend Ibn Rushd who himself was an eminent physician and had authored the prestigious 'Colliget of Medicine' *(Kulliyyāt fi al-Tibb)*. Being based mainly on his own professional experience, AL-TAYSĪR reflects Ibn Zuhr's remarkable originality and independence of thought. He had the will and the vision to take a stand against the traditionally entrenched Galenism.

Ibn Zuhr has discerned the bone feeling, itch mite Acarus-scabiei, and stands out as the first great parasitiologist in medical history, much more advanced than the ancient Alexander of Tralles. His approach was pragmatic and his motto "to try is the best policy". Like his father, Ibn Zuhr believed in the value of experiment.

His introduction to TAYSIR gives a general description of ailments and their treatments and also some "*recettes cabalistiques*". In the text, his observations reflect some of his original views such as: a description of mediastinal tumours, lithotomy, and of pericardial abscesses which he was the first to describe. Also important are the chapters on intestinal erosion *(sahdj)*, paralysis of the pharynx, and inflammation of the middle ear. He was one of the first to recommend tracheotomy, and artificial feeding via the oesophagus or the rectum. He points out the harm caused by marsh vapours. He described the agent of scabies (sarcoptes scabiei), and was among the first to do so (E.I.).

THE COMPLETE COMPENDIUM ON THE TWO ARTS OF VETERINARY AND HORSE TRAINING

Al-Baytār

كامل الصناعتين في البيطرة والزرطقة

أبو بكر بن بدر الدين المنذر البيطار

Abū Bakr b. Badr al-Dīn al-Mundhir 'al-Baytār' was born in the 2nd half of the 7th century A.H. and died in Cairo in 741 A.H. (1340 A.D.). He studied *baytarah* (Veterinary) and excelled in it. He served as chief of the grooms and veterinarians to King al- Nāsir, Muhammad Ibn Qalāwun (1309 - 1341 A.D.) for whom he wrote *Kāshif al-Wayl fi Ma'rifat Amrād al- Khayl* on diseases of horse.

Baytarah is comparable to the Greek term *hippiatrics,* but it is not a borrowed word in an arbicised form. *Baytar* as an Arabic word figures in Pre-Islamic poetry. In the 2nd half of the 3rd/9th century, Abū Yūsuf Ya'qūb b. Akhī Hizām, the stablemaster to the Abbasid Caliphs al-Mu'tasim and al-Mu'tadid, was the first to author a work on hippiatrics. Subsequently, other professional *batrās* wrote works on the subject which come under reference and some have also survived.

In professional competence, Abu Bakr had excelled his predecessors and became known as BYTĀR, 'The Veterinary Surgeon.' His work *Kāmil al-Sinā'atayn al-Baytara wa al-Zartaqa* ('The Complete Compendium on the Two Arts of Veterinary and Horse Training') is more comprehensive and profound as it deals both with the training as well as physical care of the horse.

Horse under Veterinary Diagnosis
[Royal Library, Rabāt]

He dedicated AL-KĀMIL to King al-Nāsir, Muhammad Ibn Qalāwun, and hence it was also called *al- Nāsirī.* The book discusses training of horses, their breeding, habits, colours, characteristics, age, anatomy, the equine diseases and their treatment by diet, drugs and surgery and also gives information on animal husbandry. In its ten sections the *Kāmil* represents not only the advance till then made in experimentation and expertise in veterinary medicine, but also the author's own observations and those that he had learnt from his father who was apparently a competent farrier.

THE CHOICEST OF NEWS ABOUT GENERATIONS OF PHYSICIANS.

Ibn Abi Usaybi'ah

عيون الأنباء في طبقات الأطباء

موفق الدين أبو العباس أحمد بن القاسم الخزرجي ابن أبي اصيبعة

Ibn Abī 'Usaybi'ah, Muwaffaq al-Dīn, Abu al- 'Abbās, Ahmad b. al-Qāsim b. Khalīfa b. Yūnus al- Khazrajī, the eminent physician and historian, was born in Damascus in 596 A.H. (1200 A.D.)* in a family of physicians. His father was an opthalmolojist and young Ahmad studied under him. Then he did his advanced studies in medicine under Ibn al-Baytār and other eminent physicians, and practised in the Nuri hospital of Damascus. He went to Cairo in 634 A.H. (1236 A.D.) and was appointed in the Nāsiri Hospital which was just founded by al-Malik al-Nāsir. He then entered the service of Amir 'Izz al-Din Aybk al-Mu'azzami at Sarkhad, a city in the Huran Ranges and being attracted by its climate he settled down there. He died in 688 A.H. (1269).

Ibn Abi 'Usaybi'ah won name and fame for his knowledge, intelligence and professional expertise particularly in Ophthalmology. He was also an eminent poet and had considerable verse composition to his credit.

He authored his great work *'Uyūn al-Anbā' fi Tabaqāt al-Atibbā'* in Damascus in the year 643 A.H. (1245) when he was attached to

* So according to Zirkili; according to E.I. after 590/1194.

Amin al-Dawlah, the Wazir of al-Malik al-Sālih. He used the works of his predecessors, such as Ibn Juljul's *Tabaqāt al-Atibbā'* and Qifti's *Tarīkh al-Hukamā'*, and added much fresh information. *The Al-'Uyūn* contains three hundred and eighty (E.I.) biographies of physicians, beginning with the early Greek, Roman and Hindu Physicians and then those of later periods, up to his own time. The biographies are arranged generation-wise *(tabaqāt)* and also country-wise. In the first Part *(Qism)* he mentions the Greek and other physicians, the periods when they flourished with the dates of their birth and death if available, and their works and their importance. In the Second Part are mentioned the physicians of Arabia, Iran, Hind, the Muslim West (North Africa, Spain, and Marrakush), Egypt, Syria and other countries with information on their literary and professional experiences and excellences. Notices are also recorded of great many scholars and literatuers who were not outstanding physicians but were celebrated for their achievements as poets, mystics and traditionists. Thus there is an imbalance in selection but it has preserved specimens of literary materials of the different eras.

THE BOOK OF AGRICULTURE.

Ibn Al-‘Awwām

كتاب الفلاحة

أبو زكريا يحيى بن محمد ابن العوام الاشبيلي

Abu Zakarya Yahyā b. Muhammad, known as Ibn al-‘Awwām, belonged to Ishbīl (Seville) in Muslim Spain where he flourished in the 6th century A.H. He was a scholarly person as is confirmed by his two other works - *Tarbiyat al-Karm* (Fostering Noble Conduct) and *‘Uyun al-Haa’i* etc. which have survived. His well known work is

Kitāb al-Filāhā ‘The Book on Agriculture’. He died by about 580 A.H. (1185 A.D.).

Studies in Agriculture developed consistently in Muslim Spain, beginning from the 5th century A.H. However, it was in the later decaaes in that century that a number of contemporary agronomists and botonists wrote important works on agriculture. Ibn Wāfid (d. 467 A.H.) of Toledo, Muhammad al-Tighnāri and others were eminent botonists who developed royal gardens for their patron princes and also wrote treatises which were more of a botonical nature. The pride of performance belonged to the contemporary agronomists and botonists of Seville who wrote on Agriculture. They were Abu Umar Ahmad who wrote *al-Muqni‘* in 466 A.H., and Abu al-Khayr and Muhammad b. Ibrahim ibn Bassāl (d. 1105 A.D.) who wrote specifically on Agriculture, both having written a *Kitāb al-Filāha* (Book of Agriculture). Using their works and other sources, Ibn al-‘Awwām wrote, about one hundred years later, a more comprehensive *Kitab al-Filāha* (Book of Agriculture). It would seem to have gained wider popularity and was considered important enough so that later on Ibn Khaldūn also referred to it in his Maqaddima.

While using the earlier sources, Ibn al-'Awwām cited quotations from them and thus his work became more comprehensive, an encyclopaedic one on Agriculture and agronomy providing simultaneously enough material on rural economy. His quotations from his predecessors as well as his own observations on different aspects of agriculture add to the value of his work. Vegetables (e.g. eggplants) and sorghums (cereals, millets) as well as the main crops such as Sugar-cane, Rice, Cotton and Wheat have been brought under discussion. The method and manner of growing the different crops and the use of fallowing and rotation are recorded. He observed that rice were also being grown on rain without irrigation. The manner in which cotton is grown is of special importance, because he says that cotton has been successfully grown even on waste lands. He also discusses crop rotations. According to previous practice, wheat was grown successively on the same land every year, but for better yield it should rather be combined in rotation with other crops such as barley. Fallowing, in his view, should be resorted to particularly in case of the long abandoned and newly cleared lands which being inferior and of a low fertility regain fertility through fallowing.

The ideas expressed and the views advanced by Ibn al-'Awwām in different contexts, confirm that in the Hispano-Muslim Society concern existed both for extensive and intensive agriculture.

THE SEASONAL PERIODS AND ATMOSPHERICS.

Al-Ajdābī

كتاب الأزمنة والأنواء

أبو إسحاق إبراهيم بن إسمعيل اللواتي الأجدابي

Abū Ishāq Ibrāhīm b. Isma'il, Ibn al-Ajdābī, was born by the turn of the 4th century A.H. in Ajdābiya (15 stages distance from Tripoli, Libya) and died by about 470 A.H. (c. 1077 A.D.). He was a scholar of eminence and authored books on genealogy, prosody and other subjects. His work *al-Azminah wa al- Anwā'* is the most important one on the subject.

The traditional lore of the *beduin* Arabs and desert dwellers, about the rising and the setting of moon and stars linked with atmospherics, seasonal changes and agriculture, later came to be codified by Muslim linguists and literatuers in their books specifically devoted to this subject. These became known as books on *'anwā'* or books on *azmina* and *anwā'* as al-Ajdabi's book is. Among such books which have survived and are better known may be mentioned: Kitāb al-Anwā', of Ibn Qutaiba al-Dinawari (3rd/9th century), Kitab al-Anwā', of Abu al-Hasan al-Qurtubi (4th/10th century). Kitab al-Anwā, of Ibn 'Āsim; and Kitāb al-Anwā, of al-Ajdābī (5th/11th century).

Traditionally, *ANWĀ'* meant telling the time of night by means of twenty eight lunar mansions *(manāzil al-Qamar),* and a rough estimation of the seasons by means of their helical risings or cosmic settings *(anwā)*. By codifying all that was available on the subject, a new study area was developed which though based largely on folklore, also included considerable data based on practical observations, combining the rudiments of astronomy, astrology, physical geography and agricultural calendar.

Al-Ajdābī's work would appear to be one of the latest of the series on *'Ilm al-Anwā'*, the knowledge related to the mansions of the moon and the first appearance of the light of each mansion and each lunar month, i.e. the knowledge by which was predicted meteorological phenomena as well as terrestrial events–*'naw'* being the appearance of the first light of the moon as it enters each mansion. This knowledge preserved through generations facilitated the development of astronomy in its traditional setting. The Arabs divided the trajectory of the moon into twentyeight stations, *'Manazil al-Qamar'*, a system which came to be adopted in both astronomy and astrology. It also deals with various aspects of agriculture, times of plantation, lunar and solar calendars with names of each month in Syriac and other languages.

THE RAISING OF THE SUBTERRANEAN WATERS.

Al-Karajī

أنباط المياه الخفية

أبو بكر محمّد بن الحسن الحاسب الكرجي

Abu Bakr b. Muhammad b. al-Hasan was born in the town of Karaj in the Jibāl Province of the Caliphate by the middle of the 4th century A.H. (10th A.D.). He received his early education there and went to Baghdad as a young scholar where he progressed in his advanced studies and also held high official positions. He flourished as a distinguished mathematician (al-hāsib) and engineer in Baghdad, and eventually returned to his home town where he died sometime during the later part of the first quarter of the 5th century A.H. (11th A.D).

Karaji authored about a dozen of works all of which have not survived. Besides his INBĀT in hydraulic conduits, he wrote important works on mathematics in which "he attempted to free algebra from the tulelage of geometry" (E.I.). In his *AL-Fakhri fi al-Jabr wa al-Muqābala,* besides studying further some of the problems occurring in *Arithmatica* of Diophantes, Karaji initiated the study of the successive powers of a binomial, developed it further in his second work *Al-Badī' fi al-Hisāb,* and concluded it in his yet another work now lost "through the discovery of the generation of the coefficients of $(a\text{-}b)^n$ by means of the triangle which is now named after Pascel or Tartaglia" (E.I.). In his *Al- Badī'*, he further developed "the fixed points treated by Euclid and Nicomachus and in which an important place is accorded to algebric operations"(E.I.). He wrote *Al-Kāfi fi al-Hisāb* on the use of functions. Karaji's pioneering work in the area of hydraulic engineering was *Inbāt al-Miyāh al-Khafiyya* [Raising of the

Hidden (Subterranean) Waters] which he would appear to have written approximately in the year 410 A.H. (1019 A.D), after his return from Baghdad to Karaj.

The text opens with the description of Earth which despite its mounts and ups and downs "is a globe" surrounded by water in which all is in motion according to the author. The constant need for water, and the earth's water resources and their increase and decrease due to sun's heat are underlined. The water cycle is explained: sweet water evaporating due to sun's heat and again being replenished by sun's action (drawing out sweet water from sea by evaporation). Mountains and rocks that indicate water and those that preserve ice as well as the water hidden beneath the earth, are discussed. According to Karaji, the echoes in the valleys in between hills indicate presence of water. It is pointed out that plants yield water. The mounts and lands suffering from scarcity of water are mentioned. The different kinds of water, their differing tastes, purification of water and its desalination are explained. Seasons of the year have their impact on water resources. Springs increase or decrease and change places due to earthquake. Steam inside the earth causes earth-quake.

Major part of the work, however, deals with the techniques and processes of construction of *al-Qanā* or substerranean canals, their maintenance and preservation. Gauges and measures employed for water supply are mentioned. The best kinds of gauges used in various tunnels are noted. Clearing of canals and their proper maintenance is explained. The models and instruments used are illustrated by sketches and diagrams.

THE BOOK OF INGENIOUS MECHANICAL DEVICES.

Banū Mūsā

كتاب الحيل

بنو موسى بن شاكر

Muhammad Ahmad and al-Hasan, the three talented brothers became well-known as 'Banu Musa' ('Sons of Musa'), their father being Musa b. Shākir who himself was an eminent astronomer and had gained great favour with Prince Mamun at Marw in 198 A.H. (813 A.D.). The three brothers flourished in Baghdad in the 3rd century A.H., and had received good advanced education under personal attention of the great teacher Yunus b. Mansur at the 'HOUSE OF WISDOM' *(Bayt al-Hikmat)* or 'Academy of Higher Knowledge', (founded by Caliph Mamun) in Baghdad. They were among the first graduates of The Academy who along with their other colleagues continued advanced researches, and through their observations, experiments, field studies and documentation they laid the foundations of Science and Technology for the newly emerging modern civilization.

The three brothers though highly qualified in different subjects had attained excellence particularly in Mathematics, Music, Astronomy, Medicines and Mechanical Engineering. The elderly Abu Ja'far Muhammad had specialized in Geometry and Astronomy, excelling his two brothers in all branches of knowledge except in Mechanics and Mechanical Engineering in which none was equal to Ahmad who was an engineer par excellence. The youngest Hasan was a brilliant geometrician in his own right.

Muhammad died in 259 A.H. (873 A.D.) and the other two probably survived him. When alive and together, they not only engaged themselves in scientific pursuits but patronized scientific research. As if emulating the example of the Caliph himself, MUSA SONS turned their own house into a 'Mini House of Wisdom', and spent much of their wealth in sponsoring scholars to collect and translate the works of ancient writers. They sent missions to Byzantium to seek and acquire such works, and Muhammad himself also visited Byzantium. It was on his return journey that Thābit b. Qurrā who knew Arabic, Syriac and Greek accompanied Muhammad to Baghdad and undertook translation work at Muhammad's house. The brothers patronised some of the scholars of the 'House of Wisdom' and used to pay about five hundred dinars a month to them to translate books in physical sciences and medicine. Both Hunayn b. Ishaq and Thābit b. Qurrā were under the brothers' patronage and worked on their assignments. 'Thābit wrote a report on atmospheric phenomena that had been observed by himself and the Banu Musa'.

The three brothers themselves wrote a number of works, individually and jointly, on different subjects - mainly mathematical, scientific and technological, of which about twenty have come under reference in the works of later writers, though only two or three have survived. In their works Banu Musa dealt with such problems as the first movement of the sphere; the ellipse; conic sections; measurement of plane and spherical figures; division of an angle into three equal parts and calculation of the mean proportional between two quantities; denial of a ninth sphere outside the sphere of the fixed stars demonstrated by diadactic means and by geometrical method; astronomical tables; astrolabes; the 'time'; musical automation; ingenious machines and automata; and a work on war engines.

Banu Musa became, in effect, the first group of scientists in history to work as a team in their scientific investigations and to publish their results jointly. Their *Kitāb al-Hiyal*, 'Book of Ingenious Devices', is one such example of their cooperative team work and joint authorship. This work was regarded highly in contemporary and later scientific and scholarly circles and was referred to subsequently for centuries. Thus, four hundred years later, Ibn Khaldun mentioned it as a remarkable book on mechanics. It remained unsurpassed in the domain of applied mechanics and technology until Jazarī published his work by the same name written more than three centuries later.

In *Kitab al-Hiyal*, more than one hundred models of different ingenious devices are described and demonstrated by diagrams. In the opinion of a qualified modern engineer Donald R. Hill, who has translated and annotated Banu Musa's work, "The book represents a marked advance in mechanical engineering (p.19). Further, that the authors, mainly Ahmad, had a clear understanding of mathematical and scientific principles of hydrostatic, aerostatic, pneumatics and of mechanics and they applied them intelligently in mechanical engineering and technology. Their empirical mastery of aerostatics enabled them to invent Double Concentric Siphon. They were also the first to employ the 'conical valves' component 'as a matter of course and in a wide variety of application'.*

---

* *The Book of Ingenious Devices (Kitab al-Hiyal) by the Banu (Sons of) Musa b. Shakir,* translated and annotated by Donald R. Hill, D. Reidel Publishing Company, Dordrecht, Holland, 1979, pp. 19, 31.

INTEGRATION BETWEEN THEORY AND PRACTICE IN THE APPLICATION OF MECHANICS.

Al-Jazarī

كتاب الحيل

الجزري

Badī‘ al-Zamān Abu al-‘Izz b. Ism̄‘ail b. al-Razzāz al-Jazarī belonged to al-Jazirah, the territory between the Tigris and the Euphrates in modern Iraq. Here he lived in the city of Āmid in the Diyar-Bakr country, in the second half of the 6th and the first half of lthe 7th century A.H. (12th/13th century A.D.). He entered the service of the Diyar-Bakr rulers of lthe Artuqid Dynasty in 570 A.H. (1174 A.D.), and continued on there until his death. He was commissioned to write this book by al-Malik al-Salih Nāsir al-Din Abu'l Fath Mahmud (b. Muhammad b. Qara Arslan b. Daud b. Sakamān b. Artuq), the third ruler of lthe Artuq house under whom he was now serving in his capacity as *Ra'is al-A'amāl,* Head of the Works or Chief Engineer. Thus, he must have commenced preparing this work after the accession of this monarch to the throne in 597 H. (1200 A.D.). He completed it on the 4th of Jumāda- II, 602 A.H. (January, 1206 A.D.) and died during the next three months before the end of Sha‘bān, 602 A.H. (April, 1206 A.D.).(1)

Jazari's book is the first important work of highest standard in the field of Applied Mechanics and Engineering. That he meant it to be a useful text both in theory and practice is obvious from its meaningful title AL-JĀMI‘ BAYN AL-‘ILM WA AL-‘AMAL AL-NĀFI‘ FĪ

(1) Introduction (p.9) to lthe excellent edition of the Arabic text by Ahmad Y. al-Hassan, University of Aleppo, Aleppo, 1979.

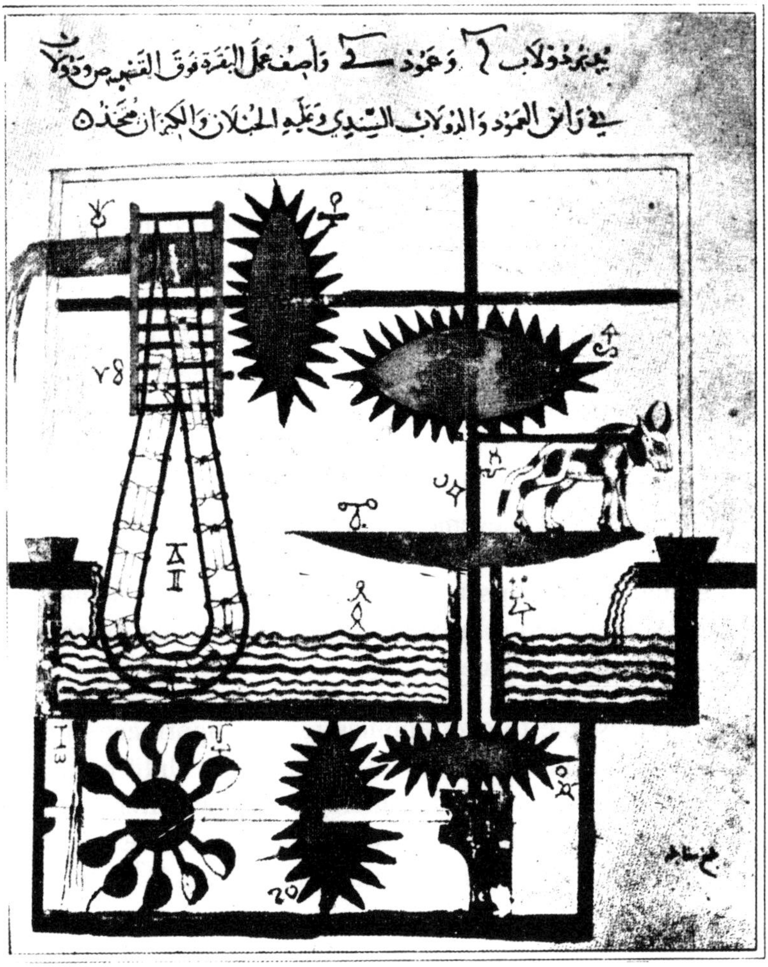

SINĀ'T AL-HIYAL, i.e. 'Integration Between Theory And Practice Useful in the Application of Mechanics'. The concept of *beneficial* application would indicate that at that time scientists like al-Jazari intended to advance technological knowledge not for commercial exploitation but for the benefit of mankind.

It is a highly technical work which has been studied by competent scholars more recently, and therefore its importance in the history of Engineering, particularly in Hydraulic technology, has not been fully appreciated. Sarton was the first (?) to underline its importance when he said: "This treatise is most elaborate of its kind and may be considered the climax of this line of Moslem achievement". More than a 'treatise, it is a full-fledged scientific work in the field of engineering, and since no other earlier or contemporary work is comparable to it, Jazari's work is to be regarded as representing the climax of this line not only of 'Muslem achievement' but 'human achievement.'

An eminent modern scholar and highly qualified engineer who has closely studied and translated al-Jazari's book has expressed his opinion on its merit of under:-

> "It is impossible to over-emphasize the importance of al-Jazari's work in the history of engineering. Until modern times there is no other document, from any cultural area, that provides a comparable wealth of instructions for the design, manufacture and assembly of machines".(2)

---

(2) Donald Hill: The Book of Knowledge of Ingenenious Mechanical Devices, Dordrecht, 1974.

THE BOOK OF INSTRUCTIONS IN PRINCIPLES OF NAVIGATION AND REGULATIONS.

Ibn Mājid

كتاب الفوائد

شهاب الدين أحمد بن ماجد النجدي

Shihāb al-Din Ahmad b. Mājid b. Muhammad b. 'Amr b. Duwaik b. Yuṣuf b. Hasan b. Husain b. Abi Ma'laq al-Sa'dī Ibn Abī al-Rakā'ib al-Najdi, belonged by descent to the Arab stock of 'Qays 'Ailān. His family, originally settled in Najd, had

migrated to Oman where Ibn Majid was born in Julfār by about the later thirtees of the 9th century A.H. (c.1432 - 7 A.D.). He died after 906/1500, some time during the first decade of the 10th/16th century.

Ahmad Ibn Mājid was the greatest navigator of his times and one of the greatest of all times. He belonged to an illustrious family of navigators and his father Mājid was known by the title of *Mu'allim al-Burrayn*, the 'navigator of the two coastlines' (of Asia and Africa). Ibn Mājid was a brilliant child and had received good general education. He was specially well versed in Arabic literature. His navigator father was his instructor and guide in navigation. Because of these fortuitous circumstances, Ibn Majid excelled all his predecessors in the theory and practice of navigation. He was a deeply religious man, and would urge the navigators to recite, in time of danger, the specific Quranic verses which he had listed. As a scientist who abhorred supertitions, he forbade the sailors to be supertitious about auspicious or unauspicious stars and planets.

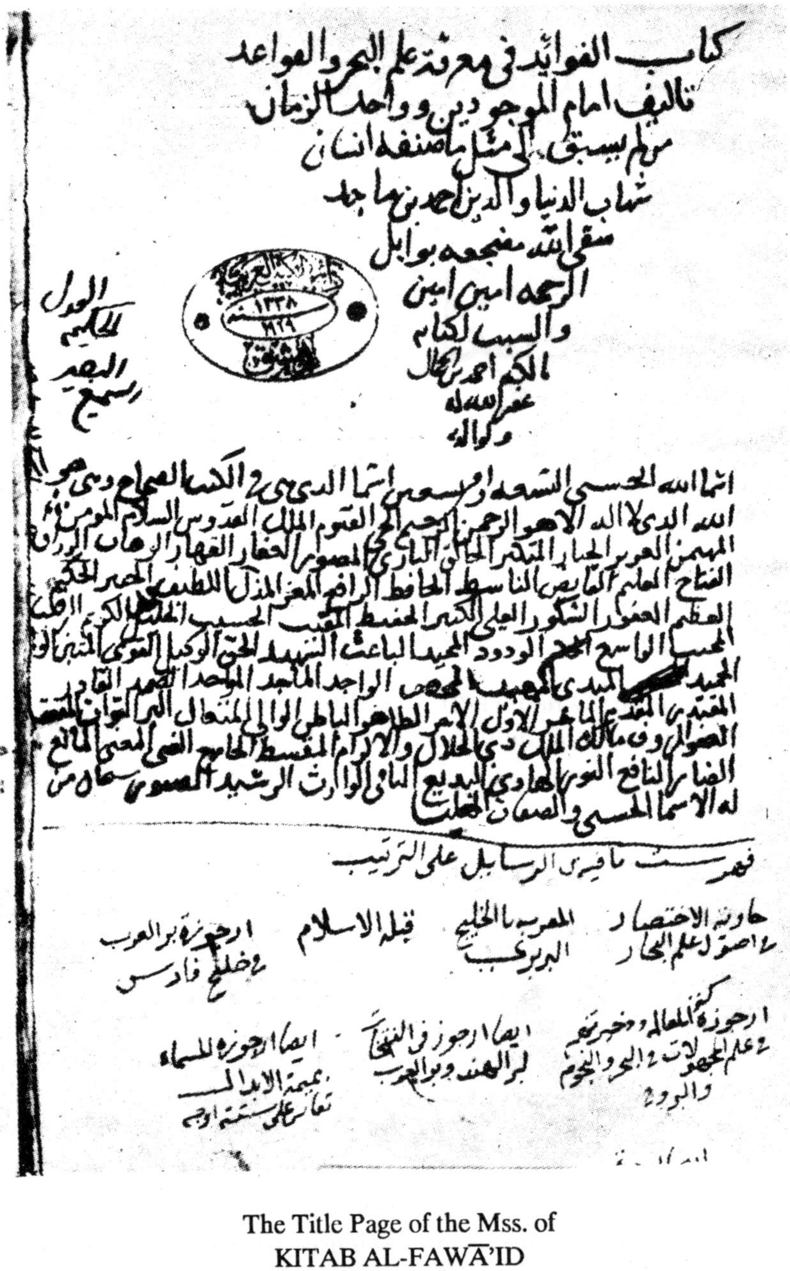

كتاب الفوائد في معرفة علم البحر والقواعد
تأليف امام الموحدين وواحد الزمان
من لم يسبق الى مثل ما صنفه انسان
شهاب الدنيا والدين احمد بن ماجد
سقى الله مضجعه بوابل
الرحمة امين امين
والسبب لكتابه

The Title Page of the Mss. of
KITAB AL-FAWĀ'ID
Preserved in the Zāhriyyah Library
Damascus, Syria

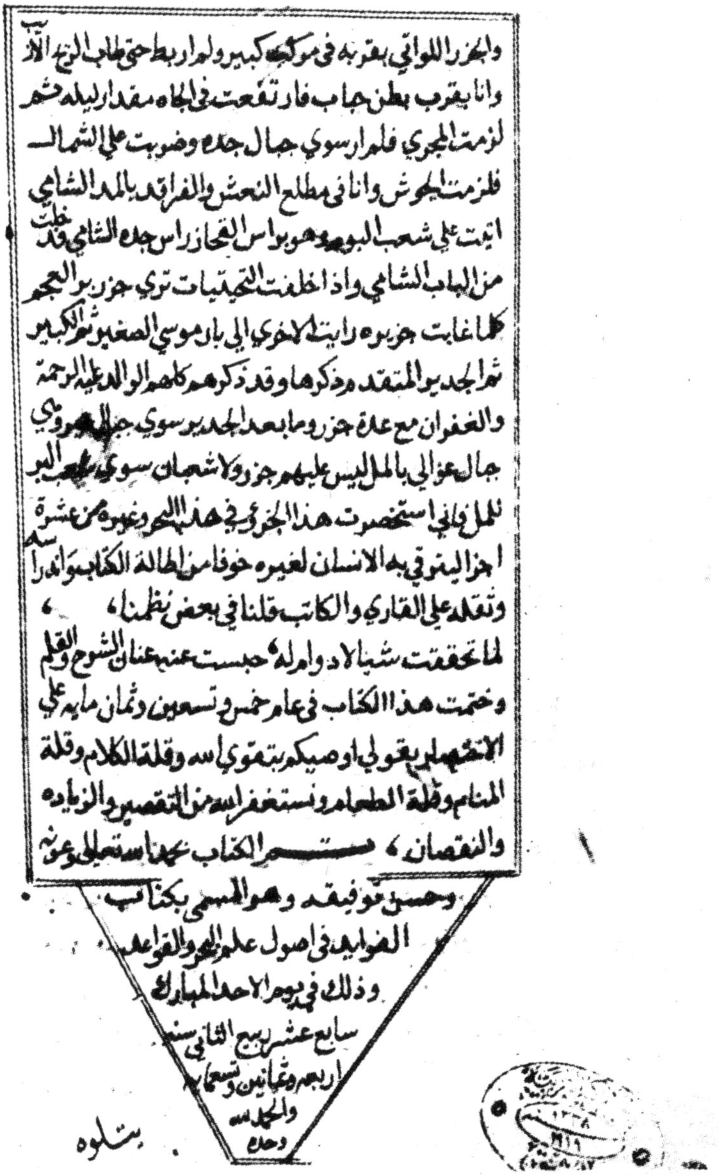
والجزر اللواتي بقربه في موكب كبير ولم ار بطا حتى طاب الريح الان
وانا بقرب بطن جباب فارتفعت في الجاه مقدار ليله ثم
لزمت المجري فلم ار سوي جبال جده وضربت على الشمال
فلزمت الجوش وانا في مطلع النعش والفرقد بالمد الشامي
اتيت على شعب البوهو وهو براس الحجاز راس جده الشامي وقد خلت
من الهاب الشامي واذا اخلفت التحيتيات تري جزر العجم
كلما غابت جزيره رايت الاخري الي بار موسي الصغير ثم الكبير
ثم الجديد المتقدم ذكرها وقد ذكرهم كلهم الوالد عليه الرحمة
والغفران مع علة جزر وما بعد الجديد سوي جبال ... مي
جبال عوالي بالمد ليس عليهم جزر ولا شعبان سوي ... البر
للمل واني استخصرت هذا الجزء في هذا البحر وغيره من عشرة
اجزا اليتوقي به الانسان لغيره خوفا من اطالة الكتاب ...
وثقله علي القاري والكاتب قلنا في بعض نظمنا
لما تحققت شيا الا دوامله حبست عنه عنان الشوح والقلم
وختمت هذا الكتاب في عام خمس وتسعين وثمان مايه على
الاخشهلي بقولي اوصيكم بتقوي الله وقلة الكلام وقلة
المنام وقلة الطعام ونستغفر الله من التقصير والزياده
والنقصان ، تم الكتاب بحمد الله تعالى وعونه
وحسن توفيقه وهو المسمي بكتاب
الفوايد في اصول علم البحر والقواعد
وذلك في يوم الاحد المبارك
سابع عشر ربيع الثاني سنه
اربعه وثمانين وتسعمايه
والحمد لله
وحده
يتلوه

Colophone of the Mss. of
KITAB AL-FAWĀ'ID
Preserved in the Zāhriyyah Library
Damascus, Syria

Ibn Mājid used charts, maps, and advanced instruments of navigation. With his expertise in the knowledge and use of the compass, he had adjusted the needle *(al-maghnātīs)* on the case and improved upon the previous model of the compass. His instruments were more advanced and accurate in the contemporary world of navigation. He has mentioned it in *Kitab al-Fawā'id* that he had shown the Portuguese an instrument which they had not seen before. In the Portuguese record, Ibn Mājid is referred to as "*Malemo Canaqua*" or "Malemo Cana", that is *Mu'allim Kanaka* meaning 'master of navigation'. He was responsible for guiding the Portuguese and showing them the way to India. As recorded by historian Qutb al-Din al-Nahrwālī (originally of Anhalwāra-Patan in Gujerat and later settled in Makka where he died in 900 A.H./1582) in his book *al-Barq al-Yamānī fi al-Fath al-'Uthmani* that Ibn Mājid had instructed the Chief of the Franks not to Sail close to the coast of Malindi (African coastline) but to sail straight across the ocean (southward?) and then turn (westward?) so that they would avoid strong waves and sale safely towards the Indian coastline.

Ibn Majid was an idefagtible writer, and he authored about forty large or small works mostly in verse form. The one on the determination of the Qibla, extending to 295 verses, was composed in 893 A.H (1488). Among his most celebrate works are, 'The Hāwiya' and 'The Fawā'id'. 'The Hawiya' is a long *urjūzā* of 1082 verses, its full title being *Hawiyat al-Ikhtisār fi Usūl 'Ilm'al-Bihār,* i.e. "A Brief Coverage of the Principles of the Science of Oceans". It was composed by him in 866 A.H. (1462 A.D.), and according to one view "represents Ibn Mājid's first attempt at a complete conspectus of navigational theory" (Tibbitt).

The Fawā'id

Kitāb al-Fawā'id fi Usūl al Bahr wa al-Qawā'id ('The Book of Instructions in Principles of Navigation And Regulations') has been estimated as a "compendium of the known knowledge of theoretical and practical navigation" (Ferrand). With his extensive knowledge of the history of navigation going back to five centuries before him, his studies in astronomy, meteorology and geography, and his perfect professional knowledge of the different types of boats and ships, of the seas and the coastlines, he formulated an advanced theory of navigation and became truly the 'Father of Nautical Science'.

'The Fawā'id' is an encyclopaedic work divided into twelve *'Fā'idās'* (Useful Information Themes), each of which is dealt with separately as a chapter by itself. Their contents may be briefly stated as under:

F. 1 Importance of Science of Navigation and introduction of the author.

F. 2 Qualifications necessary for the Pilot (Mu'allim).

F. 3 The lunar mansions.

F. 4 The compass rhumbs.

F. 5 Miscellaneous general information: the star groups, bibliography of classical works useful for the navigator, etc.

F. 6 The different types of 'routes' and their relative importance in navigational science.

F. 7 The *qitās* measurement.

F. 8 (i) *Ishārat,* recognition of 'signs' indicating landmass, and description of the western coastline of India.

(ii) *Siyāsat,* management of the ship and the well-being of the occupants by the navigator.

F. 9 Coastlines of the world.

F.10 Important Islands.

F.11 Monsoons and navigation.

F.12 Description of the Red Sea.